Voice and Nation in Plurinational Bolivia

Bloomsbury Studies in Linguistic Anthropology

Series Editors:
Sabina Perrino, Paul Manning, and Jim Wilce

Presenting and exploring new and current approaches to discourse and culture, **Bloomsbury Studies in Linguistic Anthropology** examines the most recent topics in this field. Publishing contemporary, cutting-edge research, this series investigates social life through everyday discursive practices, making these practices visible and unveiling processes that would remain concealed without careful attention to discourse.

Titles focus on specific themes to advance the field both theoretically and methodologically, such as language contact dynamics, language revitalization and reclamation, and language, migration, and social justice. Positioning linguistic anthropology at the intersection with other fields, this series will cast light on various cultural settings across the globe by viewing important linguistic ethnographies through an anthropological lens. Standing at the frontier of this growing field, **Bloomsbury Studies in Linguistic Anthropology** offers a balanced view of the current state of the discipline, as well as promoting and advancing exciting new directions for research.

Titles in the Series:

Graphic Politics in Eastern India
Nishaant Choksi

Language and Revolutionary Magic in the Orinoco Delta
Juan Luis Rodríguez

Remaking Kichwa
Michael Wroblewski

Saying and Doing in Zapotec
Mark A. Sicoli

Voice and Nation in Plurinational Bolivia

Aymara Radio and Song in an Age of Pachakuti

Karl Swinehart

BLOOMSBURY ACADEMIC
LONDON • NEW YORK • OXFORD • NEW DELHI • SYDNEY

BLOOMSBURY ACADEMIC
Bloomsbury Publishing Plc, 50 Bedford Square, London, WC1B 3DP, UK
Bloomsbury Publishing Inc, 1359 Broadway, New York, NY 10018, USA
Bloomsbury Publishing Ireland, 29 Earlsfort Terrace, Dublin 2, D02 AY28, Ireland

BLOOMSBURY, BLOOMSBURY ACADEMIC and the Diana logo
are trademarks of Bloomsbury Publishing Plc

First published in Great Britain 2024
Paperback edition published 2026

Copyright © Karl Swinehart, 2024, 2026

Karl Swinehart has asserted his right under the Copyright, Designs and
Patents Act, 1988, to be identified as Author of this work.

For legal purposes the Acknowledgments on pp. viii–xi constitute an
extension of this copyright page.

Cover design: Elena Durey
Cover image © Karl Swinehart

All rights reserved. No part of this publication may be: i) reproduced or transmitted in any form, electronic or mechanical, including photocopying, recording or by means of any information storage or retrieval system without prior permission in writing from the publishers; or ii) used or reproduced in any way for the training, development or operation of artificial intelligence (AI) technologies, including generative AI technologies. The rights holders expressly reserve this publication from the text and data mining exception as per Article 4(3) of the Digital Single Market Directive (EU) 2019/790.

Bloomsbury Publishing Plc does not have any control over, or responsibility for, any third-party websites referred to or in this book. All internet addresses given in this book were correct at the time of going to press. The author and publisher regret any inconvenience caused if addresses have changed or sites have ceased to exist, but can accept no responsibility for any such changes.

A catalogue record for this book is available from the British Library.

Library of Congress Cataloging-in-Publication Data
Names: Swinehart, Karl, author.
Title: Voice and nation in plurinational Bolivia : Aymara radio and song in an age of Pachakuti / Karl Swinehart.
Description: London ; New York : Bloomsbury Academic, 2024. |
Series: Bloomsbury studies in linguistic anthropology | Includes bibliographical references and index. |
Summary: "This ethnographic account of Indigenous language activism explores how Aymara media and cultural workers combat the threat of language obsolescence by making the language audible in diverse corners of Aymara life. Drawing on research conducted among Aymara language radio broadcasters, hip hop artists, and community members, it also examines the role Indigenous multilingualism plays in Bolivian politics"– Provided by publisher.
Identifiers: LCCN 2023048365 (print) | LCCN 2023048366 (ebook) |
ISBN 9781350324718 (hardback) | ISBN 9781350324756 (paperback) |
ISBN 9781350324732 (epub) | ISBN 9781350324725 (ebook)
Subjects: LCSH: Language maintenance–Bolivia. | Language and culture–Bolivia. |
Aymara language–Bolivia–Discourse analysis. | Aymara language–Bolivia–Social aspects. |
Radio broadcasting–Bolivia. | Music and language–Bolivia.
Classification: LCC P40.5.L322 B579 2024 (print) | LCC P40.5.L322 (ebook) |
DDC 306.442/98324–dc23/eng/20240202
LC record available at https://lccn.loc.gov/2023048365
LC ebook record available at https://lccn.loc.gov/2023048366

ISBN: HB: 978-1-3503-2471-8
PB: 978-1-3503-2475-6
ePDF: 978-1-3503-2472-5
eBook: 978-1-3503-2473-2

Series: Bloomsbury Studies in Linguistic Anthropology

Typeset by Integra Software Services Pvt. Ltd.

For product safety related questions contact productsafety@bloomsbury.com.

To find out more about our authors and books visit www.bloomsbury.com
and sign up for our newsletters.

Contents

List of Figures	vi
List of Tables	vii
Acknowledgments	viii
Note on Aymara Orthography	xii
List of Interlineal Gloss Conventions	xiii
List of Abbreviations	xiv
1 Introduction	1
Part One Radio	25
2 Redemption Radio: Dehispanicized Aymara at Radio San Gabriel	33
3 Ayllu on the Airwaves: Mediatized Metapragmatics at Radio Pacha Qamasa	55
Part Two Song	87
4 Tupak in Their Veins: Race, Nation, and Memory in Aymara Hip-Hop	95
5 Singing the National Anthem in Jesús de Machaca	121
6 Conclusion	145
Notes	155
References	165
Index	177

Figures

1.1	Map of Bolivia	3
1.2	A territorial distribution of Aymara speakers in Bolivia, Chile, and Peru	4
2.1	Radio San Gabriel in Villa Adela neighborhood of El Alto	34
3.1	Offices of Radio Pacha Qamasa	58
3.2	A campaign leaflet for Oscar Chirinos with a false 200 Boliviano note from the "National Bank of Fortune" (rather than Bank of Bolivia) on one side. Like an actual 200 Boliviano note, the bill features icons of Aymara nationhood—the ruins of Tiwanaku and the mountain Wayna Potosí	83
5.1	"The Fatherland/Qullasuyu's great name": "Patria" translated as "Qullasuyu"	132
5.2	Bolivia's two national flags raised at the commemoration of the 1921 Rebellion	137

Tables

2.1	Aymara neologisms: days of the week	47
3.1	Opening for *Akhulli Amuyt'awi* (February 26, 2010)	67
3.2	"I want to eat a little chicken"	71
3.3	The debating Aymara public	74
3.4	Dialogic toggling between speaker and audience	75
3.5	Spanish loanwords for political terms in discourse	76
3.6	"*Q'aras*" and MASistas	79
3.7	The Poetic epithet *q'ara*	82
4.1	Lyrics to *Ch'ama*	109
4.2	Metrical organization of structural sense in *Ch'ama*	109
4.3	Metrical organization of reference in *Ch'ama*	110
5.1	Spanish and Aymara versions of the Bolivian National Anthem with English	142

Acknowledgments

Like any project that has come together over many years, there have been many people and institutions who have made this book possible in both Bolivia and the United States. This project had its genesis as during my earliest days as a graduate student at both UCLA and the University of Pennsylvania, and benefitted early on from the attentive training and encouragement of dedicated faculty at both these institutions. If it were not for the initial encouragement from the late Roger Anderson to apply for a Foreign Language Area Studies (FLAS) grant to study Quechua, my life would have followed the wonderful Andean paths that it ultimately has. Although it was a crucial component to funding my MA in Applied Linguistics, the move to study Quechua was always more than just utilitarian move to cove my tuition costs, although it was also this. I was inspired by political developments in Bolivia, in particular after hearing a leader of the Cochabamba Water War, Oscar Olivera, speak during a tour of the United States in the wake of their victory for the remunicipalization of water (see Hines 2021). A language nerd through and through, not only was I thrilled to study a Native American language, but that this would fund my MA studies and potentially open up avenues to engage with Bolivians made the possibility of studying Quechua something I knew I could not pass up. Little did I know when taking classes with my Quechua teacher, Jaime Luís Daza, and studying with classmates and now colleagues, Jennifer Guzmán and Janet Stephens, how consequential the move to study Indigenous languages of the Andes would be. I am grateful to Roger Anderson, the UCLA Applied Linguistics program, and to the FLAS program. I will also thank FLAS for their support of my first visit to Bolivia to study Quechua with Monica Alcocer and my first Aymara teacher, Roman Crespo Tiritico.

Subsequent visits to Bolivia during my graduate studies were supported through funding from the Fulbright Institute for International Education, the Fulbright Hayes Dissertation Research Abroad Fellowship, and the University of Pennsylvania Center for Native American Research. This fieldwork was facilitated through collaborations with diverse Bolivian educational and research institutions and the tremendous professionals working within them. I am forever grateful to the Program for Professional Development in Bilingual

Intercultural Education for the Andean Region (PROEIB-Andes), the University of the Cordillera, the Universidad Pedagógica, and the Aymara Language and Culture Institute (ILCA). At PROEIB-Andes, I am particularly indebted to Inge Sichra, Luís Enrique López, Vicente Limachi, and the Masters students of the 2007 cohort. At the University of the Cordillera, I would like to thank Pamela Calla, whose warmth, intellect, and enthusiasm for supporting colleagues and students is a model of committed scholarship. At ILCA, I am indebted to the late Juan de Dios Yapita and to his partner and longtime collaborator Denise Arnold. Juan de Dios provided letters of invitation when this was necessary, but offered so much than logistical support. He was a one-man intellectual welcome committee to the Aymara world. His intellect, curiosity, and generosity were always a highlight of any time spent in La Paz. He was thrilled to listen to and discuss recordings and examine transcripts, and never failed to combine a generous spirit, a commitment to rigor, one tempered with patience in his approach to analysis. I thank Luz Jiménez Quispe of the Universidad Pedagógica and Franz Laime for their generosity with introducing me to community members in Jesús de Machaca, and to the people of Jesús de Machaca who, although briefly, warmly welcomed me and allowed me to participate in the commemoration of the 1921 Uprising.

I am grateful for the hospitality, warmth, and open disposition of the leadership and staff at Radio San Gabriel, in particular the late Vicente Cahuaya, who was in the leadership of the station at the time and introduced me to Hilarión Chinahuanca and the team at the station's Aymara Language Department. The host of the radio program discussed in Chapter 3, Gabriel Bonafacio, was a gracious and enthusiastic supporter of this research from the beginning. I am indebted to his openness to allowing me to attend live broadcast sessions and for his ongoing friendship. I am grateful and indebted to all of the members of the El Alto and La Paz hip-hop scene who made time to meet with me, since our first meetings back in 2006, and through the years to come in subsequent visits. I am grateful to all who were open to taking time to speak with me and let me hang out at their concerts. This is particularly true of members of Wayna Rap, Grover Quispe, Rolando Quispe, and Eber Miranda, the members of Nación Rap, and to the always sharp, insightful, and engaging Elena Tapia aka Nina Uma. My debt to Eber Miranda and Tawit Lipan is particularly great. In the early days of this project, when they were still university students in the Andean Linguistics program at the Universidad Mayor de San Andrés they worked with me in the development of transcripts and served as crucial interlocutors.

I am grateful to Nancy Hornberger for her early support of my research in Bolivia and for her encouragement in developing a research program there. As a teacher and mentor, Asif Agha has been and continues to be a source of insight, inspiration, and support. During my graduate studies, participation in the mediatization workshops he organized at the University of Pennsylvania was central in the formulation of this project. Out of these workshops I was lucky to receive Miyako Inoue's feedback on early formulations of this project. The other members of my dissertation committee, Betsy Rymes and John Jackson, were dedicated teachers, mentors, and support throughout my graduate research. I was lucky to study with a talented and supportive group of colleagues during my time at Penn including Raquel Albarrán, Cécile Evers-Traore, Mariam Durrani, Sarah Gallo, Bridget Goodman, Juan Ariel Gómez, Kathy Howard, Jennifer Leung, Holly Link, Lina Martínez Hernández, Khwezi Mkhize, Robert Moore, Jamie Schissel, and Krystal Smalls Riley Snorton, David Suisman.

An earlier version of Chapter 2 was published in a special issue of *Language and Communication* titled "Languages and Publics in Stateless Nations" that I guest co-edited together with Kathryn Graber, a volume that emerged out of a panel of a similar name at a meeting of the American Anthropological Association in 2009. Parts of Chapter 4 appeared in *Arizona Journal of Hispanic Cultural Studies* and the *Journal for the Society of American Music*.

My work has benefitted greatly from participation in a variety of workshops and conferences organized by colleagues over the years. I am grateful to David Kazanjian for introducing me to the Tepoztlán Institute for the Transnational History of the Americas where I have had the pleasure of developing my work through dialogue with colleagues including Jennifer Ponce de León, Laura Gutiérrez, Sandra Rozental, Mario Rufer, and many others. I am grateful to the participants and organizers of the Semiotics Workshop at the University of Chicago, Chris Bloechl, Summerson Carr, Susan Gal, Andrew Graan, Britta Ingebretson, Elina Hartikainen, Costas Nakassis, and Michael Silverstein for their feedback in sessions there. My fellow Harper Schmidt fellows, Fadi Bardawil, Jared Holley, Satyel Larson, Birte Löschenkohl, Poornima Paidipaty, Bettina Stoetzer, and Zhivka Valiavicharska were important interlocutors. An earlier version of Chapter 5 was presented at Linglab at the University of California at Los Angeles, I am grateful to Erin Debenport for the invitation and also for the feedback from her and the other participants at that session. At the University of Louisville, I have enjoyed the support of my colleagues in the department of Comparative Humanities and am grateful to the dynamic discussions in the Americas Research Group, the Discourse and Semiotics workshop, and the Commonwealth Center for Humanities in Society (CCHS)—Asaf Angermann, Simona Bertacco, Hilaria Cruz, Lisa Björkman, Anna Browne Ribeiro, Chris Ehrick, John Gibson, Frank Kelderman, Deborah Lutz, and Andrea Olinger. There are many others who have given me important feedback and support along the way—Netta Avineri, Jessica Bisset Perea, Jillian Cavanaugh, Aymar Christian, Galo Coca Soto, Cecilia Cutler, Aurora Donzelli, Kathryn Graber, Shane Greene, Geir Haraldseth, Aron Kantor, Bruce Mannheim, Sandhya Narayanan, Angela Reyes, Unn Røyneland, Bambi Schieffelin, Gabriel Solis, David Suisman, Daniel Suslak, Joshua Tucker, and Cecilia Urquieta.

I thank Paul Manning for his encouragement and editorial support along with his series' co-editors Sabina Perrino and Jim Wilce. Paul was the editor at the *Journal of Linguistic Anthropology* when I published my first academic article (Swinehart 2008). I am honored to have received his editorial wisdom again now on my first book project. For their support, patience, and encouragement I would also like to thank the editorial team at Bloomsbury, Morwenna Scott, Laura Gallon, and Sarah MacDonald.

Finally, I thank my parents Fred and Carole Swinehart, whose combined commitment to understanding the world and their deep sense of curiosity about it continue to be an inspiration.

Note on Aymara Orthography

Debates concerning Aymara orthography have been relatively less contentious than those in Quechua (on Quechua in Peru and Kichwa in Ecuador, see Hornberger and King 1998). To the extent that there are disagreements they tend to unfold along similar lines, including whether to limit vowels the three phonemic vowels in both languages (/a/, /i/, /u/), or to include the allophonic variants with the use of five vowels, the motivation for the latter being a similarity with Spanish orthography. Proposing instead a radical break with European writing conventions, there is also Teófilo Laime's and Virgina Mamani's (2008) proposal to write Aymara with the Japanese Hiragana syllabary. Here, I use Aymara's three phonemic vowels (/a/, /i/, /u/).

Aymara has a series of consonants and distinctions that do not exist in Spanish or English. The letter q represents a voiceless uvular stop, pronounced like a "k" but further back on the velum toward the uvula, like the sound of the letter *qaf* in Classical Arabic. All stops in Aymara are voiceless and can be a simple stop, aspirated, or ejective. The aspirated consonants are written with an h (chh, kh, ph, qh, th) and the ejective consonants are followed by an apostrophe (ch', k', p', q', t'). Ejective consonants are articulated with a quick closing of the glottis (as in the pause in middle of the English exclamation "uh-oh") and aspirated consonants are followed by a short burst of air (as in the p and t at the beginnings of the English names "Paul" and "Tom"). The letter "j" corresponds to its pronunciation in Andean Spanish as a glottal fricative (/h/). Similarly, the digraph double "ll" is pronounced as a voiced lateral approximate palatal "ll" in Andean Spanish, in contrast to elsewhere in Latin America.

Interlineal Gloss Conventions

1	First person
2	Second person
3	Third person
4	Fourth person (Speaker + Addressee)
ABL	ablative
CAUS	causative
CONT	continuous aspect
DAT	dative
DELIM	delimitative
EVID	evidential
FUT	future
IMP	imperative
INST	instantaneous aspect
LOC	locative
NEG	negator
O	object (e.g., 3S1O, third-person subject, first-person object)
PL	plural
POS	possessive
REFL	reflexive
S	subject (e.g., 3S1O, third-person subject, first-person object)

Abbreviations

CACOJMA	Cabildo de Ayllus y Comunidades Originarias de Jesús de Machaqa
	(Council of *Ayllus* and Indigenous Communities of Jesús de Machaqa)
CEA	Consejo Educativo Aymara (Aymara Education Council)
CONMERB	Confederación Nacional de Maestros de Educación Rurales de Bolivia
	(National Confederation of Rural Teachers of Bolivia)
CSUTCB	Confederación Sindical Unificado de Trabajadores y Campesinos de Bolivia (Unified Sindical Confederation of Workers and Peasants of Bolivia)
MAS	Movimiento al Socialismo (Movement to Socialism)
MPS	Moviemiento por la Soberanía (Movement for Sovereignty)
RPQ	Radio Pacha Qamasa
RSG	Radio San Gabriel
RTP	Radio y Televisión Popular

1

Introduction

The Aymara language is among the few Indigenous languages of the Americas with more than a million speakers, with estimates of the number of speakers ranging between one and a half million, to more than two million.¹ The majority of these speakers are both bilingual in Spanish and Aymara and also Bolivian citizens. Hundreds of thousands of Aymara speakers also live in neighboring Peru, and a much smaller number, though still numbering in the thousands, resides in the northernmost regions of Chile (Fig. 1.2). Aymara speakers reside in both rural communities in and adjacent to the Andean high plain, or *altiplano*, surrounding Lake Titicaca and also in the largest city of this region, El Alto (Fig. 1.1). In the city of El Alto, ethnic Aymaras constitute a majority of the population.² There are many more ethnic Aymaras than those counted as speakers, the category "speaker" being itself a complicated and complicating designation, particularly in Indigenous and minoritized language communities undergoing process of language shift (Fishman 1991, 1997). For example, many Spanish-language-dominant Aymaras may not be counted as speakers if they speak the Aymara language with limited proficiency or only understand it as so-called "passive" bilinguals, even though they still engage with the language.

Although the native or heritage language of the majority population of the Bolivian high plain is Aymara, this language, together with Quechua, the other major Indigenous language of the Andes, has been accurately described by scholars of Indigenous languages of the Andes as an "oppressed language" for how social relations of domination have unfolded along ethnolinguistic lines (Albó 1977; Mannheim 1984). As in most situations of oppression, there is not only resignation, but resistance and resilience. Aymaras have played a central, protagonist role in Bolivia's politics both historically and contemporarily, now during what has been called the *proceso de cambio*, or "process of change," of recent decades, a process which has notably included the rewriting of the constitution and the refounding of Bolivia as a plurinational republic in 2009.

The *proceso de cambio* is one way that both state and non-state actors have characterized the political period inaugurating Bolivia's twenty-first century, but another has been the term for revolution in both the Quechua and Aymara languages, *pachakuti* (Gutiérrez 2014; Hylton and Thomson 2007; Rivera Cusicanqui 2008). The reassertion of Aymara language in public, and a renewed attention to its cultivation and dissemination, has also been a part of this moment of *pachakuti*.

Despite Aymara's many speakers and its evident linguistic vitality in relation to other Indigenous languages of the Americas, trends of language shift to Spanish persist (López 2007). The long history of linguistic domination and the awareness of increasing Spanish use among younger generations combine such that an acute feeling that the language stands in an embattled relation to Spanish is shared widely across diverse corners of Aymara society. The Aymara sociolinguistic terrain is, in fact, diverse by most any metric: it spans rural and urban spaces, and stretches across class and occupational realities, including farmers, professionals, wealthy market women, artisans, and migrants to the Europe, the United States, and Latin American capitals like São Paulo and Buenos Aires. While there is much shared loyalty to the Aymara language across these dispersed and diverse contexts, there is, of course, a corresponding diversity of perspectives on the status and trajectory of the language within Bolivian society. Among Aymara speakers it is also easy to find both fears of language obsolescence, on the one hand, and, on the other, casual confidence and pride in the resilience of the language and the diversity of contexts where it remains in use. These seemingly opposed perspectives may sometimes even be articulated at different moments by the same individual. The following two encounters I had with two different Aymara speakers, one urban and one rural, one a scholar, the other a farmer, present contrasting scenarios in which each speaker articulated assessments of their relationship to their language.

The Scholar

"*Aruskipt'asipxañanakasakipunirakispawa*." The Aymara linguist's eyes lit up after he finished pronouncing this improbably long word, awaiting my response. I smiled, nodded, and responded with a simple affirmation, "*Jisa, chiqawa*" ("yes, that's right"). This was more than just a word and I had heard it before. The linguist was the late Juan De Dios Yapita (1931–2020) and we were sitting in the library of the Aymara Language and Culture Institute (ILCA). This library—walls lined from floor to ceiling with titles of Andean ethnography, history, and linguistics—situated on a steep street in the La Paz neighborhood of Sopocachi, accessible from the driveway to Yapita's home, was the site of countless encounters between Yapita and scholars both from abroad and across Bolivia. Yapita founded ILCA

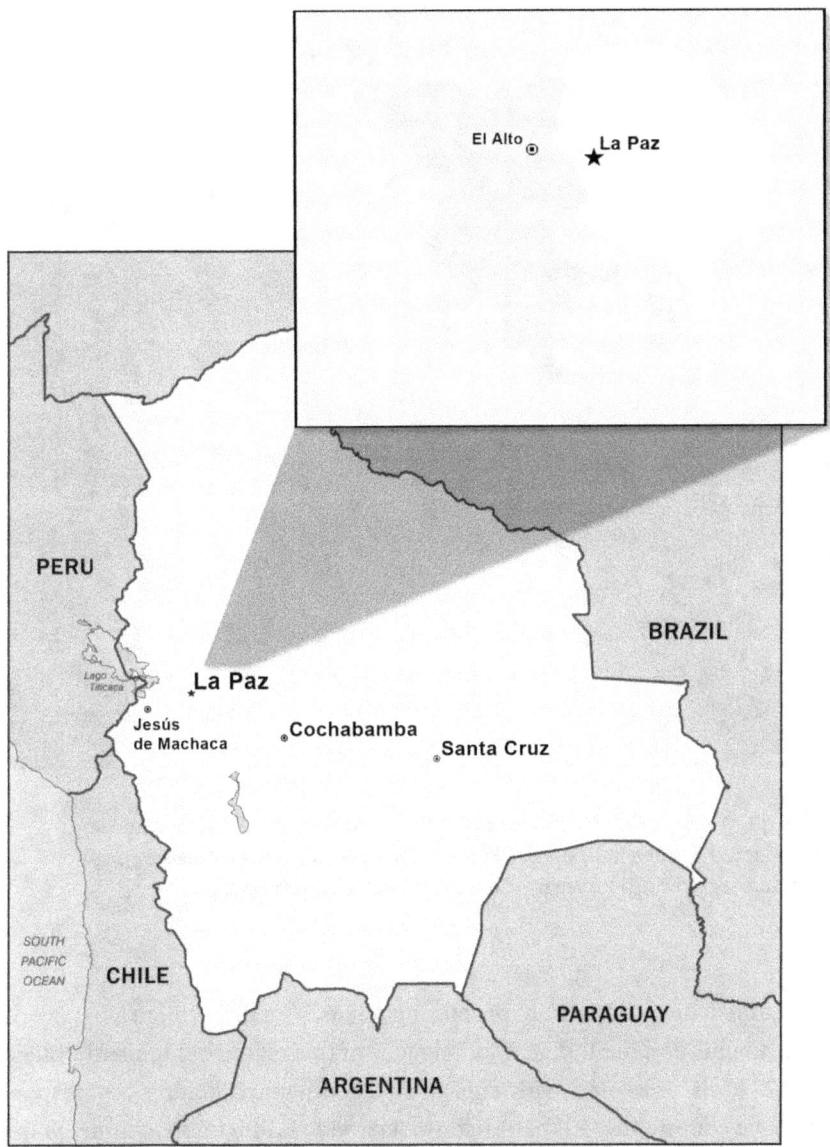

Figure 1.1 Map of Bolivia. Adapted by Shachaf Polakow from Library of Congress public domain map: https://www.loc.gov/resource/g5320.ct001884/?r=-0.581,0.234,2.161,0.996,0

Figure 1.2 A territorial distribution of Aymara speakers in Bolivia, Chile, and Peru. Adapted by Shachaf Polakow from public domain image: https://commons.wikimedia.org/wiki/File:Aymara-Language-Distributio.png#filehistory

in 1972 and dedicated his life to promoting research on the Aymara language, his mother tongue and the Indigenous language of this region of highland Bolivia.

I had been presented with this complex utterance before. My response could have communicated that I had understood and that our sentiments were aligned. I had responded appropriately, in other words. Still, he translated for me: "We should all, everyone of us, always continue to speak our languages to one another, and despite the conflict with which human beings act, resolve our problems through communication."³ How could one word not only be so long, but mean so much? Speakers of Finnish, Turkish, Mongolian, or Tamil might not find this word to be improbably long at all. Nor would speakers of other Indigenous languages of the Americas like Diné, Quechua, Nahuatl, Tsalagi, or any of the many other languages whose grammars operate similarly. These are termed agglutinative languages within linguistic typology, meaning they have large inventories of suffixes that add layers upon layers of meaning to an initial root. In this case, the word begins with *aru-*, the root for "speech" or "voice." Additional suffixes then identify who speaks to whom (we all speak to one another), and convey senses of obligation, courtesy, and deference which in English could be conveyed through modal auxiliaries (should), or adverbs (always, please, kindly). Still other suffixes contribute what linguists call evidentiality, or the degree of commitment or epistemic relation between the speaker and what is being said, whether certainty, first-hand knowledge, hearsay, supposition, or inference. Yapita also used this word to illustrate these aspects of Aymara in a 2014 essay in the Bolivian newspaper *Página Siete*: "Among the suffixes that the word contains are ones with the meaning and sense of mutual comprehension, courtesy, obligation, dialogue, etc. This word contains these and other meanings that result in reflecting a linguistic richness. In other words, it's a whole philosophy."⁴

As a philosophy of language and communication, it is a "word" about words, an example of metalanguage that demonstrates a unique quality of language as a sign system. This capacity for speakers to reflexively characterize the sign system they're using was what linguist Roman Jakobson (1960) called language's "metalinguistic function." It is also an unusually explicitly articulated example of what linguistic anthropologists call a language ideology, or a morally permeated conception of language and discursive practices (Irvine 1989; Kroskrity 2000; Silverstein 1979; Woolard and Schieffelin 1994).

By his own account, Yapita composed this word deliberately with others in the development of Aymara language teaching materials in a project headed by US linguist Martha Hardman in the early 1970s. More than just a "word," this philosophical utterance can also be understood as a morphemic poem, a deliberate and aesthetic composition. Echoes of the Greek etymology of the word poem (*poiema* "to create") can be heard in his 2014 commentary:

> It would seem some brick layer making a building had fortified this word carefully, putting first the foundation, that in linguistics we call a root, and on that he would have placed meticulously the bricks, until culminating in an

optimal way with the construction that is the suffix—*wa*, that in the study of Aymara grammar we call the sentential suffix, and also, the suffix of personal knowledge.⁵

Not only for its deliberate construction, the word is poetic also in the sense of Jakobson's (1960) poetic function. In stretching the limits of what the articulatory apparatus can achieve with one breath, this utterance itself is felt in its physicality. Jakobson called the possibility of foregrounding language's materiality the domain of the poetic function. The poetic function concerns "the palpability of signs" and "the fundamental dichotomy between signs and object" (1960: 356). Whether through rhyme, rhythm, repetition, or other means, the poetic function allows us to play with language. Both metalinguistic and poetic in Jakobson's terms, Yapita created a word designed in such a way that its very pronunciation is an achievement, comprised as it is from a series of morphemes so extravagant it can leave speakers nearly breathless.

Yapita was not the first Aymara speaker to share this tongue twister of a word with me. My first Aymara teacher, Román Crespo, and, later, other Aymara language enthusiasts in Bolivia, whether language professionals or not, rolled this word off their tongues to illustrate Aymara morphology's impressive generative capacities, and also to delight in their own command of the language. First composed for purposes of language instruction, this utterance came to function as a test to demonstrate mastery of Aymara morphology in both Yapita's courses and those of others. When shared with me, it usually came accompanied by a smile, a laugh, or other visible signs of satisfaction. This satisfaction may have been with what was being said, with pride in the speaker's command of the language, or also pride in the language itself. To articulate *aruskipt'asipxa ñanakasakipunirakispawa* in these moments conferred meaning beyond the string of words to which it corresponds in Spanish. In earlier moments, in Yapita's classes or others, it had meant that a student had "passed the test" of Aymara compositional morphology. The word also means something in terms of Jakobson's referential function, the more traditional sense of propositional meaning, namely: we should all, every single one, always continue speaking our languages. In the Bolivian context, where with each passing generation fewer Aymaras have functional fluency in the language, this word-cum-philosophy-poem becomes not just an appeal to always communicate when we have problems, but, to do this in Aymara, to continue always to speak this poetic and often challenging language.

The Farmer

Consider now the following contrast to the hyperfluency and linguistic pride expressed through Yapita's extravagant word-poem-philosophy. A rural development organization dedicated to economic development and political participation of rural Aymaras had invited me to visit their offices and their radio station. During the visit, I had the opportunity to observe a training session held for a group of rural Aymaras who had traveled many hours from remote communities in the Camacho Province north of Lake Titicaca to the organization's headquarters in the city of El Alto. They had come for training through workshops in, among other things, the marketing of hand-knit alpaca wool wares to local and international markets. While eating lunch with the workshop attendees, a man in the group advised me that, as someone interested in studying the Aymara language, I would be better served by speaking to other Aymaras, not to him or to people from his community. He suggested I should travel to areas even more remote from the capital than his own. He explained that he and his *compañeras,* and they were women who joined us at this lunch, did not speak *aymara puro,* or "pure Aymara." From his perspective, their Aymara was too thoroughly mixed with Spanish to be worthy of study. Others sitting around us chimed in and lamented that they spoke neither Spanish nor Aymara well. Although not bundled neatly in one word, he too articulated a language ideology, one that contrasted starkly to Yapita's kilometric word. This language ideology designated his and his neighbors' linguistic practices, whether in Spanish or Aymara, as deviant or inadequate with respect to his perception of a "pure" standard.

Perhaps the rural Aymaras who had come to the city for an organizational training were hoping that the US researcher joining them at lunch would kindly look elsewhere. Were they directing me toward a linguistic El Dorado, the mythical city of gold described to Spanish invaders by native Andeans in the hopes that they might continue elsewhere in their search for riches? In other words, were they saying, "Don't study *us,* please keep moving along!"? Their friendly demeanor and openness to conversation felt earnest and left me with a different impression. This group and others I spoke with were supportive and were pleased that there was interest from abroad in Aymara language and culture. Sadly, what also seemed genuine was their conviction in their linguistic shortcomings, whether in Aymara or Spanish. With regards to Spanish, this comes as less of a surprise. Spanish spoken with a Quechua or Aymara accent is highly stigmatized, and the site of much public ridicule and stigma. Vulgar characterizations of the speech of Indigenous Andeans abound in Spanish language media, both in Bolivian media (Babel 2019; Swinehart 2012a; Swinehart 2018) and in media from neighboring Peru (Huayhua 2018; Narayanan 2022). More surprising than the lack of confidence in their Spanish was the negative self-evaluation of their variety of Aymara. This was one of many occasions in which Aymara-Spanish bilinguals devalued their linguistic capabilities within a framework of semilingualism, usually expressed with degrees of shame about their supposed deficiencies in either language. If theories of bilinguals' semilingualism have been roundly discredited among scholars (cf. Cummins 1994; Hansegård 1968), these ideas persist with troubling lasting power within bilingual communities such as this one. I had heard similar sentiments expressed by urban Aymaras with regards to their own speech, but was surprised to hear rural Aymara speakers discount their Aymara as falling short of a "pure Aymara." This is because it was precisely rural Aymara speakers, such as the ones who had come in for this workshop, who were precisely the ones who so often urban Aymaras suggested to me spoke the best Aymara.

This pattern which repeatedly embeds overlapping contrasts of distinction between my interlocutors and some other, more remote speaker can be described as *fractal recursion* (Irvine and Gal 2000: 38). Identifying fractally recursive distinctions as a recurrent feature of language ideologies, Judith Irvine and Susan Gal write, "Reminiscent of fractals in geometry ... the myriad oppositions that create identity can be reproduced repeatedly, either within each side of a dichotomy or outside it" (Irvine and Gal 2000: 38). The dichotomy between being simply an Aymara speaker versus a speaker of a distinctively *pure* Aymara reappeared in a way that created a moving target, always just beyond my immediate interlocutor. The imagined speaker who holds the distinction of speaking a truly authentic Aymara recedes forever into the distance. Rather than just a ruse to dismiss a nosy foreign researcher, the notion of *Aymara puro* emerged in these interactions as a kind of El Dorado for Aymara speakers' themselves. In their imaginings of themselves and the broader Aymara sphere, *Aymara puro* remained forever just beyond reach, spoken by some other "real" Aymaras, always a bit further off in the mountainous heartland.

These scenes, of the urban intellectual in his library and the rural artisan visiting the city, involve Aymaras from different walks of life, each taking up seemingly opposite stances of evaluation toward their own speech, stances of pride and shame, respectively. Yet they both represent different responses to a set of shared experiences of being Aymaras in Bolivia, two sides of the same coin as it were. Whether urban or rural, Aymaras live in a society profoundly shaped by centuries of colonialism and an ongoing social climate of anti-Indian racism.[6] The Aymara intellectual who cultivates appreciation and prestige for his language and the rural Aymara speakers who express doubt in the worthiness of their language for study, both respond to long dominant ideologies within Bolivian society that uphold a racialized sociolinguistic hierarchy in which Aymaras, other Indigenous Bolivians, and their linguistic practices are denigrated and devalued. In the Bolivian context, to take pride in the Aymara language, to affirm its richness, complexity, and subtlety is to oppose its characterizations as a mere "dialect," not in the linguistic sense of a regional variety a language, but as something less than a language. To a certain degree, the rural Aymara speakers who suggested their language might not even count as Aymara may have internalized precisely such a view. Yet, even the rural Aymaras, filled with self-doubt in their own language, still held on to the idea that some other Aymaras could exemplify the beauty and elegance of expression they know their language can achieve. The notion of a standard against which their own Aymara speech could be measured, even if in ways that deem them deficient, remained strong.

In these interactions with the rural speakers in particular, Michael Silverstein's (2023: 160) insight about standard language ideologies operating as a widespread and pervasive framework for understanding language variation in post-Enlightenment societies resonates: "standardization as a cultural condition pervades and transforms people's consciousness of their own language. It becomes a lens through which they perceive, process, and evaluate the ubiquitous and inevitable situational variability of how language is actually used." An irony here is that the very ideology that has marginalized speakers of Indigenous and minoritized languages is often the very ideology upon which these speakers draw in projects of language reclamation. A related and similarly cruel irony is that the enlightenment ideologies foundational to notions of standard were also largely predicated on the construal of Indigenous Americans as the exemplars of the "state of nature" against which European Enlightenment theories of reason, governance, and social-contract theories would be construed, along with "terra nullis" rationalizations of the European colonization of the Americas.[7]

With this book I make no claims of having located the El Dorado of "pure Aymara" in any geographic or demographic sense. Indeed, interactions like the one above only further convinced me that such an exercise is a sociolinguistic fools-errand. This is because, as with other languages and their standard varieties, the notion of a "pure" language that serves as a normative model for expression exists primarily in the minds of speakers as an aspirational norm. These normative models often emanate from institutional sites ranging from family units, to national education systems, and national academies cultivate, develop, and enforce these models of a standard.

Prominent institutions of language standardization such as the *Académie Française* or the *Real Academia Española* were founded through royal initiatives, in 1634 and 1713, respectively, but the standardization of language they authorized and anchored came to be a hallmark of enlightenment notions of the nation-state. Language was central to Enlightenment theories of reason, science, and political order, a social order premised on multiple and interlocked exclusions of women, the rural, the propertyless, and others deemed savages (Bauman and Briggs 2000; Bauman and Briggs 2003). From the sixteenth century onward, European Enlightenment thinkers advanced ideologies and state institutions eventually enacted practices which buttressed a people-polity-language hybrid which became increasingly naturalized, despite the "natural" state of affairs nearly everywhere being much more multilingual and thoroughly varied than any such neat package presupposed or presumed to entail. The disorder of variation was precisely what enlightenment projects of homogenization aimed to overcome in order to achieve a presumably rational and ordered populace (Bauman and Briggs 2000, 2003). Language standardization was part and parcel of projecting the idea of notion of a unified and homogeneous language community-cum-People.

The emergence of a particular register of a language being taken to be a prestigious standard to which speakers normatively orient is a result of one particular variety of a broader phenomenon, a social semiotic processes linguistic anthropologists refer to as *enregisterment* (Agha 2005; Agha 2007; Silverstein 2004). Asif Agha (2007: 81) defines enregisterment as those "processes and practices whereby performable signs become recognized (and regrouped) as belonging to distinct, differentially valorized semiotic registers by a population." Itself a token of the professional lexicon (register!) of linguistic anthropology, this term embeds another technical term, *register*, at its core. *Register* as a concept within sociolinguistics has long been treated as a linguistic phenomenon of relatively limited scope pertaining to specialized vocabulary within specified social domains, that is, the *legalese* of lawyers, the jargon of skilled trades, or even thieves' argots. Thus, the slippage above between lexicon and register points to this. This earlier conception of register as a lexical, rather than more broadly semiotic, phenomenon anchored to sociological facts of class and professional stratification situates the phenomenon as a potentially static detail of linguistic variation, rather than its organizing principle. Recognizing instead that the semiotic processes underpinning the *register*-ablity, that is, the salience and cultural noticeability, of regularities of differentiation among social kinds (speaking like a lawyer, a mechanic, a thief, or a linguistic anthropologist so as to be understood as one) is more than simply a lexical question, register within linguistic anthropology has expanded to a more broadly semiotic and processual concept. Agha (2007: 145) explains that registers are "cultural models of action that link diverse behavioral signs to enactable effects, including images of persona, interpersonal relationships, and type of conduct." This more expansive view of register via enregisterment emphasizes both registers' emergence from the activity and reanalysis of human social processes (thus, the "-ment" suffix of *enregisterment* denoting process) and also foregrounds conduct and perception (thus, the noun "register" made verb, to *en*-register). Registers are both ways of being, saying and doing in the world and also ways of seeing, hearing, perceiving, and categorizing the activities of others.

The convergence of processes of language standardization with their subsequent commodification within text artifacts like newspapers and novels in the wake of the advent of print-capitalism facilitated the conditions for the rise of bourgeois secular nationalist consciousness that became dominant in the post-Enlightenment world. These, at least, are some of the key elements of Benedict Anderson's (2006) widely influential account of the rise nationalist consciousness. To read in a standard language and participate in the "unisonance" of the voice-from-nowhere of the "imagined community" of the nation was the condition which made possible a consciousness of national solidarity shared among thousands of others, all within a polity of interchangeable selves and others (Anderson 2006: 74; Silverstein 2000: 120). Not just standard languages, but literacy and commodity circulation are central to this account.

What then of notions of standard that exist in contexts like the one encountered with the Aymara farmer above, contexts in which engagements with the language are first and foremost oral rather than text-artifacts like a realist novel? A central aim of *Voice and Nation in Plurinational Bolivia* is to examine the orientation to a notion of standard within a context of oral/aural engagements with the language. The coming chapters illuminate how Aymara speakers come to make audible a register of so-called "pure Aymara," or what I will show is better described as a *dehispanicized* register of the language. This register emanates from distinct, if sometimes overlapping, institutional projects of Aymara national belonging. The voice of the book's title does not refer to voice in the sense of a metaphor for political participation, nor is this a study of radio and song "giving voice" (Fisher 2016) to Aymaras, although there is certainly a concern with and sustained attention to varied forms of politics and political participation throughout the coming chapters. Instead, a focus on the voice here refers to the voice in speech, to the voice of radio broadcasters, musicians, rappers, and community members as they engage, with their voices, in the production, replication, and dissemination of a spoken emblem of Aymara nationhood—dehispanicized Aymara.

Pachakuti

Voice and Nation in Plurinational Bolivia is the result of research conducted among Aymara language radio broadcasters, hip-hop artists, and community members during a period of radical social change in Bolivia. This research was conducted during multiple field visits over a period of thirteen years (2006–19), a timeframe that overlaps with the presidencies of Evo Morales (2006–19). Morales' electoral victory came on the heels of a series of popular insurrections in 2000, 2003, and 2005 which centered on the control of the country's natural resources, particularly water (2000) and natural gas (2003) (Bjork-James 2020; Hines 2021). These movements extended throughout Bolivian society, having broad reach both in social and geographic terms, uniting rural communities with urban middle and working classes. These were massive social upheavals that brought down the governments of Presidents Sánchez de Lozada in 2003 and Carlos Mesa in 2005. While broad in social reach, it cannot be overstated how central Aymara mobilization, both through community organizations in the rural highlands and through the neighborhood councils of El Alto, was to these movements' victories. Aymara mobilization within these struggles also evoked watershed moments in both Aymara and Bolivian history: the siege of La Paz through roadblocks was reminiscent of the tactics of the 1781 uprising of Tupak Katari, and the demands for sovereign control over the nation's natural resources echoed those of the 1952–3 Bolivian Revolution (Hylton and Thomson 2007).

During the Morales presidencies, the renegotiation of rents on natural gas during a commodities boom brought in state revenue which facilitated increased services for poor and rural Bolivians, dramatically increasing the health and quality of life for millions. The minimum wage increased, the reduction of child poverty and infant mortality were prioritized, and dramatic improvements in rural infrastructure and development were achieved. Morales' political rise began as a leader of the coca grower's union and he became the candidate for a party which united diverse social movements of Indigenous, working class and rural interests, the *Movement to Socialism—Political Instrument for the Sovereignty of Peoples (MAS-IPSP,* or simply *MAS)*. The MAS platform articulated the demands of social movements, including the creation of a constituent assembly to redraft the nation's constitution on more democratic and egalitarian grounds to recognize and empower Bolivia's Indigenous peoples. In 2009, this new constitution was ratified and Bolivia became a Plurinational Republic, with guarantees for the autonomy of Indigenous nations and the recognition of the Aymara and Quechua languages and thirty-three other Indigenous languages, mostly of the tropical lowlands, alongside Spanish as official languages.

Morales' victory was part of a broader political shift in the region which came to be known as a "pink tide" of left-wing governments across Latin America. The beginning of the twenty-first century saw left-wing governments come to power throughout the region—in Ecuador, Peru, Venezuela, Argentina, Uruguay, Brazil, and Nicaragua. This shift promised to break decades of US led neoliberal hegemony, or "Washington Consensus," which had advanced the slashing of social services and the privatization of public enterprises, and the incursion of US corporate interests. The "pink tide" represented a rejection of these policies on a broad regional scale. Understanding these developments only in regional terms, or in broad abstractions like "neoliberalism" or "globalization" obscures crucial social dynamics particular to Bolivia; notably, the long tradition of Indigenous struggle in the country.

Many Bolivians, supporters and critics of the MAS government alike, have referred to the political developments of recent years as *el proceso de cambio* "the process of change," a process also characterized as decolonization by Aymaras, other Bolivians, and scholars alike. US-based anthropological accounts of social movements in Bolivia have shared similar assessments. Bret Gustafson (2009), for example, characterizes this moment in Bolivian social history as an "indigenous resurgence" with his ethnographic account of the of Bolivian Guaranis who engage with the state, international development agencies, and hostile local elites while building their own projects of Indigenous political autonomy. Nancy Postero's (2006) ethnography of local responses to ascendant Indigenous movements and Evo Morales' electoral victory describes Bolivia's political landscape as one of "post-neoliberal multiculturalism," which, in contrast to the multiculturalism of late twentieth century (c.f. Hale 2006), aims to transform social relations rather than simply assimilating into them. A more local characterization of this period by commentators, both

Indigenous and not, draws on a term used in both Quechua and Aymara languages—*pachakuti* (Gutiérrez 2014; Hylton and Thomson 2007; Rivera-Cusicanqui 2008). Historically, *pachakuti* was used to describe the upheaval of Spanish invasion and the dissolution of the Inka Empire, but it has also been used to characterize moments of rebellion and upheaval. In both Quechua and Aymara, it is a compound word of two parts, *pacha* meaning "time" and also "space" and *kuti* meaning "return," "turn over," but also "turn" as in one's turn at cards. In this last sense, *pacha* and *kuti* both resonate with the corresponding contrast between Greek terms for "time" *chronos* and *kairos*, respectively, as the difference between secular everyday time (*chronos*) and the messianic event (*kairos*), between continuity and rupture, between flowing time and the fleeting moment. *Pachakuti*, then, is the turning over of spacetime, the overturning of the world, and has a distinctly messianic temporality. *Pachakuti* is a time when, in the words of historian Sinclair Thomson, "Indians alone will rule," an inversion of previously dominant social relations (Thomson 2004). *Pachakuti* is perhaps best translated simply as "revolution."

Aymara in Radio and Song

The opening scenes of the linguist and the farmer illustrated diverging responses to linguistic and cultural oppression—of hypervalorization on the one hand and shame on the other—that are widely recognizable beyond Bolivia. Similar dynamics have emerged elsewhere in contexts where minoritized and Indigenous languages come to mark membership in an oppressed class of people. Linguistic discrimination is a common and widespread feature of societies that have emerged from colonialism, a legacy of colonialism easily identified throughout the Americas and the globe. Speakers of Indigenous and minoritized languages find themselves increasingly embattled, but also demonstrate creativity and resilience through diverse modes of language advocacy (Davis 2018; De Korne 2021; Wroblewski 2022). *Voice and Nation* illuminates the linguistic dimensions of social change, belonging, and political conflict within the ethnographically specific context of highland Bolivia, but speaks to questions of global concern. Organized into two sections, one on radio and one on song, this book listens to Aymara language advocacy from devout Catholics, from union militants, from hip-hop artists and fans, and community members who hear in their language both the past and the future of Bolivia's Aymaras.

In many societies, educational institutions occupy privileged sites for the cultivation and valorization of standard varieties of languages. So, why pursue a focus on radio and song? As a former bilingual education teacher, I had initially come to Bolivia with an interest in the experiences of Indigenous language teachers working within the field of Intercultural Bilingual Education (IBE) (Hornberger and Swinehart 2012a; Hornberger and Swinehart 2012b). This was a logical beginning point for me, but there were a number of considerations that eventually moved my attention toward the realms of radio and music. First and foremost, I was motivated by conversations with Aymara speakers themselves who directed me quickly beyond traditional sites of education. When speaking with Aymaras from different walks of life about the status and future of the Aymara language in Bolivia, rather than directing me to remote rural towns as the farmer, and admittedly many others, had done, or to schools where Aymara was the language of instruction, as I had initially planned, many instead suggested I tune into Radio San Gabriel, the longest running Aymara language radio station in the country. According to them, this was where one could hear Aymara spoken with beauty and elegance. In terms of identifying institutions from which an "authoritative model of standard" emanated, this radio station was being identified clearly by speakers themselves as a prominent one. That such an institution would be a radio station is perhaps less surprising given the long tradition and ongoing presence of Aymara language radio (Albó 1974; Archondo 1991; Grebe and von Gleich 2001; O'Connor 2006), which contrasts to the situation of Aymara language literacy, or rather illiteracy. Well into the twentieth century up until the revolution of 1952, literacy for many Aymaras in any language was actively suppressed under conditions of servitude, or what was referred to as *pongeaje* within the hacienda system prior to the 1952 revolution (Machaca 2007; Pérez 1992).[8] Mass literacy among Aymaras is first and foremost in Spanish and literacy in the Aymara language remains a recent, uneven, and still often aspirational phenomenon.

In addition to radio broadcasting, discussions with Aymara speakers about contexts in which Aymara language cultural production was most dynamic often led them to bring up an even more surprising context, the hip-hop scene in El Alto. People beamed with pride and optimism in mentioning that Aymara youth were composing and performing rhymes in the language. Reorienting from classroom contexts to settings more in the realm of "education, broadly conceived," I became convinced that comparative ethnographic study of these different Aymara institutions' could convey the complexities of sociocultural process unfolding in Bolivia along the axes of language, culture, and Aymara national belonging. Rather than the more traditional educational settings I had become familiar with in my own professional life, the contexts of radio broadcasting and musical sociality stood out as dynamic arenas of Aymara language cultural production, each offering rich possibilities to study how notions of linguistic prestige were being consolidated, differentially valued, and disseminated among Aymara speakers.

Organization of the Book

The book's first section brings us to two radio stations, the prominent Jesuit-run radio station, Radio San Gabriel, in Chapter 2 and, in Chapter 3, an examination of a popular political talk-show run by members of the Aymara rural teacher's union on the radio station of the Aymara Education Council. The first of these two chapters offers a linguistic ethnographic account of how the longest running Aymara language radio station in Bolivia cultivates its prestige as a center of Aymara linguistic authority. This chapter examines the procedures of the radio station's Aymara Language Department as its members write and approve the scripts of all broadcasts to ensure the dissemination of dehispanicized Aymara, free of any traces of bilingual speech. Through interviews with members of the radio station's Aymara Language Department about their experiences at the station, this chapter illuminates how the recruiting and hiring of members of this department upends otherwise dominant regimes of value within Bolivian society by privileging rural Aymara women as model speakers of dehispanicized Aymara. Analysis of the opening segments of a program called "Aymara language" offers concrete examples of the use of neologisms for time, revealing a conflict between the Gregorian calendar and Aymara modes of time reckoning.

Chapter 3 takes us to the flagship program of the radio station of the *Consejo Educativo Aymara* "Aymara Education Council" (CEA), an organization of Aymara bilingual rural teachers, in which a speech genre of deliberative discourse surrounding the chewing of coca, called *akhulli* in Aymara, serves as the inspiration for the show, in both its name and format. This multilingual program is often mostly in Spanish, yet the show's host opens, closes, and provides summaries and commentary in fully dehispanicized Aymara. When the host quotes the Aymara public, however, this public speaks Spanish. This chapter demonstrates how not just speaking Aymara qua linguistic code, but also adopting an orientation to ideas about what constitutes distinctively Aymara norms of speaking, or a distinctively Aymara *metapragmatics* (Silverstein 1976), becomes a point of commentary among Aymaras. Evaluations of what counts as stereotypically Aymara also provide a focus of attention throughout this chapter as both the host and his guests articulate stereotypes of Aymara personhood in the course of the show. This chapter presents a case where represented speech and political representation converge through typifications of the Aymara and broader Bolivian public made by the show's host and guests, politicians courting the Aymara vote.

The second section of the book examines the politics of Aymara language in song, and in particular, kinds of song that have not traditionally been sung in Aymara: hip-hop and the national anthem. The La Paz/El Alto metropolitan region is home to a vibrant hip-hop scene which includes Aymara rappers (Hornberger and Swinehart 2012a; Swinehart 2012c; Swinehart 2019b). Drawing on interviews, ethnographic accounts of performances, and analysis of lyrics, the first chapter in the book's second section examines Aymara hip-hop as an intervention in the sociolinguistic terrain of the city that unsettles prevailing assumptions about the nature of language shift among the children of rural migrants to the city. These artists disseminate models of Aymara subjectivity which overlap with those discussed in earlier chapters, but also diverge in important ways. While lyrically establishing connections between contemporary Aymara struggles with historic ones, these artists also situate Aymaras in relation to African American and Black diasporic freedom struggles both lyrically and through their embrace of transnational hip-hop material culture (Swinehart 2019b).

The second part of the section on song, Chapter 5, examines the translation of the Bolivian national anthem into Aymara and its performance at the commemoration of a 1921 massacre of Aymaras by the Bolivian army (Choque Canqui 2010). My analysis in this chapter foregrounds latent tensions within Bolivian plurinationalism through a combined consideration of the indeterminacies of translation alongside an ethnographic account of the anthem's performance at a site of racial state violence. Sung at the site of a massacre, the militaristic lyrics take on uneasy valences and raise questions about how an Aymara nation is situated within the now plurinational republic. Questions of linguistic commensurability confront political projects as the new Aymara anthem translates *la patria* "fatherland" as *Qullasuyu*, a political unit from the era of the Inca Empire, and, in the process, semantically rescales the political aspirations of Aymara nationalism. As a performative, public enactment of citizenship, singing the anthem in the newly official Aymara confronts language ideologies that have long excluded Aymaras as citizens, but also challenges anti-statist Aymara political currents which previously rejected Bolivian nationalism (Alvizuri 2009).

These chapters correspond to different demographic groups of Aymaras living in and near the city of El Alto. The key figures involved in the Catholic radio station discussed in Chapter 2, Radio San Gabriel, while urban professionals living in El Alto, are migrants who have moved to the city from small communities across the Andean high plain. The participants in the El Alto hip-hop scene discussed in Chapter 4 are largely the children of such migrants to El Alto from the high plain. The teachers involved in the radio program in Chapter 4, and also the politicians whose interviews will be discussed, are urban Aymaras from El Alto and La Paz. The participants in the commemoration examined in Chapter 5 bridge the countryside and the urban periphery. These contrasts along lines of age and occupational affiliation motivated the selection of these sites for this study and, indeed, there are important ways that these cases diverge.

In the traditional social-science conception of field site, what follows is a straightforwardly comparative multi-sited ethnography organized around four case studies, each offering perspectives from diverse corners of Bolivian Aymara life. The motivation for such an approach was to abandon the pretense of treating "the Aymaras" as an ethnological monolith (cf. LaBarre 1948) with the hope of achieving an anti-essentialist ethnography of what are often essentialist projects.[9] While comparative and multi-sited, there is another sense in which this study looks and listens from one "site"—dehispanicized Aymara—from the perspective of the semiotic construct of a putatively pure Aymara language.[10] The aim instead is to offer comparative views from actors, individuals, and institutions, who take language as a deliberate object of poetic attention.

Poetics as Both Object and Analytic

The radio programmers and hip-hop artists, much like the linguist Juan de Dios Yapita with his morphemic poem, embrace Aymara's poetic possibilities as they make aesthetic decisions to foreground its distinctiveness, particularly, but not only, vis-a-vis Spanish. The poetic organization of language in this regard will constitute both an object of study and also a method for its approach (Silverstein 1976;

Silverstein 2004). The mid-twentieth-century linguist Roman Jakobson's work on the relationship between linguistics and poetics drew attention to the porous borders between literary and non-literary language, asserting a correspondence between "linguistic phenomena expanding in space and time and the spatial and temporal spread of literary models" (Jakobson 1960: 351). Jakobson's insights into the dialectic interplay of literary and non-literary language are particularly relevant when considering the global expansion of hip-hop. His proposition that poetic metricality was not limited to the genre of poetry but a feature of verbal interaction generally became a productive point of departure for linguistic anthropologists such as Dell Hymes, who drew on Jakobson's work to develop "ethnopoetics" as a means to analyze Native American oral narratives (Hymes 2003; 2004), and Michael Silverstein who drew on poetics as a method to diagram real-time negotiations between conversation participants (2004). For Silverstein, the poetic function "consists of a set of indexical relationships of utterance-segment to utterance segment that emerge from a superimposition of cardinal (*not* ordinal) metricality onto denotational text ..." (Silverstein 1993: 50). Silverstein's (1984, 1993, 2004) examinations of parallelism, repetition, and cohesive structure in conversation, and the indexicalities these serve to organize, demonstrated poetics as a productive methodological tool for illuminating interpersonal and propositional alignments and disalignments in discourse. The metrical organization of sound form through parallelism and repetition are not the only aspects of poetics to emerge as salient in the following cases. The aestheticization of speech, the drawing attention to the sound form of the spoken sign itself, has been referred to as poetics since perhaps the third-century BC when Aristotle wrote *Poetics*. He argued that the use of unfamiliar words and the alteration of familiar ones were key elements for establishing *distinction* in poetic speech:

> Foreign words, metaphor, ornamental words, and all the other varieties will ensure that it is not commonplace or low, and the common element will ensure clarity ... for being different from the regular form and thus varying the accustomed pattern, it will produce an effect of distinction, while at the same time by virtue of its overlapping with normal usage it will promote clarity.
>
> (59)

This insight will resonate with the cases examined in the coming chapters as we encounter archaicisms, neologisms, hispanicisms, and "foreign words" in broadcast discourse, but also in the speech of both rappers and hip-hop fans. These deployments of poetic language often function to delineate contrasting linguistic registers and, crucially, contrast as voices enregistered as belonging to distinct and locatable figures of personhood.

Some Introductions before We Begin: Q'aras, 2Pac, and Coca(ine)

There are technical concepts from linguistic anthropology that will reappear in the coming chapters which will be useful to introduce and explain here: *metapragmatics, emblems, rhematization,* and *figures of personhood*. These concepts undergird and relate to the notion, discussed above, of *enregisterment,* the term used to describe semiotic processes that group linguistic signs with non-linguistic ones, bundling diverse signs across modalities. In closing this introduction, I will discuss each of these in an introductory fashion through an anticipatory examination of a set of three cases, or semiotic objects, that will reappear at different points in the coming chapters: a racial slur, coca/cocaine, and the name 2Pac/Tupak. *Q'ara* is a powerful epithet that makes cameo appearances in Chapters 3 and 4. A derogatory term for whites, *q'aras,* provides an opportunity for understanding both *figures of personhood* and *rhematization,* or the tying of abstract qualities to observable ones. From stereotypic models of personhood, we move to a pair of biographic individuals by way of introducing of an important name that appears at multiple moments throughout the book: 2Pac/Tupak. This name's differential enregisterment underscores the important point that such processes unfold along particular trajectories within specific populations, but also ones that overlap and converge in ways that illuminate connections across time, space, and people. Finally, we come to one of the most potentially taboo, or at least illegal, and politically charged materials to come from the Andes—cocaine. An account of the political valences of coca and its contrasting modes of consumption, chewing coca or using cocaine, provides an opportunity for explaining coca's role as an *emblem* of Indigenous sovereignty and also the *metapragmatics* of Aymara speech and conduct surrounding its consumption, topics which return in Chapters 3 and 4.

Q'aras

Figures of personhood are social kinds that, as enregistered signs do generally, become perceivable through figure-ground contrasts of comparison within semiotic fields (Babel 2019) organized along axes of differentiation (Gal and Irvine 2019). In other words, figures of personhood may be defined not only with the qualities attributed to them, but also negatively, by what they are defined against, by what is presumed to be their opposite. In this chapter introducing readers to Aymaras, let me introduce the figure who is understood by many Bolivians to be their opposite—the *q'ara*.

Ask a Bolivian to translate the word *q'ara* to English and they would likely say "white," not in reference to the color, but to the racial category. The word is widely recognized in Bolivia among Spanish speakers and used untranslated within Spanish discourse. This raises the question of whether this translation would be from Aymara or Spanish?[11] Whereas *blanco* "white" purports to describe the physiognomy of light skin, Aymaras will explain that this is not an accurate translation, and that a better gloss would be "naked" (*pelado* in Spanish). The explanation that follows is that colonizers arrived with nothing and had to take everything from the Natives in order to live, including the labor and wealth of others. Silvia Rivera-Cusicanqui suggests the term implies a subject who is culturally stripped and living off the efforts of others (Rivera Cusicanqui 2012: 105).[12] It is not just that the person is of a different ethnicity or skin color, the term suggests that they embody a strange and sinister combination of vulnerability, neediness, laziness, and greed.[13]

Q'ara invokes historical and ongoing inequalities with a single harsh two-syllable word laden with both contempt and resentment. The word begins with an unvoiced post-velar ejective stop /q'/. This sound is not only absent from Spanish, but also widely perceived by Spanish speakers as difficult and harsh. Difficult, harsh, contemptuous, and resentful, are all qualities that figure into the negative stereotypes of Aymaras that circulate in Bolivia (Swinehart 2012a). Conflating the quality of a language's sounds (difficult and harsh) with the character of its speakers provides a clear example of *rhematization* (Gal and Irvine 2019: 19). Taken on a whole, *q'ara* is linguistic sign that affords a particularly nasty and potent double indexicality. In two short syllables, the term denigrates the person to whom it refers while simultaneously confirming and replicating the negative attributes (harsh, difficult) presumed to belong to the speaker who utters it.

2Pac and Tupak

These homophonous names, 2Pac and Tupak, are distinguished on this page through orthography, but also by the reader's prior exposure to hip-hop, Andean history, or both. That is to say, each has been "enregistered among a specific population" delimited by their prior encounters with these signs, the names 2Pac and Tupak. The first, 2Pac, is the name of one of the greatest selling hip-hop artists of all time, even years after his death. The second is a name shared by Indigenous Andean revolutionaries from the late eighteenth century, the Quechua Tupak Amaru II and the Aymara Tupak Katari, and others before them (Stern 1987; Thomson 2004). A reader familiar with the history of hip-hop or the Black Panther party may also know these names are linked by more than homophony.[14] The history of anti-colonial uprisings in the Andes inspired Afeni Shakur, a member of the Black Panther Party, to name her son after one of its leaders, Tupak Amaru II (Hoye and Ali 2003). For her, the name Tupak was also an emblem, a sign of antiracist, anticolonial resistance recognized by millions of Indigenous people across the Andes. Born Alice Faye Williams, the name she took as an adult identified lineages other than kinship, of political stance and religious affiliation, and expressive of aspirational qualities, Afeni, from Yoruba for "lover of people," and Shakur, from Arabic for "thankful" (Colin 2019).

The Tupaks of the eighteenth century had also changed their names for similar reasons. Tupak Katari was born Julián Apaza and Tupak Amaru II was born José Gabriel Condorcanqui. In taking these names they both honored the sixteenth century Tupak Amaru, the last Inca leader to assert this title, and also invoked aspirational qualities through the very name, *tupaj* "shinging" meaning "brilliant or shining" in Quechua, and *amaru* (Quechua) and *katari* (Aymara) meaning serpent, invoking both phallic and subterranean powers associated with the animal. Multiple *rhematizations* are afforded by Shakur's and the Tupak's renaming, both the referential/denotational attributions of abstract qualities ("grateful love of the people" for Shakur; "brilliant male leadership" for the Tupaks) and also, maybe more crucially, by adopting of African and Indian names under regimes of white supremacist colonial violence, these names operate as signs of anti-racist confrontation and solidarity with the colonized. In Hoye and Ali's 2003 biography of Shakur, they quote him as having said, "I was named after this Inca chief whose name was Tupac Amaru ... He was a deep dude. If I go to South America, they gonna love me. I'm telling you. They know Tupac" (Hoye and Ali 2003: 8). We will read more in Chapter 3 how right he was. When Tupac Shakur insisted, "Holla if ya hear me!" they answered. One of the things that we will hear them call out in Chapter 4 is, "*La coca, ce n'est pas cocaína.*"

Coca/Cocaine

¡La coca no es cocaína! "Coca is not cocaine" is a slogan that be found on shirts, mugs, stickers, and other souvenirs sold to tourists across Bolivia. This is not only to get the tourist dollar, but also to educate foreigners who conflate the coca with its alkaloid derivative and are ignorant of both the plant's legal ubiquity in the Andes and the devastating human cost of the efforts at its eradication. A highly politicized leaf, coca is also banal, or sacred, a cure-all, or a curse, depending on who one asks. Chewing coca is a widespread practice in Bolivia and throughout the central Andes. Coca leaves are also central to a range of religious and ritual practices of Aymara, Quechua and non-native Andeans alike.[15] More everyday contexts include the infusion of coca leaves for tea and also as medicinal remedy for many, seemingly any, ailments. It is also chewed as a stimulant in work situations requiring endurance, whether in mines, construction sites, agriculture, or behind the wheel of a taxi. The alert but relaxed bodily state can help facilitate work, stave off hunger, and during community meetings, for example, help participants maintain a meditative, philosophical disposition and be attentive to the contributions of one's interlocutors.[16] Coca undergirds a broad range of activities and their accompanying modes of sociality. How people navigate and adjust the norms operative within these diverse scenes of social life concerns *metapragmatics*, not just the effects of language per se, but also the act of typifying these effects, whether as polite or impolite, Aymara or *q'ara*, or within any other possible axis of differentiation. Metapragmatic expectations of the communicative conduct expected within a stereotypical scene of Aymara coca chewing and of what is metapragmatically normative for Aymaras versus *q'aras* are central topics in Chapter 3.

In the face of US-led efforts to eradicate the plant, the coca leaf became an emblem of both Bolivian national sovereignty and of the resilience of Indigenous Andean cultural practices. Rather than on souvenirs, in the years and decades before the election of Morales, the slogan would just as likely be found on banners or shouted at demonstrations by *cocaleros*, coca farmers and their supporters opposing US-backed coca eradication projects, which involved the presence of the US Drug Enforcement Agency in Bolivia. In Chapter 4, we will encounter this slogan again, and now as a refrain in a song, transformed yet again, not only in verse but in French.

In its status as a slogan, repeated across modalities (shirts, mugs, banners, etc.), the slogan is itself is an *emblem*, an indexical icon of a political stance against coca eradication and in support of Bolivian sovereignty in the face of US overreach. For some, the practice of chewing coca serves as a metonym for Aymara resilience and of national sovereignty. For others, it is a reminder of Bolivia's proximity to a transnational trafficking of cocaine. Morales' detractors accuse him and his supporters of being lowlifes and *narraficantes* and also use *comecoca* "coca-eater" as an insult. This insult also projects a figure of personhood, albeit a negative one, a figure who, with a cheek swollen from a wad of coca and speech distorted from chewing it, hurls back a reciprocal and opposing epithet—*q'ara*.

Figures of personhood are emblematic models, stereotypes of nameable social kinds (such as *q'ara*, above) to which individuals and groups may take up different forms of alignment and disalignment. They may aspire to embody and represent such a figure, just as well as they may reject and differentiate themselves from the qualities presumed to belong to such a character, or may simply become topics of commentary and debate. In this way, they are central for understanding the metapragmatic protocols surrounding the social contours of belonging and exclusion. As stereotypes, figures of personhood necessarily are ideational, not flesh and blood people, even though they rely on materiality, including human material. Their enregisterment depends on identifiable embodied representatives. They ideologically recruit materiality for that simple fact that signs require perceivable vehicles, whether the sensuousness of sound (the harsh /q'a/ of *q'ara*), articles of clothing, or a speaking body, a person who may come to stand in as an embodied representative of a social kind (Shankar and Cavanaugh 2012, 2017). Figures of personhood group together perceivable signs including bodies, language, work habits, occupation, gender, and others, and unify within apparently discrete categories of social personhood. Without prior processes of enregisterment having taken place, such a diverse array of signs would otherwise seem unrelated. For outsiders unfamiliar with such register formations, they are just that, unmoored from frameworks of stereotypy. Once these semiotic bundles (Keane 2003) are perceivable and are taken to be naturalized and congruent by a social group, that is, enregistered, people negotiate footings with them, and with other people through them. This is why understanding how ongoing processes of the Aymara language's enregisterment unfold cannot be separated from questions of how notions of race and nation are structured in Bolivian society. In a plurinational society marked by wide-scale multilingualism, there is a near kaleidoscopic array of orientations to how linguistic practices become semiotically tied up with politics and personhood. The aim in the coming chapters is to listen to some of the ways that Aymara linguistic practices have become implicated in models of social personhood in this transformative period of resurgent Indigenous political power.

Part One

Radio

Radio broadcast is distinctive among media for both its immediacy and the sense of intimacy it is able to convey. For listening audiences, the mobility and relative low cost of radio has made it a popular companion to people in solitary work, farmers in remote fields, and truckers on long drives. Radio has been a prominent media form in Bolivia, and among Aymaras in La Paz and throughout the broader high plain region in particular, since it first appeared in the early twentieth century. Both historically and today, radio enjoys a higher profile in Bolivia than in many Latin American countries, a prominence that is likely a result of the intimate relationship between radio and political mobilization throughout Bolivia's tumultuous twentieth century, a relationship that has continued into the twenty-first century (Albó 1974; Archondo 1991; Grebe and von Gleich 2001; O'Connor 2006). In the first half of the last century, during the inaugural period of radio's presence in Bolivia, it arrived as a source of hope for both state modernizers and Christian proselytizers for their respective projects of making citizens and saving the souls of Bolivia's geographically dispersed and largely Indigenous rural population. Radio broadcast promised to facilitate the reaching of these populations spread over a massive and geographically challenging terrain. The low cost and wide reach of radio emissions made it a medium of particular utility in Bolivia's mountainous and extensive territory.

By the 1940s, there were thirty radio stations throughout the country and sixteen in La Paz alone (Quisbert 2003: 26). Radio began shaping the sonic imaginary of this large and diverse country. The state-sponsored Radio Illimani, founded in 1933, played an important role in bringing Indigenous Andean musical genres into the homes of urban creoles and allowed for this music to begin to sound "national" and "folkloric" to urban audiences, rather than being musical genres narrowly associated with rural and Indian contexts (Bigenho 2005: 69–70).

As Brian Larkin has shown in his work on colonial infrastructure and media in northern Nigeria (2008), the adoption of new technologies and their eventual use often exceeds and rarely neatly calibrates with the intentions of those who introduce them. Upon adopting and making use of the novel medium of radio, rural and working-class Bolivians set about using it for their own ends. A particularly prominent example of this is the case of worker at the center of Bolivia's most profitable economic sector, the mining of tin and other minerals. Miners' radios played a crucial role in the dissemination of Marxist and anarchist ideas in the decades leading up to the 1952 revolution (O'Conner 2004, 2006).

In the decades following the 1952 revolution, Aymara language broadcasting expanded from serving audiences primarily in a utilitarian modality of providing news to become increasingly a source of entertainment and a realm for the development of Aymara language expressive culture. Radio theater in the Aymara language became popular on the Jesuit radio station Radio San Gabriel, with serial performances that would have their finales performed for live audiences in El Alto (Fujita 2011: 3). During the military governments of the 1960s and 1970s, Aymara language programing served as an important vehicle for political education, even under conditions of state surveillance and censure. Camouflaged through both allegory and the Aymara language itself, radio programmers were able to engage in political programming in Aymara, where in the Spanish language they might not have been able. One program, called *Los Cuentos del Achachila*, or "Tales of the Ancestor,"[1] disguised reports and commentary on contemporary events as folktales (Fujita 2011: 5). One radio technician who worked on this program recounted this experience as follows: "Before 1980 during the Banzer dictatorship, programs came out more camouflaged ... stories with scenes in which animals portrayed situations that the peasantry was living through at the time ... One letter sent from the countryside, about *Los Cuentos del Achachila,* said literally: 'The lion is Banzer, the dogs are his military, we are the sheep ... ' Naturally, we couldn't reproduce it like that on the radio" (Gianotten 2006: 70–1, cited in Fujita 2011: 5).

In the two decades following the return to democratic government in 1982, radio played a central role in a crucial political development of the period among Aymaras, the broader La Paz region, and, ultimately, the Bolivian national stage. The first electoral party to successfully address Aymaras as Aymaras in Bolivia, Conciencia de Patria (Condepa), emerged from the success of a prominent radio figure, Carlos Palenque (1944–97). Palenque began as a musician and subsequently became a popular media personality and founder of Radio y Televisión Popular (RTP). His successful program *La tribuna libre del pueblo*, simultaneously broadcast on radio and television, became a forum for denouncing corruption, poverty, and social issues in La Paz and Bolivia. Media anthropologist Jeff Himpele describes Palenque's political efficacy at transforming his program's audience into a political base as arising from the dynamic between the direct participation of the public in the program and the political analysis he offered as host. "As if [Palenque] were able to stem the social crisis, after the presentation of each case Palenque would take the participants' (often incoherent) testimonies and provide for them and viewers a soothing and therapeutically coherent framework of understanding" (Himpele 2002: 305). While his programming was primarily in Spanish, it was not monolingual. Palenque addressed a bilingual audience and engaged them through the notable and prominent participation of a bilingual cohost, Remedios Loza. Loza was not only bilingual, but an Aymara *chola*, or urban Indigenous woman.[2] Loza fielded calls from listeners who called in speaking Aymara and otherwise served as an Aymara translator on the program (Archondo 1991: 109). Condepa's founding congress was held at the ruins of Tiwanaku and its campaigns prominently incorporated Aymara iconography, including the *wiphala* flag of the Indigenous movements, moves that attracted some voters but also raised the ire of diverse critics. Aymara nationalists, for example, leveled the accusation that these were cynical gestures of ethnic opportunism (Archondo 1991: 203). In an upset of the elections of 1989, Condepa secured enough votes (13 percent nationally and 28.15 percent nationally) for Condepa to secure seats in Congress. Remedios Loza became the first Aymara woman "*de pollera*" (who wears clothing typical of urban Aymara women) to hold a seat in Congress (Himpele 2002: 314). His wife, Mónica Medina, was elected mayor of La Paz in 1994; but only three years later, the same year Palenque would run for president, his political trajectory was tragically cut short by a fatal heart attack.

The legacy and history of both miners' radios and the political interventions of RTP inform both radio audiences and radio broadcasters' understandings of local radio in Bolivia. The commercial radio of RTP in the 1980s and 1990s and the radio broadcasts of militant miners decades before it represent different modes of radiophonic politics than the two radio stations in the coming two chapters. Like these historic cases, both Radio San Gabriel and Radio Pacha Qamasa stand in the tradition of Aymara political media protagonism, if in different ways. While Radio Pacha Qamasa (Chapter 3) is clearly aligned with the class protagonism of miners' radio from decades earlier, Radio San Gabriel (Chapter 2) operates in alignment with a stance of public service and commitment to the poor and working classes, if in an idiom of Jesuit piety rather than the charismatic populism of Palenque and Condepa. The two cases in the coming section stand out, however, for their explicit address of Aymaras as a people. While neither of these radio stations are commercial in the same fashion as Palenque's was, both Radio San Gabriel and Radio Pacha Qamasa operate on a scale that exceeds what "independent radio" might evoke for many readers. Neither are they "independent" per se, either. Radio San Gabriel is a Catholic radio station, operating within the context of the diocese of La Paz, while Radio Pacha Qamasa has operated as an extension of an organization of Aymara rural teachers, the Aymara Education Council.

The long history of Aymara language broadcasting contrasts sharply with the paucity of Aymara in television, film, and print media. There are notable and prominent exceptions. While some films have been made in the Aymara language, like *Ukamau* (1966) by the neorealist director Jorge Sanjinés (Himpele 2004, 2007; Schiwy 2008), and Bolivian state television has developed occasional, and often short-lived, Aymara language programs, such as the *Entre Culturas* (Between Cultures), these serve as exceptions that prove the rule of Spanish language dominance within Bolivian film and television. Aymara texts circulate in educational settings, particularly at the primary-level Aymara where intercultural bilingual education (IBE) emphasizes textual literacy (Arnold and Yapita 2005; López 2007), and in those corners of higher education tied to IBE (Hornberger and Hult 2008; Hornberger and Swinehart 2012). Still, the number of Aymara speakers who regularly engage with their language in written form remains very few. Considering this range of Aymara language media, both historically and today, radio has been and continues to be the Aymara language media form with the greatest reach among Aymara speakers, making it of particular interest as a site from which notions of a standard have emanated.

That the speech of the radio broadcasters whom we will encounter in the coming chapters is articulated under conditions of professional distinction is important for a number of reasons. Verbal dexterity, linguistic ability, and the very quality of one's voice combine not simply as incidental features of characteristic of one's speech, but as the prerequisite, achievement, and result of their professional practice. In contrast to media forms like television or film, radio broadcast is an exclusively auditory medium. Where enticing good looks may play an important role in securing fame for the television star, it is the ear not the eye that must be seduced in order to draw in a listener. Of course, many professions rely on the cultivation of linguistic skills for their practice. This is clearly the case for lawyers, clergy, academics, journalists, and other writers.

Some of these professions, like clergy or academics, involve considerable mastery of verbal communication and demand mastery of profession-specific genres of oratory, such as the sermon or the university lecture. Still, among professions, few rely on the voice alone to cultivate an audience in the way that a radio personality must.

Analyzing spoken language that is both directed to a target audience and produced within a framework of professional distinction leads me to draw on the concept of *mediatization*. Asif Agha (2011) defines mediatization as what occurs when communicative process becomes embedded within moments of commodity formulation, or, "institutional practices that reflexively link processes of communication to processes of commoditization" (Agha 2011: 163). This conception of mediatization differs from other conceptualizations of the same term within media studies literature (cf. Hjalvard 2008) where often it refers more broadly to an omnipresence of mediation, a saturated mediascape that results in political actors' orientation to "the media" rather than to a deliberating public of their voting constituents (Hjalvard 2008). These formulations of "mediatization" often replicate anxieties about public disenfranchisement while failing to provide an analytic for understanding communicative process within capitalist societies. These anxieties often echo Jürgen Habermas's laments of the demise of "the public sphere," laments which overestimate the extent to which a "rational critical liberal subject" existed in the first place, and obscures the exclusions such a formulation of a public sphere presupposed, of women, the propertyless, and the enslaved. Such formulations also ignore the extent to which early moments of democratic discourse were facilitated by commodity circulation in the first place. We may consider, for example, that the *print capitalism* of Anderson's (2006) account was a circulation of ideas facilitated through an exchange of commodities, newspapers, pamphlets, and other print.

Aymara language radio presents a case where mediatized discourse facilitates the consolidation of a public that is cast within a nationalist frame, but through in an oral/aural modality rather than through the circulation of print media, the novels and newspapers discussed by Habermas (1989) or Anderson (2006). Still, there are similarities to Anderson's account, particularly when one considers the centrality of temporality, real and imagined, of simultaneity. The simultaneity of broadcast, the spoken address to a nation, and the aural experience of hearing one's nation via broadcast are the analogous formative discursive interventions here. While speech on the radio has a different durability than a print artifact, as spoken texts, these still emerge through processes in which language, the command of not just a linguistic code but a particular register combined with verbal skill and quality, enters into moments of commodity formulation through the labor market. The speech practices examined in the coming chapters come under scrutiny within institutional frameworks by speakers who are professionally accountable for their linguistic performance, making their language more than simply unselfconscious, "natural" behavior. Rather than removing such talk from the purview of linguistic scholarship, an interlocked set of aims combine in providing accounts of the Aymara language's mediatization: to illuminate the social relations both informing and emerging out of these cultural workers' linguistic labor, and to describe how this reflexive process shapes notions of standard, that is, enregisters a dehispanicized register of the Aymara language for the airwaves.

To speak in such a way that demonstrates a masterful command of a prestige register of a language, while also executing an elocution that attracts and holds the attention of a listening audience is no small feat. While journalists, radio hosts, and most other media professionals are held to linguistic standards in ways that the rest of us are not in our everyday lives, this is often even more starkly the case for those working in Indigenous and minoritized language contexts. Examining this dynamic with respect to Buryat-language journalists in post-Soviet Siberian Russia, Kathryn Graber (2020) writes that "when the language in which journalists work is itself a strong marker of ethnonational identity, their status as language workers takes on new importance and scrutiny—especially when that language is in jeopardy" (Graber 2020: 144). In the Buryat case, a literary standard had been developed during the early Soviet period that served as reference point not only for print media, but also for radio. The mediatization of the literary standard in the context of radio broadcast came to provide a source model for standard language fluency, something which carried with it unintended consequences. "Radio and television interviews in particular … are sites of public performance in which ideas about what it means to speak Buryat 'correctly' become clear. Ultimately, language shift, uneven control of the standard, and racialized expectations of 'good' public performance conspire to produce a kind of performance anxiety in people" (Graber 2020: 171). In other words, the hyperfluency of language professionals in the public sphere can also make degrees of semifluency of listening audiences even more conspicuous, and even introduce feelings of inadequacy at odds with the official aims of language revival efforts. This need not necessarily be the case, and there are also examples where radio broadcasts in Indigenous and minoritized languages accommodate and even promote dialectal diversity, rather than adherence to a standard (see Ennis 2019 and Urla 1995, 2012 for Kichwa and Basque examples, respectively).

In an influential study of New Zealand radio announcer's talk, sociolinguist Alan Bell (1984) coined the term "audience design" to describe how broadcasters adjust their speech when addressing in-studio guests as compared to their listening audience beyond the studios. Radio serves as more than a repository of naturalistic speech available to sociolinguistic study. Audiences are not simply a priori entities, but are also constituted through the very act of address. Whether constituting audiences as modern consuming subjects, as Debra Spitulnik has shown in Zambia (1996), or as anti-capitalist opposition to the state, in the case of Basque free radio (Urla 1995), radio programmers orient to their listeners, not simply as vague and passive audiences, but also orient to them as presupposed social groups who, through being hailed as audiences, come to embody the possibility-cum-promise of an agentive community.

In the process of addressing audiences, the presuppositions that radio broadcasters hold about their audiences, and the discursive events which they believe to be compelling, become analytically available through the public nature of broadcasts. A famous example from the history of US radio provides an example of the powerful interdiscursive potential of radio broadcast within a framework of political address. Shortly following the advent of a mass radio listening audience in the United States, President Franklin Delano Roosevelt framed his broadcasts to the nation in a paternal framework of hearth and home by calling these "fireside chats." By the final five years of his presidency these broadcasts reached an estimated fifty percent of US households (Craig 2005: 156). Radio is a media form in which speech genres themselves regularly become mediatized and foregrounded as the interpretive frame for broadcasts. While not a presidential address, the radio broadcasts examined in Chapter 3 appear to have a similar aspiration, to address an Aymara nation while invoking an interactional scene external and distant from the recording studio, but one evocative and iconicly suggestive of Aymara political sovereignty—the chewing of coca during deliberative community meetings. This involves not only invoking familiar scenes and practices, but also invoking particular metapragmatic frameworks, that is, particular expectations and norms about the conditions, constraints, and effects of how participants will speak. Similar to what Tamar Katriel has demonstrated with "dugri speech" on Israeli radio invoking metapragmatic tropes about the earnestness and directness, in Chapter 3, we will see that the implications of invoking the scene of coca chewing on the radio goes beyond sociolinguistic norms and into the realm of Aymara metapragmatics. In the cases that follow, there is an address of Aymaras as a people. In the first case, Radio San Gabriel, they are hailed as a faithful flock of devout Catholics and, in the second, Radio Pacha Qamasa, they are addressed as politically engaged citizens participating in deliberative dialogue and debate. In both instances, they are also addressed as Aymaras within frameworks of national belonging.

2

Redemption Radio: Dehispanicized Aymara at Radio San Gabriel

The city of El Alto, Bolivia, is perched at the edge of the Andean high plain, or *altiplano*, overlooking neighboring La Paz, Bolivia's administrative capital, in the valley below. El Alto, or *Patamarka* in Aymara, sits at an altitude approaching 4000 meters above sea level. El Alto is not only among the highest cities in the world, it is also among the most densely Indigenous, with more than 80 percent of the population consisting of Aymara migrants from the surrounding high plain and their descendants (INE 2001). As home to nearly half of all ethnic Aymaras in the greater Lake Titicaca region, many consider El Alto the capital of the Aymaras (Albó 2006). The views here are as breathtaking as the very atmosphere, which leaves many visitors wanting for air. This rarely poses a problem for El Alto's residents, some of whom can be heard in busier neighborhoods as they loudly beckon to potential riders as they hold open the side doors of the minibuses that serve as one mode of collective transport here. They call out the names of avenues, landmarks, and neighborhoods to passing crowds of pedestrians—teenagers in school uniforms, men in suits with briefcases, and women wearing the heavily pleated skirts and bowler hats typical of Aymara women. Upon boarding one of these vans, most of the conversations among the riders would likely be in Spanish, but might also be in Aymara. There is a good chance that the language heard coming from the driver's radio will be Aymara, particularly if it is tuned in to Radio San Gabriel (RSG), "The Voice of the Aymara People." There is also a chance that "Radio San Gabriel" was among the destinations called out by the driver's helper as he solicits passengers. This well-known Jesuit-affiliated radio station's building serves as a landmark in this sprawling city (see Figure 2.1) and, with its exclusively Aymara language broadcasting, stands out in the city's soundscape. There are other radio stations with Aymara language programs, but such programming is often limited to early mornings, targeting agricultural and manual laborers.

Figure 2.1 Radio San Gabriel in Villa Adela neighborhood of El Alto.

If RSG serves as a landmark for commuters navigating their way through the city, RSG also provides an orienting role as the preeminent station from which models of eloquent Aymara speech are broadcast. A well-elaborated regime of metadiscursive practices at RSG orients projects of multiple scales—from individuals' own projects of personal and professional transformation, to broader interventions, including the expansion of a linguistic register of dehispanicized Aymara. This chapter examines the work of the division of RSG responsible for the quality of broadcast speech, the Aymara Language Department, focusing on two of its members, who find themselves situated at the intersection of multiple and intertwined sources of authority—the Catholic Church, disciplinary linguistics, and the Aymara people. The protocols of metadiscursive scrutiny they maintain at RSG constitute a key site in the constitution, maintenance, and diffusion of dehispanicized Aymara. By following the individuals who enforce this metadiscursive regime, how they enter into and enact its authority, this chapter demonstrates how this nexus of institutional, moral, and scientific authority converges within RSG's Aymara Language Department to secure a register of dehispanicized Aymara as a complex icon of Aymara personhood emanating from the station's airwaves.

Aymar Markan Arupa, "The Voice of the Aymara People"

Radio San Gabriel was founded shortly after the Bolivian National Revolution of 1952, a major social upheaval in which miners' militias played a crucial role. Jesuit priests had founded radio stations in mining communities within a wider broadcasting milieu dominated by radical and communist political currents (O'Connor 2006). Although miners are remembered as the central protagonists in the 1952 revolution, also crucial to its victory were the highland Aymara and Quechua communities who overturned nearly feudal relations in the countryside, often through insurrectionary land expropriations (Dunkerley 1984; Winchell 2022). In 1955, Maryknoll Jesuit priests founded RSG in the small Aymara community of Peñas near the shores of Lake Titicaca, later moving it to El Alto. The principal aims of the radio station were Spanish language literacy and Christian evangelization. Bolivian social historian Javier Hurtado (1987) writes in his history of RSG:

> The Maryknoll Fathers' principal motivation for their work among the Indians was, obviously, the evangelization of a population that despite five centuries of Christianization continued being pagan and still far from a monotheistic Christian faith. It was this situation that induced them to thinking about teaching them Spanish, through literacy, as an indispensable means for evangelism: to receive the Word of God.[1]
>
> (Hurtado 1987: 18 as cited in Ccama 2006: 149, translation mine)

Within a broader framework of evangelism, RSG understood the Aymara language as a bridge to Spanish language literacy and integration into the mainstream of the Catholic faith. Such an approach was in line with the post-1952 revolution MNR government's modernizing projects and with earlier formulations by the Catholic Church of "the Indian problem" as a problem of national integration (Orta 2004). Yet these initially assimilationist orientations would quickly shift due to political ferment in Bolivia and changes in the Catholic Church. The Second Vatican Council (1962–5) made an opening, particularly in Latin America, for a social justice-oriented evangelism of "liberation theology" (Orta 2004).

During the 1960s and 1970s, radical currents of Aymara nationalism arose, Indianism (*indianismo*) and katarism (*katarismo*). Indianismo, in particular, was associated with work of Fausto Reinaga and the *Partido Indio de Aymaras y Keswas* (PIAK), founded in 1962 and later renamed *Partido Indio de Bolivia* in 1966 (Macusaya 2018; Reinaga 1970). *Katarismo* took its name from the eighteenth-century revolutionary Tupak Katari and found institutional expression through organizations like the *Movimiento Revolucionario Tupak Katari* (MRTK, "Revolutionary Movement Tupak Katari"). Katarismo became most influential with the founding of the *Confederación Sindical Única de Trabajadores Campesinos Bolivianos* (CSUTCB, "Trade Union Confederation of Rural Workers of Bolivia") under *katarista* leadership in 1979. Indianismo and Katarismo were critical of the assimilationist projects of the post 1952 Bolivian governments, which only recognized Aymaras as *campesinos*.

The influence of Aymara nationalism on RSG during this period was profound. During this period, RSG made a dramatic shift in orientation toward Aymara language and culture, adopting an Aymara-centric idiom that resonated with these other nationalist currents in Aymara communities, while remaining within Maryknoll Jesuit discourses of social justice and service to the poor by reformulating "liberation theology" as a "theology of inculturation" (Orta 2004). Practices earlier demonized by the Catholic Church as "being pagan and still far from a monotheistic Christian faith" were now celebrated as being essentially Christian—with the spilled blood of a sacrificed llama, for example, recast as analogous to the wine of the sacrament. Pre-Colombian iconography such as the motif of the *chakana*, an iconic representation of the Southern Cross constellation, and also a symbol of the Inca Empire, *Tawantinsuyu*, with its four political units, or *suyu*, was adopted as a homologous representation of the Christian cross.

In 1971, RSG established the *Centro Aymarista de Comunicación Social* ("The Aymaraist Center of Social Communication"), its literacy campaigns became bilingual, and all radio programming from that point on was designed to "recognize, value and promote cultural expressions of the people" (Ccama 2006: 150, translation mine). By the radio's own account in their fiftieth-anniversary commemorative history, these changes represented "a relationship with the Aymara people marked by horizontality, self-education and socioeconomics, defining a transcendental change in the policy of RSG" (Radio San Gabriel 2005: 80, translation mine). Here we find the confluence of a Jesuit discourse of egalitarianism with a recognition of the Aymara as a people (*el Pueblo Aymara*).

It is with this authority, or to assert it, that Radio San Gabriel describes itself as "The Voice of the Aymara People." The voices, and language, its listeners hear broadcast on its airwaves are linked to both polity and deity. Consider the station's namesake link to divine authority; the Archangel Gabriel is the messenger of God. Rather than narrowly a voice of religious authority, "the voice of the Aymara people" draws on multiple institutional projects, including the authority of religion, the authority of disciplinary linguistics, and the moral, collective authority evoked through appeals to Aymara nationhood.

A Register for the Radio

A new orientation to the Aymara language was a central feature of the shift in policy during this period and in the decades to follow. It would be difficult, however, to characterize this new orientation as being simply "horizontal" or democratic. While there is an undeniably democratic appeal in the promotion of a vernacular via mass media, the Aymara spoken on RSG's airwaves differs from the daily speech of most Aymara speakers of any regional variety. These differences exceed the divergences that might be anticipated from radio genre norms, such as the exaggeration of both enunciation and prosodic contours. The Aymara spoken on RSG also differs from what Lucy Therina Briggs described as "Radio Aymara" in her 1976 doctoral thesis on dialectal variation in Aymara. Analyzing Aymara language radio broadcasts in the 1970s, Briggs identified Radio Aymara as a "translation dialect" because of its imposition of Spanish SVO word order on the SOV preferred word order of Aymara. Briggs also characterized Radio Aymara as having a heavy presence of Spanish loanwords (Briggs 1976: 675–713). Rather than differing from other varieties of Aymara for the presence of Spanish features of lexicon and syntax, the Aymara on RSG today is notable for precisely the opposite: a conspicuous absence of Spanish loanwords and their replacement with neologisms.

The maintenance of this register provides a central focus for RSG's Aymara Language Department, which occupies a prominent position within RSG's organizational infrastructure. This department plays a central role in the production, revision, and approval of scripts for the radio station, serving as Aymara language authorities, as a collective epicenter of "pure Aymara." In many ways this could be seen as what has been termed corpus planning (Ferguson 1968). Corpus planning studies have often focused on written texts as opposed to *spoken language* and have tended to examine interventions at the nation-state or policy or educational institutions (Canagarajah 2005; Hornberger 1994). An examination of RSG's Aymara Language Department, however, provides an account of both the metadiscourse surrounding the "pure" register, or the *idiom of purism*, and actual instances of its use, or *discourse purism* (Neustupny 1989). Insofar as this is also an instance of the mass-mediatization of a register formation (Agha 2011), what follows illuminates the processes that make dehispanicized Aymara audible on a large scale for Bolivian Aymaras.

Recruiting the Model Speaker

The question of who can be counted as a speaker of a language can be a vexing question for linguists and state authorities alike (Moore, Pietikäinen and Blommaert 2010; Muehlmann 2012), but also for members of minoritized language communities and language advocates who belong to them (Smalls 2012). Does a grandchild who can understand and answer questions from her grandmother in Aymara, but only speaks with her classmates in Spanish count as an "Aymara speaker"? What of the speakers who even doubt whether their variety of Aymara is "pure enough" to count as true Aymara? As an enterprise which relies on the quality and appeal of its spokespersons' speech and voices, RSG places a premium on the selection of its audible vocal representatives. The recruitment of broadcasters for RSG is accomplished in part through advertised competitions for employment at the radio. Unlike the language competitions examined by Alexandra Jaffe (1999) on the island of Corsica, these competitions are not public but happen behind the scenes. They are gatekeeping devices for entrance onto the radiophonic "stage" of RSG. Yet the recruitment of the initial labor pool is not completely hidden from the public. The availability of positions is publicized by the radio station itself. Once candidates arrive at the El Alto radio station offices, their proficiency in reading, composition, and elocution in Aymara is evaluated together with assessments of content areas of expertise.

One member of the Aymara Language Department, Celia Colque Quispe, explained to me her experience of being hired through such a competition:

> There was a notice right here at the radio, they published it, so I listened to it, one noon on the announcements program, *Aruntawi*, I heard it on that program. And I, I said to myself, "Why can't I go?" The notice said that (you'd) have to know how to read and write Aymara, to translate, and also you'd have to know how to type. So, why can't I go? I came directly on a Monday and they gave the test, for the competition. I came and there we were. We were thirty. They were there from the UMSA (*the prestigious state university*) too. There had been a certain communication with UMSA's linguistics department. They had also come from other radio stations. When we came they gave us a sheet written in Spanish and we had to read it in Aymara, to speak directly into Aymara—

translation. And another was how many words per minute you could write, and later elocution, how you spoke in Aymara ... all that, they asked me if we could speak on the radio and after that ... those who run this radio, the bosses, the staff, they decided.[2]

Competing against trained linguists from Bolivia's most prestigious university and against others with radio work experience, a young woman, a native speaker of Aymara from a community near Lake Titicaca, won the contest. This competition inverted the general tendencies that otherwise predominate within Bolivia's linguistic market (Bourdieu 1991) by privileging the rural, native speaker over urban and university-educated ones. Celia's command of the language, both in writing and speech, and her ability to express herself eloquently in Aymara, secured her employment in a salaried position at a prestigious institution. This point is not lost on Celia. From her experience of being hired and through her experience at the station, her Aymara identity and language has afforded her prestige rather than contempt. The value of her language became evident within the interactional sequence of the interview I conducted with her. She responded to my first question, posed in Spanish, in Aymara, effectively switching the code from Spanish to Aymara:[3]

Karl:	¿*Cómo es que llegaste a la radio?*	"How did you come (to work) at the radio?"
Celia:	¿*Aka radiorux?* ¿*En Aymara* Castallanuti? (*se ríe*)	"Here to the radio? In Aymara? or Spanish? (laughing)"
K:	*Como quieras, yo como... Como quieras.*	"As you please, because I... As you please."
C:	*En Aymara y Castellano.*	"In Aymara and Spanish."
K:	*Como quieras, como quieras. Radio San Gabriel radiorux qallta...*	"As you please, as you please. You began at RSG radio..."
C:	¿*Kunjamas purinta?*	"How did I end up here?"
K:	¿*Kunjamas purinta?*	"How did you end you up here?"

Celia proceeded to explain her experience participating in the Aymara language competition mentioned above. Her confidence in responding to my Spanish question in Aymara bears no resemblance to the behavior of someone looking to accommodate another's lack of Aymara fluency. Celia knew I could speak Aymara, even if with limited proficiency, and challenged me to conduct the interview in Aymara. Celia's interactional style here contrasts sharply with that of Aymara speakers who may deny speaking the language out of fear of being negatively evaluated. One stereotype held by urban Aymaras of recent migrants to the city from the countryside is that recent transplants would deny their Aymara fluency in order to assume a more "urban" or "sophisticated" presentation of self. Yet this interactional stance is completely counter to Celia's own, and one incompatible with her experience at RSG. Indeed, when I asked her what she liked most about her job, she responded simply, "Claro, aquí ser Aymara. Me gusta ser Aymara." ("Clearly, here, being Aymara. I like being Aymara.")

Laying Down the (Lexical) Law

The Aymara Language Department is one of many departments at the radio. Although relatively small, with only seven employees during my fieldwork, its role to ensure the use of "pure Aymara" across all radio broadcasts afforded it considerable authority. The department's work followed the trajectory of all broadcasts, often including follow-up. The department intervened prior to each broadcast by either writing or editing scripts, and was responsible, along with the radio's director, for these scripts' ultimate approval. Yet, its responsibilities were not limited to the development of scripts. The department also was responsible for the implementation of a protocol extending through and beyond the broadcasts called *seguimiento*, or "following."

Seguimiento involves two procedures: the real-time monitoring of broadcasts for "aberrations" and a follow-up interaction with those who utter them on air. "Aberrations" is not a term of my choosing, but comes from the very protocol of *seguimiento*. Rather than scrutinizing programs for the appropriateness of the topics of discussion, aberrations here concern not purity of content, but of linguistic form. This is not a theological or political department but the Aymara Language Department and its charge is to enforce norms for the Aymara language in broadcasts. A central practice in the *seguimiento* protocol is the use of a ledger which department members use to record aberrations, propose corrections, and educate the culprits of said aberrations. The ledgers contain four columns on each page. Each column has a Spanish heading: aberración ("aberration"), léxico aymara ("Aymara lexeme"), fecha ("date"), and firma ("signature"). Members of the Aymara Language Department record aberrations uttered on air, and in the column next to it write Aymara word (lexeme) which should be said in its place in future broadcasts, and then the member of the department who recorded the aberration finds the offending party to have them sign the ledger to affirm that they know of their error and agree to speak in accordance with the department's norm in the future. This real-time monitoring of broadcasters' utterances with its attendant follow-up protocol organizes RSG's internal regime of metadiscursive normativity as a speech chain (Agha 2007), one in which the Aymara Language Department decides what legitimately should be heard or not heard on the airwaves as authentic Aymara speech.

How is the monitoring phase of *seguimiento* conducted? If you were to enter the Aymara Language Department's offices at RSG, you would invariably hear a radio playing, tuned to RSG, with at least one of the department's seven members listening in with a *seguimiento* ledger close at hand. This institutional form of transcription exerts a sole focus on the aberration, removing it from the larger context of the utterance. Even the most skilled department members operate with human limitations on auditory acuity and attention. However hard department members listen, the flow of speech inevitably exceeds the complete capture of every last lexeme. As a literacy practice tied to listening, this initial step of *seguimiento* may be considered a form of stenography, or "a technology that faithfully turns physically-audible speech into a precise and permanent written record at the real-time moment at which the recorded speech is uttered" (Inoue 2011: xx). The social arrangement into which this stenographic practice is introduced, however, is completely the opposite of the one described by Miyako Inoue in the reproduction of court speech in Meiji-era Japan, or, for that matter, more familiar contemporary contexts of court or office stenography. In this instance of stenography, we also find asymmetrical power relations between transcriber and speaker, but within *seguimiento*'s division of labor, it is the authority who transcribes the voice of the subordinate.

In the follow-up phase of *seguimiento*, this same power asymmetry obtains a performative character between those who commit aberrations and those who track them down through signing the ledger, but with an added twist. There is an inversion not only of the institutional relations defining other types of stenography, but also of the confession model: rather than bringing a list of sins to the priest, the language authority compiles the list of sins to deliver to the sinner. Standing before the authority and a list of aberrations with their appropriate remedies (léxico aymara), and the date of sinning, the sinners performatively confess with their signatures to those sins and promise a change in future linguistic behavior.

The Aymara Language Department is invested with authority within this speech chain, but who are the authorities for the authorities? The institutional counter-valorizing of rural Aymara speakers' linguistic abilities in the language competitions, as described above, lets us know that one source of authority are the rural Aymara communities from which many of the competition winners, like Celia, hail. Other more institutionally consolidated centers of authority also play a role within the department—particularly the discipline of linguistics. The director of the department, Hilarión Chinahuanca Siñani, described the process of self-education among the employees of the Aymara Language Department (himself included), which they undertake upon their employment at RSG:

> They've arrived at the radio, not having thought to study linguistics but from necessity itself—my people ask this of me, and they tell me to clarify this, "Where does this come from?" … We know how to speak but we still don't understand. People have reflected on those things with me. I've placed myself over there at the "house of linguistics" at the Universidad Mayor de San Andrés. We've even studied in short courses on Saturdays and Sundays, Saturdays and Fridays in the afternoon … I dedicate myself to this, to studying.[4]

His account reveals more than a story of self-improvement through education or the pursuit of individual interest or passion, although it may surely also be these things. Embedded in this narrative is an ethical and moral sense of responsibility that responds to the Aymara collectivity. He makes explicit what Gal and Irvine refer to as an anchor (2019: 38, 120–2) which provides an ideological ground for his discursive interventions as department head. The enforcement of the linguistic norms through his work at the department answers a request of him and his colleagues from the Aymara people (*mi pueblo me pide*, "my people ask this of me").

In a similar vein, the compiling of the materials which buttress the authorities' authority within the practice of seguimiento was explained in the same interview as itself a process of Aymara nationalist consolidation. The gathering of reference grammars and linguistic texts was explained as a collective project of the department members which moved beyond a task of professional necessity to become imbued with both moral and nationalist value. Hilarión explained this crucial precursor to the department's activity within a framework of Aymara traditional community practice, namely, the Aymara concept of mutual aid and reciprocity, or *ayni*:

> So, each one bring his own text with reference to linguistics. Even though at the radio, the radio is very big and the so is its library but we still don't have all these texts … So this is a type of *ayni* that we do. It's not to say, "I have it home, why bring it in?" No. It's that the people, the very population with one little word encourage us, give us strength. That's why we're here.[5]

The development of metalinguistic expertise through study is one route to authority. The authority of study draws on the technical expertise of disciplinary linguistics, sometimes mediated through educational and academic materials compiled by members of the radio. This practice of compiling materials expands beyond linguists within or affiliated to the department to include "the people." The authority of disciplinary linguistics and educational materials is understood as being incorporated into the department's practice alongside and within the framework of community authority and the collaborative practice *ayni*, itself a practice steeped with a sense of moral obligation. Those who contribute sometimes do so, if not with books, even "with one little word" (*con una palabrita*) in unbeknownst acts of *ayni*.

Among reference grammars, an important text for the work of this department is Ludovico Bertonio's 1612 Aymara dictionary. Bertonio's 1612 dictionary predates those of most modern European languages, coming more than a century before Samuel Johnson's 1755 English dictionary, and decades before *L'Academie Française*'s publication of its first dictionary in 1694. Here we find some historical continuity with the Catholic Church playing a prominent role in corpus planning for the Aymara language. From colonialism's earliest days in the Andes, the Catholic Church recognized the necessity of mastering local languages, particularly Quechua and Aymara, which remained in wide use in the wake of the Spanish invasion. Describing the city and province of La Paz, where contemporary El Alto is located, the Jesuit Priest José de Acosta stated in 1591: "All the Indians of this province and city speak the general language which is called Aymara, although many of them also speak and understand the Quechua language, which is the general language of the Inca"[6] (cited in Torero 1975: 225, translation mine).

Other languages throughout the Americas that gained the status of "general language of Indians" for colonial projects throughout the Americas included Quechua, Nahuatl, and Guarani. It may come as a surprise to many today, given the colonial legacy of anti-Indian racism, that Spanish nor Portuguese suppression of Indigenous languages remained a constant feature of the colonial enterprise. Languages such as Nahuatl, Guarani, Quechua, and Guarani were meticulously studied, documented, taught, and even promoted throughout long periods of colonial history (Bessa Freire and Rosa 2000; Hanks 2010; Heath 1972; Mannheim 1984; Rafael 1993). It is within this context that Aymara became a central vehicle for Catholic missionization in the central Andes during the seventeenth century. Bertonio's dictionary was the central Andean component of a larger metadiscursive project of Jesuit and Franciscan production of dictionaries and grammars in the service of colonialism and evangelism in the Americas and beyond (Bessa Freire and Rosa 2000; Hanks 2010; Heath 1972; Mannheim 1984; Rafael 1993).

Bertonio's dictionary continues to play an authoritative role within the metadiscursive matrix of *seguimiento*. When encountering a Spanish loanword, a decision must be made by the lexical authorities concerning which word provides the proper remedy for the "aberration." Before resorting to the invention of neologisms, the question arises whether a word can be "rescued" (*rescatado*) through the inclusion of archaicisms in seguiento ledger's corrective column of *léxico aymara*. "Rescue" as a concept in relation to lexical items suggests that they are capable of facing danger, rather than simply falling out of use. Here is one place where a notion of endangerment, in other words, is embedded within the metadiscourse of *seguimiento*. Within this framework, the place of refuge where the lost lexemes hide is Bertonio's dictionary. The dictionary as text-artifact is not just a repository of words, but a linguistic time capsule of words used by Aymara speakers 400 years ago. This notion is graphically illustrated on the cover of Radio San Gabriel's 1993 edition of Bertonio's dictionary. The cover illustration depicts a muscular man wearing a knit *lluch'u* hat laboriously unearthing a time-capsule like box from the earth. Written on the box is not "Aymar Aru" (Aymara language) but the nearly homophonous *Jaya mara aru*, "distant year language," a popular folk-etymology of the language's name. Behind him is a demonstrating crowd, mouths open, carrying two banners, one reading *nuestra cultura es milenaria*, "our culture is millenial," and the other *lengua antigua*, "ancient language."

The point of entry of archaicisms into broadcasts comes primarily through the expulsion of loanwords, the providing of remedies for any "aberration" in radio broadcasters' speech being the principal focus of *seguimiento*. The director of the department accounted for this when discussing the most common errors heard on the radio's programs:

> Hilarión: "More on the radio it's always the incursion of the loan. Even me sometimes, I don't even realize it, but it comes out, 'you've said this.' They also are in the same situation. So they listen to the radio and it strikes us which is the Spanish word being borrowed. There's no problem with names but there are words that are there and they get borrowed. That's the problem. For example, they say minutes *minutus*. They say *Chika urutxa tunka minutunakampixiw* ('ten minutes past noon'). But in Aymara we already have *q'ata*. *Chika urutxa tunka q'atanakampixiw* and people understand, it's not that they don't understand … My mother says it, my family says it, uses those words. So we can't continue *minutus, minutus*."[7]

In the opening of this passage, the director reanimates the voice of a coworker disciplining him, "You've said this." This representation of an interaction provides a mini-diagram of one link in the speech chain of the metadiscursive regime operative at the radio station, except in this case the culprit breaking the standard of purity to which RSG aspires is the director himself. In speaking with me, he indulges in an act of self-deprecation that inverts the power dynamic the institution normatively dictates. When the Aymara language authority and enforcer of linguistic norms admits that he too is guilty of using Spanish loans, we encounter the gap between what Neustupny (1989) called *idioms of purism* (the metadiscourses of language purity) and *discourse purism* (the adoption of dehispanicized forms within the object-discourse). We encounter the distance between prescribed and actual behavior: exemplary speakers themselves find it difficult to follow the standard to which they aspire. Here is the awkward recognition that the standard itself is something that no one speaker fully commands.

He then continues to provide what for him is a prototypical aberration concerning the denotation of time—"it's ten past noon." The sentence in question contains the phonologically assimilated, or what Hardman (2001) calls *aymarized*, word for "minutes"—*minutus*. The director would have preferred the broadcaster to say *q'ata*. This was the term he wrote in the column headed *léxico aymara* ("Aymara lexeme") and beside the aberration *minutu*. Rather than calling on the authority of the Bertonio dictionary, instead, he invokes the linguistic practices of his rural family as authoritative—"My mother says it, my family says it, uses those words." The anchors of rural provenance and the intimacy of kinship justify the corrective practice of the department's protocol—"so we can't continue *minutus, minutus*."

When I asked other Aymara speakers what *q'ata* meant, including a linguist and native Aymara speaker, Juan de Dios Yapita, who is familiar with many varieties of Aymara, no one replied with "minute" or any unit of time. Whether or not the director has given an accurate depiction of his own family's linguistic practices is less important here than is his appeal to their authority: rural speakers serve as the model speakers of the register in this account; and the use of his own family as a sample of model speakers anchors his own practice of *seguimiento* in the mantle of authority.

In this same discussion, the director showed me his own ledger with further examples uttered during a news broadcast earlier that morning, "*Kasta, kasta* is a loan, it comes from Spanish. *May maya* in Aymara [he] has to say. *Phasilakiwa* from *fácil es* ('it's easy') but here *yachaykiwa* in Aymara. The Aymara lexical [item] and the aberration [he] has committed, then the responsible party is aware and signs. Like that for everyone who has a program."[8]

Both *kasta* and *phasil* are loans from Spanish, but loans of different types. The second example, *phasil*, is another aymarized loan, the phonological assimilation of *fácil* (easy). Without the labiodental voiceless fricative /f/ in their phonemic inventory, Aymara speakers have used the closest phoneme available, the aspirated voiceless bilabial stop /ph/. *Kasta* (type) is a loan of a different type, coming from the archaic Spanish *casta*, which would contemporarily be expressed in Spanish with *tipo* ("type") or *variedad* ("variety"). Other loans like this in Aymara, including very common words (such as the verb "to speak," *parlaña*, from the sixteenth-century Spanish *parlar*), are testament to 500 years of contact with Spanish. Many loans denote referents introduced to Andean society since Spanish invasion. Livestock like sheep, for example, now common throughout the high plain, were unknown before conquest; the Aymara word *uwija* "sheep" is an aymarized rendering of the Spanish *oveja*. Like sheep, units of time like minutes, hours, seven-day weeks, and the twelve-month year were introduced through colonial imposition, even very shortly following Spanish invasion. The following entry from Ludovico Bertonio's 1612 dictionary gives us some sense of this: "Day and its parts: Vide: Parts of time, where they are found the names of the hours, almost all correspond to ours"[9] (Bertonio 2006 (1612): 197).

While Bertonio's dictionary includes entries for day (*uru*), month (*phaxsi*), year (*mara*), and time (*pacha*), absent are entries for hour, minute, second, or the names of the days of the week. Were these the parts of time that "correspond to ours"? Despite the absence of widespread use of timepieces in the sixteenth century, the sexagesimal division of hours into minutes and seconds would not have been unknown to Bertonio, but were perhaps more within the esoteric domains of mathematics. There are aymarized loanwords for the days of week (Table 2.1) and for the seven-day week itself, *simana* from the Spanish *semana* ("week"). The neologism to replace *simana* is nearly homophonous with the Aymara word form "seven," *päqalq*, becoming *päqanaka* when replacing *simanas* "weeks" with the addition of the plural marker—*naka*. Interestingly, the neologisms for the days of the week share etyma with the European terms: "sun day," "moon day," etc. These draw not only from Spanish etymology but even from English and Norse: *illapa uru* "lightening day" alludes to the lightening associated with the Norse god Thor, the source deity for the English word "Thursday" (Table 2.1).

When asked, Aymara speakers indicated some familiarity with these neologisms (Table 2.1), but only those tied to educational organizations (like RSG, the Aymara Educational Council, or those involved with bilingual education) claimed to use them regularly. Whether or not the aymarized loanwords for days of the week were adopted by Aymara speakers at the time of Bertonio's writing, these have long been a part of the daily speech of Aymara speakers. Still, they persist as conspicuous targets for lexical reform at RSG.

Table 2.1 Aymara neologisms: days of the week

Spanish day	Aymarized loan	Neologism	Direct gloss	English gloss
lunes	Lunis	phaxsi uru	moon day	Monday
martes	Martis	saxra uru	war day	Tuesday
miércoles	Mirculis	wara uru	star day	Wednesday
jueves	Jwivis	illapa uru	lightning day	Thursday
viernes	Wirnis	ch'aska uru	Venus (star) day	Friday
sábado	Sawaru	kurami uru	rainbow day	Saturday
domingo	Tuminku	inti uru	sun day	Sunday

Days of the week feature prominently in the opening segments of many radio programs. The convention announcing the date and time establishes for the audience that it is a live, not prerecorded program. In the following transcript from the May 10, 2007, opening of the Aymara Language Department's flagship program, *Lengua Aymara* ("Aymara Language"), we encounter an interface between the use of neologisms and the particular discourse genre of the radio program, resulting in a surprising tension with how calendric time and its denotation are handled.

1. CELIA: *Kamisaki jilata kullakanakax?* — How are you brothers and sisters?
2. *Jallakipaxa nayasa jumanakaruwa arumt'tatapxta* — I'd like to welcome you as always
3. Lengua Aymara *wakichaypunirakiniwa* — with the program Aymara Language
4. *wasitat* <u>radio</u> *tuqin qamart'asipkarakta* — here at the <u>radio</u>. You're living with
5. <u>Radio San Gabriel</u> *ist'apkarapta pätunka* — Radio San Gabriel, listening in twenty
6. provincia*nakaxa aruntt'atarakiwa* — provinces you're greeted
7. *qhirwanakana suntanakana* [????] *nakana* — in valleys, in the heights, in the [????]
8. *thayampis wichhumpi, chikt'ataw* — with the cold and wind
9. *jumanakax ist'iraksta* radio *jallakipanaya* — you're listening to the radio's message
10. *sasina arunt'atapta.* — saying you are greeted [welcome].

11. HILARIÓN: Jallakipana achachila awicha	Grandfathers and grandmothers
12. kamaraki ^^mama t'alla^^ mallku kawnirinakas	even ^^mama t'allas^^ and mallkus
13. jilata kullaka kamaraki wayna tawaqunakaraki	brother, sister and even young boys, girls
14. jisk'alalanaka jumanakasa arumtt'atxaraptawa	and little ones you are all welcome
15. jichhurux niyaw ukaxa ^^**illapüru**^^ ukjamaxraki	Now that it's ^^Thursday^^, like that
16. aka <u>llamayu</u> phaxsin niyaw akaxa tunka urunaka	in this month of **May**, ten days
17. mäkiptawayxi. urunakas **päqanakas**	are almost done. The days, **the weeks**
18. phaxsinakas jalakpun jaliwa	the months are always running, flying.
19. chikamaru puriñanixa	We're arriving at the middle
20. aka <u>Calendario Gregoriano</u>	of this <u>Gregorian Calendar</u>
21. ukanxa utjiti wasa yatiqsta	in that you know
22. machax maraxa jak'achasinkaraki.	the new year is approaching.
23. Jilata Martín Tarki jupampi chikañtasiñani	Together with brother Martín Tarki
24. ukjamaxa sapumayniw arumt'atapta	every one of you is welcomed
25. qallantañaniwa wakichawisampi.	we'll start with our program.

An apparent incongruence arises in lines 19–22: how does the middle of the calendric year reveal that "the new year is approaching"? There is a tension here between the Western, Christian, Gregorian calendar and a solar, agricultural, Aymara calendar. This dissonance highlights the very neologisms Hilarión uses to refer to units of time—the neologism *illapüru* instead of *jwivis* "Thursday" (line 15), *llamayu* instead of *mayu* "May"[10] (line 16), and *päqanaka* instead of *simanas* "weeks" (line 17). *Illapüru* denotes "Thursday" in Aymara (at the lexemic level), but situates it within two distinct frameworks of time reckoning: (1) the Western, Christian calendar ("it is now the month of May" [line 16] and "the middle of the Gregorian Calendar" [line 20]) and (2) the upcoming Aymara New Year tied to the southern hemispheric winter solstice ("you know the new year is approaching" [lines 21–2]). The broadcaster orients the listeners to two distinct frameworks of time reckoning—one Western and one Aymara. The incongruity of these two distinct frames brings the denotation of temporal neologisms into discursive focus. Furthermore, that the words "Gregorian Calendar" are the only words Hilarión utters in Spanish within this stretch of talk only further underscores its distinctiveness. Announcing the date in this way does more than just situate the listener with respect to the simultaneous character of the program's broadcast; it foregrounds the act of reckoning with two competing, or at least copresent, semiotic frameworks for time.

A second type of lamination concerns the prosodic conventions of the radio genre and Hilarión's use of the lexical register. Exaggerated prosody can be found in many radio discourse genres. In the example above, Hilarión uses it to bring focus to the use of a neologism. Two words share a salient prosodic contour: *mama t'alla* and *illapüru* (lines 12 and 15). These words are uttered more slowly and with parallel prosodic contours; the first three syllables are high pitch (H) and the final syllable low pitch (L), a parallel (H-H-H-L) contour motivating a relation of equivalence between the two (Jakobson 1960). The equivalence here is not that these are both neologisms—*mama t'alla* is a rotating position of political authority for women within traditional Aymara communities. Poetically linking the neologism *illapüru*[11] with a title emblematic of traditional Aymara political organization configures it within a discursive diagram of Aymara authenticity as parallel to *mama t'alla*, co-textually imbuing the neologism with values of tradition and authority.

Despite their best efforts, the eradication of Spanish loans is incomplete and the audience hears *provincianaka* (line 6), *provincia* being a loan from Spanish and—*naka* the Aymara plural marker. In this case, there is a potential Aymara equivalent, as there were political administrative subdivisions in preconquest times, the aforementioned *suyu*. If ever challenged to account for her use of a Spanish loan here, perhaps Celia might resort to the confessional discourse we encountered with Hilarion's earlier admission that *no me doy cuenta pero sale* ("I don't realize it but it comes out"). Indeed, no one is perfect; no one is free of sin. Even the language authorities commit *aberraciones*.

Combating Colonialism (i.e., "Contact") through Correction?

The Aymara Language Department's efforts to enforce purity in their language may remind readers of the figure of a schoolmarm correcting others' grammar. Language purism projects necessarily involve language correction, demarcating what constitutes legitimate and illegitimate forms of speech, making this an Aymara variety of verbal hygiene (Cameron 1995). The schoolmarm comparison would be misguided in this case, however, obscuring the sociohistorical matrix in which these metadiscursive practices unfold. The conflation of language and ethnic identity may be accompanied by a sense of moral obligation to defend and uphold the language as a metonym for "the people" within contexts of social oppression. Language purist discourses often respond to perceived or real pressures on minority communities as a kind of "battle cry" (Jernudd 1989: 3). Speaking to the moral discourse within some language revitalization projects, Fishman (1997) writes: "Since the beloved language is closely and inseparably associated with other verities, the moral imperatives that exist to defend the latter also directly and obviously apply to the language as well. Not to do so would be unthinkable and clearly morally reprehensible" (Fishman 1997: 73). For some at the station, the loanword seemed to reflect this process, and they perceived the introduction of neologisms and maintenance of a distinct lexical register as part of protecting the language. Recall Hilarión's view that his job implied a responsibility to his people (*mi pueblo*) and his invocation of an Aymara cultural norm of reciprocity (*ayni*) in explaining the compiling of work materials. The link between morality and linguistic practice was even echoed in his impatient admonition "we cannot continue *minutus, minutus.*"

The threat of a large-scale language shift from Aymara to Spanish concerns others besides Aymara organizations like RSG. The central Andes has been identified by linguists employing language endangerment discourses as one of the world's "hotspots" of language endangerment, together with other regions such as Siberia and northern Australia[12] (Harrison 2007). Another way to understand these "hotspots," however, might be as areas of linguistic resilience, as regions where indigenous peoples have managed to maintain their languages and life ways in the face of colonial domination and subjugation. In Bolivia's case, it is one of the only nation-states of the Americas with a majority indigenous population (the other being Guatemala). This unique status is not the result of somehow escaping the ravages of colonialism. Hardly isolated from the world economy, Aymara communities have been linked to a global economy since the sixteenth century, when gold mined by conscripted laborers left the Andes for Europe to put the gold in "the Golden Age." Andean indigenous communities' asymmetrical relationship with the world economy did not end with colonialism, continuing through the twentieth century with extractive industries taking Bolivian tin to factories from Detroit to Dresden. The plundering of natural resources for foreigners' benefit, together with the historical backdrop of genocide, features prominently in Aymara historical narratives. One Aymara radio broadcaster told me that Aymaras were the "Jews of the Andes" because, like the Jews of Europe, the Aymara maintained their language and culture despite attempts to eradicate them as a people. The sentiment behind this surprising analogy echoed through other conversations with Aymara Bolivians who on varied occasions expressed their desire never to become an "extinct tribe."[13] This was the prognosis, or worse, the hope one century ago of Bolivian intellectuals like Alcides Arguedas, who, in his hopes of a "modern" Bolivia, predicted the disappearance of the Aymara as a distinct ethnic group through linguistic and cultural assimilation (Arguedas 1979 [1909]). A century later, discourses of "endangerment" continue to resonate with narratives of Aymara nationhood.

If protecting the language is commensurate with protecting the people, at RSG this means targeting loanwords that are reminders of the painful processes of colonialism to which the Aymara have been subjected. Further evidence of this is found in the Aymara Language Department's selectivity in its attention to which loanwords are purged. Aymara has been in contact with Quechua for much longer than Spanish, yet Quechua loans are not the focus of *seguimiento*.[14] This selective purging is not unique or surprising; it simply underscores the sociohistorical situatedness of such purist efforts. Neustupny (1989: 218) provides Czech purism as another example of selective purging of loanwords, where German loans were subject to replacement but not French or Latin loans. In post-Soviet Tatarstan, home to a Muslim and Turkic minority group in the Volga region, Tatar language purists purge Russian loans but embrace the re-adoption of Arabic and Persian loans (Wertheim 2003).

If there were any attempt to purge Aymara of Quechua loanwords, there would be at least two problems. The first would be the large percentage of the southern Quechua and Aymara lexicon that is shared, and the second would be determining the directionality of the loans (Cerrón Palomino 1994). Words as common as door (*punku*), wall (*pirqa*), and the numbers three (*kimsa*), five, (*phisqa*), six (*suxta*), and ten (*tunka*) almost surely came into the Aymara lexicon from contact with Quechua. Reciprocally, there is a compelling theory that the ejective consonants of southern Quechua emerged as an areal feature from contact with Aymara (Adelaar 2004). The point here, however, concerns not the feasibility of a different purist project but why the Spanish loanword is a target and not the Quechua loanword. This concerns Spanish invasion; the *aberración* is both a metonym for and the indexical residue of Spanish invasion, or what more frequently, and euphemistically, is called "contact."

Conclusion

The consolidation and maintenance of a distinct register of pure Aymara on RSG's airwaves is considered by its promoters to be part of a larger historical process of decolonization. Yet its source materials derive from Catholic institutions, an issue not without its historical ironies. The Catholic Church's interest in developing expertise in Indigenous languages was fundamental to the colonial project, and animated the work of the sixteenth- and seventeenth-century Jesuits and Franciscans discussed above (see also Hanks 2010; Heath 1972; Mannheim 1984; Rafael 1993). Aside from the Catholic Church's complicity in the very processes that the actors at RSG aim to reverse, there are other residues of colonial hierarchies lurking within the metadiscursive regime examined here. In Bertonio's 1612 dictionary, Spanish remains the matrix language in which Aymara is framed and commented upon. Today, the Aymara Language Department's flagship program has a Spanish name—*Lengua Aymara*. And the ledgers of *seguimiento* bear column headings' words that are in Spanish (*aberración, léxico aymara, fecha, firma*), not Aymara. Despite the decolonizing aims of this protocol, Spanish remains the authoritative language within this framework (see also Meek and Messing 2007). In addition to the framing of Aymara by Spanish in the ledgers of *seguimiento* or in the title of *Lengua Aymara*, there are traces of translation in the neologisms for the days of the week we encountered above.

Might there be unforeseen consequences from emergent asymmetries of competence between those who are familiar with the neologisms deployed on RSG and those who are not? In any language there are asymmetries of competence, with speakers recognizing more registers than they are able to command with any fluency (Agha 2007: Chapter 3), and all standardization projects introduce new asymmetries (Gal 2006). Researchers like Yapita and Arnold (2005) and Canessa

(2000) discuss the distance between a register of Aymara purged of Spanish loans and the daily varieties used by Aymara speakers as harmful in educational contexts. Canessa (2000) describes rural Aymara children becoming discouraged upon encountering written Aymara that is foreign to them, feeding into already circulating ideas of semilingualism; that is, that they don't speak "real" Aymara. Arnold and Yapita (2005) note that many of the neologisms confused students and sometimes shared unfortunate homonyms with local varieties (Arnold and Yapita 2005). Elsewhere in the Andes, among Quechua speakers, Coronel-Molina (2008) examines a similar case in which register bifurcation is cultivated by the Academy of Quechua Language between *qhapaq simi* (rich language) and *runasimi* (people's language). Coronel-Molina (2008) argues that, despite claims to the contrary, the asymmetries of competence resulting from the Academy's interventions do more to curtail Quechua language use than to promote it, with the primary result being the formation of a new, self-appointed class of language experts. "The sense of prestige derived from using the 'authentic' Quechua boosts the perception of their own status among Academy members. This in turn reinforces their feeling of authority *vis-à-vis* the communities" (Coronel-Molina 2008: 333–4).

These are all compelling accounts, but I am hesitant to draw similar conclusions—or to see in any of these other cases easy analogues to the metadiscursive regime in place at RSG. The metadiscursive "heavy lifting" required to maintain a distinct lexical register of Aymara audible on RSG's airwaves should not be misinterpreted as "exposing" or "deconstructing" practices of an "invented authenticity" that serves only to reinforce the authority of those enforcing the register itself. That could be one conclusion, and may indeed be the case in other seemingly similar scenarios (e.g., Coronel-Molina 2008). In the case of RSG, however, a simple pro-vernacular critique—for example, of *seguimiento* as a form of Foucauldian "governmentality"—might well be misguided, especially if it ends up divesting authority from actors in societies still wrestling with colonial legacies (Briggs 1996); new forms of discursive authority are an important part of what they are fighting to establish.

Furthermore, such conclusions run the risk of sidestepping the potentially awkward, but necessary, reflexive move to consider how research such as this, and the academic disciplines they address also constitute metadiscursive practices bestowing authority to those engaged in them (Briggs 1996). The development of authority in language and communication, per se, whether among researchers or radio broadcasters, need not be problematic, but demands reflexivity and, perhaps equally challenging, increased *ayni* among those engaged with and studying these processes. Certainly, the "voice of the Aymara people" has every right to develop its voice and authority over how it will sound, just as the Aymara people may decide whether or not to listen. There is more going on here, however, than simply the extension of an RSG brand or attention to a slice of the radio market.

There are individual, social, and linguistic consequences of the processes unfolding at RSG. We may recognize in RSG what Foucault (1988) called "technologies of the self," or those technologies which "permit individuals to effect by their own means or with the help of others a certain number of operations on their own bodies and souls, thoughts, conduct, and way of being, so as to transform themselves in order to attain a certain state of happiness, purity, wisdom, perfection, or immortality" (18). Foucault discussed technologies of the self as distinct from, if at times overlapping with, technologies of sign systems—technologies "which permit us to use signs, meanings, symbols, or signification" (18). For those involved in maintaining the metadiscursive regime within RSG, however, the development and reproduction of metalinguistic expertise combines with metadiscursive protocols to create a nearly complete overlap of technologies of the self and technologies of sign systems. In a country where even today to hear an Aymara voice is for many to hear the voice of the poor, the anti-modern, the rural people, who are worthy only of contempt or fear, the metadiscursive regime at RSG contributes to Celia's reporting with ease that the best thing about working at RSG is "being Aymara." While the regime in place at RSG is evidently transformative for those involved, it extends beyond a project of personal accomplishment, or of individual linguistic intervention, to one of a broader—and, from Celia and Hilarión's perspective, more emancipatory—scope.

3

Ayllu on the Airwaves: Mediatized Metapragmatics at Radio Pacha Qamasa

I first heard of the radio program *Akhulli Amuyt'awi* from Franz Laime, the founding director of the radio station on which it is broadcast, *Radio Pacha Qamasa*. I met him after his tenure as director of the radio while he was a student enrolled in an international master's program for Indigenous bilingual teachers from across the Americas. He was one of the half-dozen Aymara students in the program and I was a visiting scholar. I had recently finished a Master's in Applied Linguistics and had before that been working as a bilingual teacher in Los Angeles, California. When I was told that he had worked for the Aymara Education Council as director of their radio station during the insurrectionary movement in El Alto that was the "Gas War," I knew I wanted to interview him about these experiences and, gladly, he was happy to talk about them. An early and obvious question in the course of the interview concerned the radio station's name. The term *pacha* I knew. This is a much commented word in both Aymara and Quechua that is translated as both time and space, and approximates the notion of spacetime in physics (Swinehart 2019a). It was *qamasa* that I was less sure of and asked for his explanation. His explanation was surprising:

> Karl: What does *Pacha Qamasa* mean?
> Franz: It's, let's see, *Pacha* is time and space, it includes all that. *Qamasa* is another, separate word that means courage, or courage of time. Courage, energy …
> Karl: That's why the program has the name *Times of Courage*. (referring to another program on the radio) It's almost a direct translation of Pacha Qamasa.
> Franz: Exactly. But if I had to explain *qamasa* to you … Have you ever seen, let's see … What animal are you afraid of?
> Karl: uhhhhh …

Franz: A bear suddenly appears at your back. There it is—a bear! You don't realize it but when you turn around, and the bear has taken all that energy that you have and has psychologically diminished you, he's reduced you. That's what the bear has, it's *qamasa*, energy. Do you understand me? That's *qamasa*.

I did and I didn't understand. On the one hand, I was correct in identifying "time of courage" as a possible translation of *pacha qamasa*. On the other hand, I had never considered fright as the loss of a vital force, a leak in one's reserve of courage. What Laime was describing sounded like what others had described as a dangerous, potentially illness-causing *susto* "fright," a phenomenon known throughout Spanish-speaking America (Rubel 1964). What Laime describes is a related concept, but distinct. Qamasa is the force that one might have over others, the ability to provoke *susto* in them, the power that the imagined bear would have over me. I will also admit that the Spanish translation, *coraje*, still gives me pause. While cognate with the English "courage," it can also be translated as "anger," two concepts that few English speakers would describe as synonymous.

In his explanation of the radio station's name and of the word *qamasa*, Laime also articulated a discourse of "recuperating" Aymara words. "Qamasa" was one of these words. He attributes the CEA and its radio with introducing this term into circulation in the public sphere in a way reminiscent of the work of the Aymara language department at Radio San Gabriel in the previous chapter. He told me, "The concept of *qamasa* has been recuperated by *Radio Pacha Qamasa* and later many radios began to use that word in their spaces. And it makes us happy because the Aymara Education Council has made it such that that word is recuperated." Laime credited his father, Félix Laime Pairumani, a well-known Aymara linguist in Bolivia, for having worked with other intellectuals and the leadership of the CEA in adopting "qamasa" for the radio station's name.

As a "recuperated" concept, it is a term that presumably requires explanation to other Aymara speakers and not just foreigners like myself. That *qamasa* is almost but not exactly like *coraje*, which is, in turn, similar to but also more than the English "courage," is a kind of incommensurability that opens up possibilities of explanation, stances of authority, and also essentializations. More than simply "time of courage," the name *Pacha Qamasa* facilitated for Laime a footing of authority to explain Aymara metaphysics, the unified notion of spacetime *pacha*, and a vital force of being, *qamasa*.

A conceit lurking in these metalinguistic explanations is that they reveal more than just semantics, offering insight on some essence of the language and by extension its speakers. Consider how many words across languages are explained as being "untranslatable" and, thus, held as precious to the community of speakers. The voice of another, a speaker of another language, comes through in the act of uttering these words. One hears a Brazilian with *saudade* for home, a Dane longing for *hygge*, a Jewish evaluation of someone's *chutzpah*, or a Japanese delight for an *umami* broth. In this mode, the discourse surrounding these words produces a rhematization, in that they project a link between a language and an essence associated with, or at least privileged by, its community of speakers (Gal 2013; Gal and Irvine 2019; Keane 2003; Shankar and Cavanaugh 2012, 2017).

This chapter examines such rhematizations in the discourse of the host and participants of a political talk show on Radio Qacha Qamasa. Linguistic and political representation come together in the political talk show called *Akhulli Amuyt'awi*. We will see in the transcripts of this show examined in this chapter that rhematizations of Aymaras and their Others are projected from discursive units of different scales. The show's host opens his show with a chronotopic projection of idealized kinds of Aymara subjects depicted within an Aymara national territory, all within the show's invocation of an Indigenous Andean speech genre associated with chewing coca. Another rhematization occurs through the voicing effects of codeswitching between Aymara and Spanish, done within represented speech that quotes an opinionated Aymara public. Another rhematization coheres through a voicing effect performed by one of the show's guests in his use of an Aymara epithet in otherwise Spanish language political speech, speech in which he diagrams the outlines of his idealized model of Aymara personhood.

In the last chapter, we encountered broadcasters at Radio San Gabriel who approached the Aymara language itself as a metonym for the Aymara nation, a terrain to be recovered through lexical rescue and innovation, closely monitored and protected from encroach. Radio Pacha Qamasa similarly foregrounds the Aymara language as an emblem of Aymara identity. We also hear the Aymara language as the language spoken by the voice of authority. The host's eloquent dehispanicized Aymara provides the matrix language, the audible framework for the program in which other voices, whether speaking in Spanish or Aymara, are heard and evaluated. It is the host's Aymara voice that frames the discussions, poses questions, summarizes contributions, and opens and closes the show. The first and last words are Aymara. While much of what makes this an "Aymara program" is the language heard on it, the show is multilingual and often mostly in Spanish. The Aymara language is foregrounded, but along with other Aymara emblems, most notably the coca leaf, coca chewing, and the speech genre associated with this practice and the metapragmatic norms governing it.

The Aymara language functions as an emblem of Aymaraness, but so too does the speech genre of the *akhulli*, a model of interactional communicative conduct associated with chewing coca. Not limited to Aymaras but also practiced by Quechuas and encountered throughout the Andes, *akhulli* is a conversation organized through the sharing and chewing of coca leaves. Normatively, the *akhuklli* is a civil, ethically grounded, multiparty, deliberative, and non-hierarchical exchange of ideas. In modeling itself after the deliberative conversation tied to the sharing and chewing of coca leaves, the radio program examined here is an example of the mediatization of Aymara metapragmatics. The chewing of coca leaves is a practice that occurs within a broad range of contexts throughout the Andes, from the most banal to the most ritualized and sacred, in cities and the country, by Quechuas, Aymaras, and non-Indian Bolivians alike. Chewing coca, and the coca leaf itself, came to be an overdetermined symbol of nationalist and Indianist politics alike because of its relationship to the international political economy of cocaine production. That the foundation for a communicative practice of community deliberation and the raw material for international narcotics trade are one and the same is a strange accident of history. The program examined in this chapter, *Akhulli Amuyt'awi*, rose to prominence in El Alto because of how it served as a forum for debating

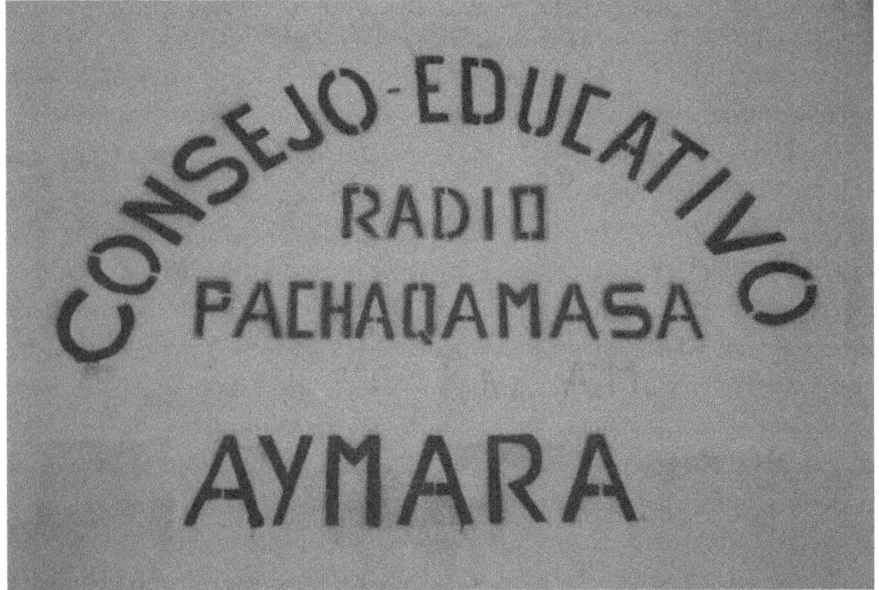

Figure 3.1 Offices of Radio Pacha Qamasa.

and organizing around the very issues that underlie "the coca problem"— Indigenous autonomy and the control of natural resources.

Following some background on the CEA, Radio Pacha Qamasa, and the program *Akhulli Amut'awi,* this chapter analyzes textual examples of broadcast discourse from the program in which participants advance competing discourses of what it means to be Aymara and to engage in Aymara cultural practices. Various bids for the representation of Aymaras come through the broadcasts examined in this chapter, from both the host and his guests. We will hear the host of the show both describe and quote the Aymara listening public he addresses through his program. Candidates for elected office speak on the show in their own campaigns to represent Aymaras politically and, in the process, offer models of what it means to be Aymara.

The Aymara Education Council, Radio Pacha Qamasa, and Akhulli Amuyt'awi

Radio Pacha Qamasa is not just a radio station, but also the public voice of the Aymara Education Council (CEA), the political and professional organization of Aymara bilingual teachers in Bolivia. Emerging from Aymara teachers' activism around bilingual education in the teachers union, the CEA as an organization embodies both Bolivian trade union traditions and Indianist and Katarista political traditions. The CEA is recognized as a semi-autonomous organization of Aymaras alongside other indigenous First Peoples' Education Councils (CEPOs, *Consejos Educativos de Pueblos Originarios*). The media workers of Radio Pacha Qamasa, like those at Radio San Gabriel, commit themselves to the cultivation of the Aymara language in the public sphere through concerted institutional intervention. This project is one with language at its core and is fundamentally reflexive for how it both presupposes an Aymara speaking audience while reflexively aiming to transform that very audience.

Educators, educational institutions, and the fight for access to education itself have all figured prominently within Aymara history, a historical legacy that the CEA situates itself within. This legacy includes the movements of the *caciques apoderados* who used Spanish language literacy to read, maintain, and use colonial era documents to defend communal lands in courts (Ari 2014; Choque and Quispe 2010; Rivera-Cusicanqui 1987). Because of the successes of Aymara communities in defending their lands in courts, large landowners, or *latifundistas,* enforced illiteracy among Aymaras in areas where the latifundistas held political power. Aymaras were banned from reading newspapers or books and corporal punishment was delivered if Aymara farm workers were found reading (López 2005; Pérez 1992). In response to this situation, and in the context of the renewed mobilization of the Caciques Apoderados, Aymara communities organized the education of their children through itinerant teachers. An Aymara elder who lived through this period is quoted by education scholar Luís Enrique López (2005) describing the conditions in which Aymara education operated during the early twentieth century: "Educating our children was a kind of contraband, we had to hide, pay out of pocket, selling our products that was how we taught ... We had to watch like guards ... From those two hills we would watch to see if soldiers were coming, and we'd yell if they were coming" (Choque 1994, as cited in López 2005, translated by author).

The experiences of itinerant clandestine teachers formed the basis for an experiment in Aymara education, the *Escuela-Ayllu Warisata*. Founded in 1931, this school emerged as a collaboration between former itinerant Aymara educators, most notably Avelino Siñani, and a socialist educator from La Paz, Elizardo Pérez. The Warisata Ayllu-School would serve as a reference point for generations to come and its leaders also contributed to international initiatives in Indigenous education, participating in the 1940 Pátzcuaro congress, for example Perez (1992). That questions of education and literacy animated struggles in the early twentieth century figures into how Aymara educators view their own contemporary activism as coming in the wake of earlier generations' struggles.

The roots of the CEA reach back less to the days of Warisata, however, as much as to the period following the fall of the military governments of the early 1980s and the wave of working class and Aymara militancy that surged in their wake. In 1983, the Confederation of Rural Teachers of Bolivia (CONMERB) began demanding the implementation of intercultural bilingual education as "a decolonizing educational project in the context of our ethnic majority's process of social liberation" with the aim of "overcoming and definitely liquidating the still existing remnants of colonialism" (cited in Machaca 2007: 21, translation by author). Less than a decade later, in 1991, the Unified Sindical Confederation of Workers and Peasants of Bolivia (CSUTCB) convened committees on a national basis composed of teachers and parents with the goal of advancing the goal of community control of education. In highland Bolivian Aymara communities, these committees would participate in councils created with the 1994 Education Reform (Law 1565) and ultimately came to form the basis of a newly formed CEA. The CEA was one of nine First Peoples' Education Councils (Consejos Educativos de Pueblos Originarios, CEPOs) formed in order to facilitate the participation of Indigenous communities in the development and implementation of intercultural bilingual education. While legally recognized by the Bolivian state and granted significant powers in the development of educational policies for their respective communities, the CEPOs operated as largely autonomous organizations. In addition to the publication of pamphlets, informational and educational materials, and a regular newsletter, a central vehicle for communicating with its constituents, both educators and families, is the CEA's radio station, Radio Pacha Qamasa.

The founding director Franz Laime explained that prior to Radio Pacha Qamasa's founding in 2003, the CEA rented studio time from Radio San Gabriel to broadcast regular programming. At the high rate of nearly eighty US dollars for a two-hour slot, this ultimately consumed a large portion of the CEA's budget. Instead of abandoning radio broadcasting altogether, the CEA's leadership remained committed to this medium for communicating with its constituency and decided to invest that money toward launching its own radio station. They ultimately saved enough money to buy the transmitter of Radio Mundial, a radio station that had been owned by a prominent sports announcer and Quechua Bolivian, Alfonso Arévalo, who was a sympathizer and supporter of Indigenous organizations like the CEA.

Laime explained to me how having their own radio station was important not only because of the organization's finances, but also to establish independence from the religiously oriented Radio San Gabriel. His historical narrative of RPQ's beginnings lays out this contrast between the two radio stations:

> Radio San Gabriel was said to belong to the Aymaras but it put in a lot of evangelical content ... they were holding on to the same policy of the SIL, the same contents, get a hold of a song, a rhythm from your culture, and put in the content of evangelization, to get the people dizzy. And in Pacha Qamasa we saw that very clearly. At Pacha Qamasa one couldn't say "God bless you," please, no, *Pacha Mama jumampi jichhuruxa irnaqtpa* ('May Mother Earth work with you today'). With the blessing of *Pacha Mama*. Trying a little bit not to deviate from that form of devotion for mother nature, before all that about god is imposed ... Pacha Qamasa was the opposite of San Gabriel. Precisely for that little detail we had a large audience. That is what differentiated us.

Laime discussed the Christian messaging of the Jesuit radio station as taking the same approach as the US evangelicals associated with the Summer Institute of Linguistics (SIL). The effect of reinterpreting evangelical hymns with Andean rhythms on the listening audience is one that he describes as dizzying (*"marear a la gente"*) to Aymara listeners. Laime and others at RPQ were interested not necessarily in a secular outlook per se, but rather they were interested in programming with more distinctly Aymara cultural content.

Having been founded in 2003, it was only months before Franz, the staff of RPQ, and the residents of El Alto confronted challenges that required and demonstrated their deep reserves of *qamasa*. In October of that year a major conflict broke out in which the residents of El Alto and the surrounding high plain played a decisively protagonist role. The Gas War, as the conflict of 2003 came to be known, was not just about gas. Outrage at the death of a young girl at the hands of government forces during an attack on demonstrators in the Aymara community of Warisata, the same Warisata of historic fame, combined with anger over then President Gonzalo "Goni" Sánchez de Lozada's plans to sell Bolivian natural gas at low cost to the United States and Chile. Protestors set up roadblocks and marches filled the streets; the situation escalated to full-scale fighting with government forces.

Laime explained the outrage with the Sánchez de Lozada government in terms of Indigenous sovereignty claims and in terms of Aymara norms of resource management citing the practice of *pirwa*, or "storage," of potatoes. Here too, like *qamasa* discussed at the opening of the chapter, his explanation of an Aymara word provided an opportunity for articulating what he held to be an Aymara cultural norm, a "logic" of conservation. The scene of authority in his account below is the practice of rural farmers in how they store their potato crop. This logic was the one being violated by the Sánchez de Lozada government:

> It was the demand of the rights as Indigenous people over natural resources, right? Because the logic that we advanced in the *Akhulli Amuyt'awi* was the following: for example, for us as Indigenous people, what's the logic? When we sow potatoes and we harvest, in a year that went well, we take (some potatoes) and we divide the produce. One part that we select goes to be the seed, or the *jatha*, as we call it. Another part that we select goes to the *pirwa* or storage as we could call it Spanish. That doesn't completely fill the concept of *pirwa* in Aymara, for the bad times, and another *jatha*, another little bit that's left for food—*manq'añataki*, for eating, and another part that's left over, but that's there, well, sell it. But that's the logic that we've set out. Why don't we first help people with natural resources, with the gas, the people here? And secondly, our reserve as a country, what are we thinking? And third, what's left, to sell it. That same logic, even though it's a non-renewable resource—double the reason still! Right? So, that more or less had been the focus from our perspective.

Laime brings up the program *Akhulli Amut'awi* as having advanced a particular discussion, as a space of political deliberation in the lead-up to the conflict of October 2003. The program was not simply a megaphone for the CEA, but instead was considered as a space of dialogue and deliberation. Following a format similar to many talk radio programs in the United States, the show's host invites specialists and public figures to discuss pressing issues and to field questions and comments from callers and an in-studio audience. The program aired every Friday night and became a site for vigorous debate of politics and strategy through a formative social upheaval and brought together diverse sectors of Aymara political life. Laime explained this dynamic as such:

> The *Akhulli Amuyt'awi* are what made history on Friday nights. The idea was that we should take advantage, we do everything but finally to be realists, we're people, we work, but we'll educate ourselves [nos capacitaremos]. There aren't institutes. We'll do it here. … We would bring Aymara intellectuals principally. That was what we did. Aymara intellectuals, I tell you, Roberto Choque, Esteban Ticona, Felipe Quispe, one time Evo Morales.

During the events of October 2003, RPQ came under attack from the de Lozada government. The radio station's newly, and dearly, acquired transmitter was riddled with bullets by the military police while pro-government stations' transmitters, located adjacent to RPQ's, were left unharmed. This did not stop RPQ, however, as they were able to quickly repair the transmitter and continue broadcasts. RPQ was among the few radio stations to have mobile reporters informing the public of events from barricades and battles around the city of El Alto. Laime and another radio announcer received death threats from anonymous callers who would menace "o callas o mueres" (either you shut up or you die) and "silencio o muerte" (silence or death). These threats did not stop the radio from running new programs, and *Akhulli Amuyt'awi* was never canceled due to the unrest in the city.

> *Akhulli Amuyt'awi* didn't shut up for one Friday during that whole time. So, I can say that we sowed a seed of consciousness more than simply the sense of being rebellious or of going to fight for something that has nothing to do with us. It was the demand of the rights as Indigenous people over natural resources.

From its beginnings in the tumultuous events of 2003, *Akhulli Amuyt'awi* has continued in its mission as a site for political commentary and debate.

Upon arriving in La Paz/El Alto to conduct field work, I was able to meet Gabriel Bonifacio Flores, the host of *Akhulli Amuyt'awi*, and other members of the CEA through Franz Laime and my connections with people working in the field of intercultural bilingual education. During my field visits in La Paz/El Alto, I would make my way to the offices of the CEA to attend the live sessions of

Akhulli Amuyt'awi on Friday nights. The CEA's offices are located in a four-story brick building at the edge of El Alto, just a few blocks off the dusty highway that connects El Alto to the industrial suburb of Viacha. The offices share the plaza with two weekly markets, a middle school, and some small businesses. The first two floors of the building house large meeting spaces, with the main offices on the top floor overlooking the surrounding city and mountain peaks. The third floor is dedicated to the offices and studios of their radio station, one of which is open to the public on Friday's to listen and participate to Flores and the guests he interviews in the weekly broadcast. Some Fridays there would be three or four men and women coming in to listen, and other days there would be an overflow crowd, with people also sitting outside of the studios, listening to the broadcast from the waiting room.

Flores is a charismatic and eloquently bilingual host, with a rich baritone voice and the clear enunciation of a radio announcer. True to the character of the CEA, Flores is also an educator himself, his primary employment being a middle school teacher in El Alto. In addition to his teaching job, he works throughout the week to ensure the success of the show's program, to secure a steady agenda of guests participating in the show. Flores revealed to me that he knew he had a talent for using his voice to draw a crowd from a young age when he worked as a street vendor, projecting his voice loudly and clearly selling *salteñas* (a Bolivian savory pastry). He eventually was able to study at the Bolivian Catholic University and received scholarships to study community radio abroad, first in Venezuela and then later in Seville, Spain. His experiences living abroad raised his awareness of not being just Bolivian, but increased his sense of being Aymara. When he returned to Bolivia he arrived motivated to expand the use of Aymara in the media, beyond the "morning programming" that targeted laborers and farmers, usually for purposes of evangelism and literacy. He addressed the issue of limited Aymara language programming in an interview with me:

> They only came on in the morning in Aymara. And later? *Chhaqataw* (' It's lost'). There wasn't anything. And how can a majority population be reduced to some few hours of communication? That for me was something foolish. A majority population with the largest linguistic population being Aymara, or Indigenous people. No. Here we require mass media (Sp: *medios de comunicación*) that dedicate the whole blessed day in their language. And at the same time speaking the same language that people understand best.

In Spain, Flores had participated in a radio debate program on a Catholic radio station, but felt that too often the issues discussed were driven by questions of religious practice that were of little interest to him, such as whether wearing a cross as jewelry to a club was sacrilegious. Upon returning to Bolivia he wanted to debate, "*temas e intereses del pueblo y en lengua nativa*" (topics and interests of the people in native language).

The first recording of the program was unlike subsequent recordings in that, rather than being recorded in the radio studio, it was a recording of Aymara elders in a rural *ayllu* as they met to discuss issues facing their community. Flores explained to me how this became the baptismal event of the show:

> We sat down there and we said, "What? What do we call it?" and we remembered the countryside. At ten in the morning did an *akhulliku* and in the meantime people sat down in the *akhulliku*, began to dialogue and talk, right? And it's in Aymara. *Akhamakiwa* (Aym: Just like this): What's good? What's bad? What's delicious? Etc. So, we functioned for about a month with the name *Akhulli*. Later we said this isn't only *akhulli*, philosophy is being generated here so it's *Akhulli Amuyt'awi*.

Akhulli is not only the act of chewing coca, a nominalized form of the Aymara verb *akhulliña* "to chew coca," but also a speech genre associated with the sharing of coca. The second part to the program's name, *amuyt'awi*, is derived from the verb *amuyt'aña*, "to think," "to reflect," made a noun by the ending "*-wi*," a nominalizer for a place or location where the root verb is enacted. The program's name could be translated as "place for chewing coca and thinking," or in Flores' words, "generating philosophy." The program's name provides a metacommunicative frame that suggests the kind of talk the listener can expect. It also does more than this. The name offers an example of what Susan Gal and Judith Irvine call a "metamove" of modeling or anchoring, where one site, here a radio program, is modeled by another, the rural *akhulli* with elders, in such a way that the radio show is presented as a diagrammatic icon of the *akhulli* in the countryside (Gal and Irvine 2019: 215). We will see below that this is achieved not only through the show's title, but also through the host's talk in the course of the show.

A Mediatized *Akhulli*

The *akhulli* among Aymara elders in the rural *ayllu* was more than a trope invoked through the program's name, but also an account of the show's baptismal event. While only the inaugural show was recorded in the countryside, subsequent programs were recorded in the studios of RPQ. The setup for the sessions is similar to recording studios elsewhere, with two studios equipped with microphones separated by a sound booth housing the sound equipment, internet, telephone lines, and a sound technician. One studio was for the host, Flores, and his guests; while the second studio had benches for a live, listening audience. The *akhulli* became transformed in multiple ways, from rural to urban, from face-to-face interaction, to one situated in a studio, connected to participants through microphones, radio waves, and telephone lines. Coca remained, in both studios, and quite likely in the homes and mouths of those tuning in to the program. The *akhulli* as a chronotope of Aymara political life, deliberative democratic dialogue, became projected across the city of El Alto and out over the surrounding high plain.

Akhulli Amuyt'awi had been on the air for four years during my first visits to the radio station in 2007. This was still early in the presidency of Evo Morales and in the lead-up to the rewriting of the nation's constitution. From its beginnings in the uprising of 2003 and through the election of Evo Morales, and in the lead-up to and the wake of the rewriting of the nation's constitution, which was ratified in 2009, the program remained a vibrant clearing house for activists, politicians, and commentators in the city of El Alto and the broader Aymara sphere through a period of intense political debate. The program had a political profile through its association with the CEA, and its host himself was a working teacher. Still, the very nature and aim of the program was to have a diversity of voices from the Aymara public, a space for Aymara intellectuals and activists to discuss, assess, and educate the broader Aymara public about the issues facing the nation. We find this laid out explicitly by the host himself below in an opening segment of the program, where he asks, *Kunjamas aka markasanxa?* "How is it here in our nation?" (line 6) and then reminds the listener, with a poetic repetition, this is why they've tuned in, "*yatiyawinakasa utjki, amtawinakas utjki, amuyt'awinakas utjki, taqi ukanakata aruskipt'añataki Akhulli Amuyt'awi wakichawinxa* / 'there's lessons, there's memories, there's philosophies, in order to talk about all these things is the program *Akhulli Amuyt'awi*'" (lines 7–8).

The opening segment below (Table 3.1) is worth examining in its entirety to hear how the host discursively projects portraits of the listening "nation" as he convenes the *akhulli*. Because this is done in Aymara, the audience is already presupposed as being an Aymara listening public, but Flores also depicts the contours of Aymara territory and characterological figures of the Aymara people who inhabit this territory. This space is evoked within a temporal framework in that he also establishes the simultaneity of broadcast through reference to the weather (lines 18–19), and the fact that he's hungry for an evening supper—wishing for a bowl of soup on a cold night (lines 37–40). He acknowledges possible participants, situates them with respect to one another, and invites them

Table 3.1 Opening for *Akhulli Amuyt'awi* (February 26, 2010)

(1:12)		
1G:	Kamisaki? Kamisaki jilanaka kullakanaka?	How are you? How are you brothers and sisters?
2	Pacha Qamasa Radio ist'irinaka mä jach'a arunta purt'ayataptaw jumanakaru.	Pacha Qamasa Radio listeners, a big greeting we (exclusive) send to you
3	Jallallakipanaya sasina Akhulli Amuyt'awi wakichawitpacha	saying Greetings! from the program Akhulli Amuyt'awi
4	Pacha Qamasa Radio ist'irinaka	Pacha Qamasa Radio listeners
5	jumanakampiw jichhaxa chikañchasiñani.	with you now we (inclusive) come together.
6	Kunjamasa akaaaa markasanxa?	How is it in this country of ours?
7	Yatiyawinakasa utjki, amtawinakas utjki, amuyt'awinakasa utjki,	There's lessons There's memories There's philosophies
8	Taqi ukanakata aruskipt'añataki Akhulli Amuyt'awi wakichawinxa.	In order to talk about all these things is the program Akhulli Amuyt'awi.
9	Niyaw purt'anipxi jilata kullakanakasa.	They're almost arriving, brothers and sisters.
10	Jupanakasa amuyt'apxaniwa arst'apxarakchini.	They'll be thinking and be speaking too.
11	A ver kunanaka amuykipt'añachi kunanakaya aruskipt'añachi.	Let's see what things they're thinking, what they'll be speaking about
12	Ukhamawa. jichhaxa aksa tuqinxa chikañt'asipxañani.	That's how it is. Now over here we (inclusive) will all get together
13	Jilata kullakanaka markachirinakaxa niyawa pata tuqinakansa	Brothers, sisters, citizens almost up in the heights
14	uuywampi yapumpi sarnaqirinakaki jupanakaxa	those just walking with animals and fields
15	yamakisa uka qarwanakasa ant'ata wakanakas jikt'asita	you almost have the llamas and cows gathered
16	uywa, uwijanakasa ant'asata ukjam utjaw tuqiru kut'atakarakchi	animals, sheep gathered like that and also perhaps you've returned home
17	yaqhipanakaxa niyaw uyu tuqirusa jist'ant'apkarakchi ukhamapachawa	Others are maybe holed up and maybe closed in too
18	Alalalalayyyyyy aka jalluxa aka taqi jalluntaskakistï	brrrrrrrrrrr this rain over here, it is raaaaining!
19	Yaqhip tuqinakana sapxarakpachapï	In other places they must be saying (this) too!

(*continued*)

20	Qhatunkirinakaxa jichas qarit qarit inasa sarantapkchi	The market vendors are now coming in very tired.
21	Radios it'asita Pacha Qamasa ist'asa	Carrying radios listening to Pacha Qamasa
22	Bueno jumanakaruwa mä jach'a qhumanta purt'ayatapxarakta	Alright, to you (plural) a big hug we (ex.) also send.
23	Aka El Alto Pata Markata Tupak Katari markapatxa	Here, El Alto (Spanish) from El Alto (Aymara), from Tupac Katari's city
24	waljaninakawa ist'apxixa	there are many listening.
25	Radio Pacha Qamasa jumanakaru arut'atapxarakta	We at Radio Pacha Qamasa also greet you
26	Khithinakatix khaysa Chukiyaqu markana Calacoto, a?	And those down there in La Paz Calacoto, eh?
27	Jisa, Calacoto tuqina ist'apxiya	Yes, over in Calacoto they're listening
28	Jilata kullakanakaxa uksa tuqin wali sumaya	The brothers and sisters over there also are good
29	q'aycht'apxarakixa Radio Pacha Qamasa.	at carrying around Radio Pacha Qamasa.
30	Jumanakarusa jallallt'atapxaraktawa taqi tuqinakana.	to you we also send greetings everywhere
31	Khaysa yungas junt' uraqina	There in the yungas in the tropics (hot lands)
32	uksa tuqin yaqipanakaxa	and others elswhere
33	inasa kuka yapuchawimpi sarantawayapchi.	maybe they're walking off into their coca harvests.
34	Jichhuruxa ukat yaqha irnaqawinakampi	Today later with other jobs
35	inas phuqt'awayapxarakchi (2:50)	maybe they've also completed
36	ukhamaxa jichhax qarit qaritaki ampi	like that now a little bit tired right
37	A ver, Max, jichhax caldito manq't'asiñ muntxa	Let's see, Max, now I'd like to eat soup.
38	Janiwa nayax phiri munktixa. Jas ukhama ampi	I don't want crackers (phiri). Like that yes.
39	Sapxakirakpachaya ampï ¿No? Quiero comer un pollito	They would probably also say it, yes, no? I want to eat a little chicken.
40	Jas ukham yaqhipax sapxarakchi.	That's also probably how others would say it.
41	Bueno, ukañkamaxa yanakaxa Irjatta ukhamakiskiw.	Alright, your being there things have gotten bigger and that's how it is.
42	waliki jallallapana	Alright, greetings.

(continued)

43	ee Akhullt'asiñani.	Uh Lets chew coca.
44	Jisa, jilirinakas kawkhankisa kuka tari?	Yes. Gentleman (elders). Where's my cloth for laying out the coca?
45	Kawkhankisa ch'uspa? Kuka ch'uspaxa kawkhankisa?	Where's my coca bag? The coca bag where is it?
46	wal apst'asiñan ukhamaxa (3:16)	We'll raise a lot that way.
47	Aksa tuqin niyawa Inal Mamaxa [aptaq..] apnuqt'ataxi.	Over here Inal Mama is almost laid out.
48	Akhullt'asiñani Jilata Nelson Guarachi	Let's chew coca brother Nelson Guarachi
49	Akhullt'asiñani jilata Edwin Mamani	Let's chew coca brother Edwin Mamani.
50	Akhullt'asiñani. Jupanakaxa purt'anipxi akhullt'iri, no?	Let's chew coca. They arrived chewing coca, no?
51	Jilataaa Edwin? Edwin Condori.	Brother Edwin? Edwin Condori
52	Janiwa Edwin Mamani, Edwin Condori.	No. Edwin Mamani. Edwin Condori.
53	Ukhamakiti? Pantjasta nayapï.	Isn't it like that? I made a mistake.
54	Bueno jupanakaw aksankapxi.	Alright they're here
55	Ukatxa yaqha jilatanakas purt'anipxarakiniwa	Later some other brothers will also be arriving
56	Aksankapxaniwa jilata aka Ejecutivo Departamental	They'll be here the brother this Departmental Executive
57	de Federación Departamental de Maestros Rurales	of the Departmental Federation of Rural Teachers
58	de La Paz. Jupas aksa tuqiru purt'anirakini	of La Paz. He'll arrive here.
59	Jupanakampisa aruskipt'arakiñaniw.	We'll be speaking with them too.
60	Bueno jichhakucha qallant'añani.	Alright now we'll begin. [Pause 2.0]

to join him and others in chewing coca and considering the problems facing the country together with his guests, soon to arrive.

The title *Akhulli Amuyt'awi* itself serves as a metacommunicative frame for the program. We hear in this opening that the invitation to chew coca and reflect on the issues of the day is not achieved by the title of the program alone. The host invites listeners at home to join, to chew coca, to consider the issues and the contributions of the program's guests, and perhaps even call in and participate themselves. Flores also projects discursive images of an Aymara listening public, invoking a range of social types that the listener may imagine as copresent through the mediation of the airwaves. He expands the *akhulli* from the recording studio out across the high plains and city below to encompass a range of characters the listeners can imagine as prototypically Aymara subjects—farmers in the high plains and mountains (lines 13–17), vendors in markets (lines 20–2), residents of El Alto, which he calls "Tupak Katari's city" (lines 23–5), and Aymara speakers in La Paz, even in its wealthy southern neighborhoods like Calacoto (lines 26–30), and coca growers in the Yungas (lines 31–6). We might consider this list a portrait of Aymara social types, and simultaneously also a kind of salutation, a welcoming of participants present in the act of tuning in. In making this list, he enables possible footings of role alignment by listeners who might feel interpellated in this act of recognition. This listing of imagined listeners also resonates with a practice of acknowledgment common in another, analogous context with which Flores has practice in his role as a trade unionist—the acknowledgment of notable attendees at the opening of a meeting, a practice common at the inauguration of many gatherings in Bolivia, whether civic, political, educational, or otherwise.

His opening greeting also follows a spatial, even territorial, logic. Flores diagrams an expanse of Aymara territory from the high plain, the *altiplano*, in the west, through El Alto, "Tupak Katari's city," down through the city of La Paz, its lower wealthy suburbs, and beyond the city to the east and north to the "hot lands" of the Yungas. His mention of listeners in La Paz and the wealthy southern neighborhood of Calacoto comes with a question of incredulity (line 26) and an affirmation (line 27) that, yes, even there the show has listeners tuning in. La Paz and Calacoto are situated as remote in relation to Flores through his use of the distal/remote spatial deictic *khaysa*, "over there/yonder." Those tuning into the show may know that the studio where Flores is located is in El Alto, but his use of deictics further diagrams the social space surrounding the broadcast. Calacoto is "over there" while the proximal spatial deictic (*aka*, "here," line 23) is used in reference to El Alto establishing it as the deictic center of the broadcast, the place from which he speaks. He takes up a multiply authoritative footing by speaking not only for himself, but speaking on behalf of the radio station (line 25), taking on the participant role that Erving Goffman called the principal (Goffman 1981). This comes within an interesting identification of the city itself that comes out with a triple voicing of the city's name. In line 23 he says the city's name in Spanish (El Alto), in Aymara (*Pata Marka*), and then also Tupak Katari's city (*Tupak Katari Markapa*). When he situates himself geographically, he also situates himself institutionally ("We at Radio Pacha Qamasa greet you") and in terms of Aymara history and authority ("from Tupak Katari's city").

After having greeted his audience, Flores closes this stretch of the opening with a greeting, "*Waliki jallallapana*/Good greetings" (line 42) and transition into the *akhulli* itself, with an inclusive-we inflected "*akhullt'asiñani*/let's chew coca" (line 43). He describes the process of arranging coca in lines 44 through 47, looking for the cloth where the coca to be shared can be laid out (*kuka tari*) and locating his coca pouch (*kuka chuspa*). He is audibly chewing coca already at this time. He uses the name of coca which designates her as an animate female being, *Inal Mama*, and affirms that she is present (line 47). He announces the names of the guests as he repeats the call of, "let's chew coca" (lines 48–9), noticing then that the guests had arrived already chewing coca (line 50). In fact, one of the guests, Nelson Guarachi, audibly chews coca throughout the entire broadcast, an ample wad of coca in his mouth leaving his speech with a distinctive distortion. Having convened the participants in the *akhulli*, from the listeners in the mountains, city, and valleys, to the guests in studio, and, crucially, Inal Mama herself, the host has established that "the gang's all here" and can declare "qallantañani/let's begin" (line 56).

Vox Populi, Vox Aymarensis/The Voice of the Aymara Public

After greeting the listening public and before interviewing his guests, Flores continues with his monologue but shifts into a segment in which he animates the voices of the Aymara public and outlines the political landscape as he sees it, or rather as he hears it, and then repeats this for the listening public. Where earlier in the broadcast he presented characterological types, the farmer, the market vendor, in this section we hear the voices of an unnamed public through

Table 3.2 "I want to eat a little chicken"

37	A ver, Max, jichhax caldito manq't'asiñ muntxa	Let's see, Max, now I'd like to eat soup.
38	Janiwa nayax phiri munktixa.	I don't want crackers.
	Jas ukhama ampi	Like that yes.
39	Sapxakirakpachaya ampï	They would probably also just say it, yes,
	¿No? Quiero comer un pollito	No? I want to eat a little chicken. (Spanish)
40	Jas ukham yaqhipax sapxarakchi.	That's also probably how others might say it.

represented speech. The contrast between his narrating voice and the narrated voice of another within his own speech is a contrast he often marks through a switch from Aymara to Spanish. We encountered this voicing effect produced through codeswitching at the close of the previous section in lines 37 through 40, when Flores discussed his own hunger and the likelihood that his listeners might also want something more substantial than just a cracker at that hour (Table 3.2).

When Flores animates the voice of the hungry Aymara listener, we can hear this both as an invitation for the listener to identify with the host and also as a marker of simultaneous broadcast, a move that underscores the live nature of the dinner-hour transmission. There are at least two interesting things to note additionally. One is that, even though a single utterance, Flores cites a plurality, something said by many listeners. In quoting a voice, the verb in the matrix clause, *saña* "to say," is conjugated not in the singular but in the plural (*-px*—plural marker)—*sapxakirakpachaya* "they would probably also just say." Furthermore, the way "they would probably also just say it" would not be in Aymara, but in Spanish, "*quiero comer un pollito.*" The voicing of the hungry listener is dialogic in yet another way. He introduces this speculation with a questioning "no?" inviting the listener to reflect both on how others in the listening public are feeling and what they might say if asked. The pragmatic effect of producing a multilingual, dialogic exchange within what is, in fact, one radio broadcaster's monologue, is a discursive convening of an Aymara public. This public is bilingual, and here, when quoted, it is a public that speaks Spanish.

In discussing the phenomenon of quoting others' speech in one's own, I follow Asif Agha (2007) in referring to represented speech rather than reported speech, as is common in literature on the subject. "Report" suggests that the citation of another's speech is in some way accurate, traceable to an author and a past moment of interaction, while, in fact, representations of speech "need not deictically formulate their pragmatic objects as having occurred in past time, or even in an interaction distinct from the current one" (Agha 2007: 32). In what follows, we find speech that is either represented as concurrent with Flores' own broadcast, like the wish for a chicken dinner, or in a non-specified, ongoing present. Rather than a report of the past, Flores performs an animation of ongoing political dialogue. Sometimes the speech is tied to individually locatable persons, like politicians in the case below, but often he represents unnamed voices of the public.

The embedding of others' speech into one's own is a form of metalanguage that opens windows onto the social and historical relations in which a speaker is enmeshed. How a speaker calibrates the ongoing context of their own speech with the voices and contexts of others reveals a view from within discourse itself, a glimpse into the life-world of the speaker. The literary and sociological promise of this form of metalanguage made it the focus of commentary from the Soviet literary theorist V. N. Volosinov who wrote about this phenomenon in terms of indirect and direct discourse. Volosinov described the shifts between narrating and narrated voices within a text as sites where fragments of subjectivity became pictorially available, if only partially, illuminating the presence of another within the voice of the narrator. He describes these effects as comparable to the sculptures of Auguste Rodin, where "the figure is left only partially emerged from the stone," with only the suggestion of full presence (Volosinov 1986: 132).

For Volosinov, how the voice emerges as a figure that contrasts against the ground, or "stone," of the narrator's voice is that the second voice is somehow "made strange" (Volosinov 1986: 131). One way Flores achieves this is through the contrastive use of Spanish. This contrastive use of Spanish to bring other voices into his own commentary continues through the following segment of this program as he animates diverse voices from within the Aymara public. On a show discussing upcoming local elections, he animates voices who assess the merits and shortcomings of different candidates, of whether or not they are worthy of carrying on the legacy of Tupak Katari, of whether or not they are worthy bearers of the torch of *katarismo*. Flores moves between citing nameless others ("it's said," "elsewhere it's said") and quotes named individuals, such as the Aymara politician, Simón Yampara, who criticizes the president Evo Morales. He then quotes unnamed others who are, in turn, critical of Yampara and his party, the *Movimiento Sin Miedo* ["Movement without Fear"], and Yampara's alliance with a white politician, Juan del Granado, aka Juan Sin Miedo. The speculations on the risks of cross ethnic alliances is a theme that will be examined further below with an extended critique offered by another guest, and toward a different target, Evo Morales and his party. Note in Table 3.3 the role that codeswitching between Spanish and Aymara plays in producing the pragmatic effect of a dialogic exchange among members of an Aymara public.

The exchange that Flores will have soon with his guests, and later still with listeners calling in, is modeled in his own dialogic voicing of "what people are saying." Not only is there direct quotation of other's speech, but there is also a dialogue internal to his own discourse, the posing of possibilities and the asking of questions. Throughout this portion of the program, Flores poses questions directly to his audience about these circulating evaluations of the various candidates. They are at once the public whose speech he is representing and the audience who will verify or refute these assertions—the *akhulli* participants who, through dialogue, will clarify the situation. We hear two examples of this

Table 3.3 The debating Aymara public

Akhulli Amuyt'awi, Feb. 26, 2010, 10:42	
*_underlined_=Spanish	
1 Maysa tuqitxa saw	Elsewhere it's said
2 _dice que Evo no está con Tupak Katari_ jas ukham sasaw tata Simón Yampara.	_It's said Evo isn't for Tupak Katari_ that's how Mr. Simon Yampara is saying it.
3 Jupax arsux yaqhipa chiqanakanxa siwa. Sapxarakiwa heeee Movimiento Sin Miedo ukaxa	He says his other truths, it's said. They also say heeeee Movement Without Fear it
4 _es un partido de la derecha. Movimiento Sin Miedo no origina en el pueblo campesino_	_is a party of the right, Mvt. Without Fear doesn't originate in the farming people,_
5 _Movimiento Sin Miedo_ ukaxa janiwa aka _pueblo obrero campesino_ tuqita yurikiti	_Movimiento Sin Miedo_ it's not born of this _people of workers farmers_.
6 jas ukhama sasawa sapxixa. Kunatsa jupaxa sari uka tuqita.	That is how they say it. Because that's where he comes from.
7 Ukaw k'umiwinakaxa. Jan wali _negativo_ tuqinxa uñsti.	Those are the criticisms. On the not good _negative_ side it appears.
8 ukxarux saskakiwa. Ukxarux saskakiwa.	To that it's being said. To that it's being said.
9 hee _su plan de gobierno no es tan difundido_. Janikiwa yatipkti siw.	hee _his governmental plan is not so disseminated_ they don't know it's said.
10 markachirinakaxa mmm? Taqi tuqinakana _él es utilizado por Juan del Granado_	Citizens mmmm? In every place _He's used by Juan de Granado_
11 Jas ukhamawa. Chiqat janicha? Jumanakankiw.	That's how it is. Is it true or not? (the decision) It's yours.

above in lines 1 and 11 where he asks the audience *Ukhamat janicha?* "Is it like that or not?" (line 1) *Chiqati janicha?* "Is it true or not?" (line 11). In Table 3.4, we see that Flores does this elsewhere throughout this portion of the program.

The kind of dialogic toggling between assertion and request for affirmation that we hear in Flores's broadcast is a feature that Bruce Mannheim and Krista VanVleet (1998) have identified as a fundamental feature of Southern Quechua discourse. Given the many areal features shared between Aymara and Quechua, it makes sense that this discourse style would also appear in this context. In the third example above, we see that, in addition to including the audience through this posing of questions, Flores also achieves inclusion through the first-person plural inclusive (as opposed to the first-person plural exclusive

Table 3.4 Dialogic toggling between speaker and audience

1. Ukham siwa "*es muy oportunista. Mm? Se auto proclamó por el MAS.*" Chiqat janicha? Jumanakawa uka tuqita sapxäta.

    That's how it's said, "*He's very opportunistic. Mm? He declared himself for the MAS.*" True or not? You (pl) out there will say.

2. Jaqixa janiw q'ariskit ampi? Ukhamat janicha? Jumanakawa yatipxta.

    People don't lie, right? Is it like that or not? You (pl) know.

3. Kamsañs muni akampixa? Anchhitawa qhanacht'añani.

    "What's meant by this? Right now we (inc) will make it clear."

used in the opening section, lines 2 and 22; Table 3.1) when he states that, with regards to the many different positions and circulating opinions regarding the candidates, we (speaker and addressees) are going to achieve clarity on the issue. In his questions to the listening audience, and his inclusion of them through first-person inclusive verbal reference (*qhanacht'añani* "let's make it clear"), the interactional text evokes more than a monologue delivered by a lone host, but instead a multiparty exchange with the listening, if not physically copresent, audience. When Flores poses these types of questions within this monologue, he follows with shows of deference to his audience, reassuring them that they are, ultimately, the authorities in these matters.

A Balance of Bilingualism

How do we understand Spanish vis-à-vis Aymara here? Flores distinguishes his voice from the voice of the public by representing this public as a Spanish-speaking one. This may seem counterintuitive for a broadcaster, and a representative of a media institution, who has the promotion of Aymara language as one of his central aims. If to characterize Spanish a "prestige language" associated with power and politics within a sociolinguistic situation of diglossia (cf. Ferguson 1968) seems accurate for Bolivia more broadly, such a characterization does not account for what we hear here. If anything, Aymara on this program is the language of authority. The eloquently dehispanicized Aymara of the show's host opens and closes the show is the voice that frames the discussion, summarizes contributions, and wraps things up.

That Flores represents the speech of the listeners as Spanish may be, in part, a form of linguistic realism, an accurate representation of how much of his audience does usually speak when they do. Many, if not most, of the program's audience is bilingual and even Spanish dominant. This is also true of the show's guests. When guests arrive to the show, they are greeted in Aymara, and they greet the host and the listeners in Aymara, but the conversation often transitions quickly to Spanish with only occasional stretches of Aymara. The host, the guests, and callers alternate between Spanish and Aymara during the program. Even during the previously examined broadcast roughly a quarter of the total program was in Aymara (approximately 33 of 120 minutes). The following program we will hear from below had even less Aymara spoken on air, just fifteen of the ninety minutes of the program.

The clear delineation between Spanish and Aymara in Flores' speech that contributed to the voicing effects was, in part, possible by the thoroughly dehispanicized nature of Flores's Aymara. Like his colleagues at Radio San Gabriel, Flores avoids hispanicisms and adopts neologisms to avoid them. Such a clear delineation between codes is not shared by most of the guests on his show, however, who rarely speak the media-standard dehispanicized Aymara but, rather, Aymara more typical of bilingual speakers that employs Spanish lexical items phonologically assimilated into Aymara, or simply incorporates Spanish lexemes into Aymara morphosyntax. This is if the guests have much fluency in Aymara at all. One of the guests on the program discussed above, for example, incorporated Spanish loanwords for key terms in the topic of that evening's discussion, terms like *politician, candidate, convincing, discourse,* and *elect* (Table 3.5).

Table 3.5 Spanish loanwords for political terms in discourse

20:53		
E = Edwin Condori	F = Gabriel Flores	Spanish or Spanish loanword
1E	Janiwa suma discurso utjkiti	There's not a good discourse
2	porque mä político,	because a politician
3	Kandidatox kunjamañapasa?	How does a candidate have to be?
4	Chiqasa taqi jaqina,	Truly in each person,
5	taqi wawanakana,	in all the children,
6	taqpacha khititix ilijkani	in everyone who will elect him,
7	khititixa juparu uñt'askanixa	to everyone who will know him,
8	convencedorañapawa.	he has to be convincing
9	Chiqanasa chuymaru puriñapawa	Truly he has to enter their hearts,
10	puriñapawa sapa mayniru	to enter each one of them
11	puriñapawa amuyt'awinakampi	he has to enter with ideas.
12F:	Aymara arunxa sisnawa ukxa	F: In the Aymara language we'd call
13	yäqaña	that yäqaña
14E:	Yäqañ jay ukham	E: Yäqañ, yes, like that.

In this bit of talk where we hear Condori speaking Aymara with many Spanish loanwords, we also find Flores staking out a clear footing of a language expert. Whether as a correction or an elaboration, Flores says "in the Aymara language we'd call that 'yäqaña'" in response, or as an "adjacency pair" (Schegloff and Sacks 1973), to Condori's assertion that a politician needs to enter the mind of the electorate "with philosophies" (*amuyt'awinakampi*). The suggestion is taken up and affirmed by the interviewee. Other Aymara speakers I spoke with provided me with three distinct, if related, glosses for *yäqaña*—to realize, to learn, and to pay attention. A similarly cognitive sense of *yäqaña* appears in Gregorio Calisaya's 2007 list of Aymara Neologisms where it is listed as "to ponder." I bring up these varied but overlapping definitions of *yäqaña* not to resolve them, but to point out a moment in which language authority is enacted on the part of Flores. In his metalinguistic commentary, Flores takes up a footing of authority vis-à-vis his guest, but also to the broader public. This mediatized moment, for those listening to it, gives meaning to this word similar to my asking a native Aymara speaker, or looking it up in a dictionary.

Flores' status as a representative of the CEA and a teacher himself may be enough to establish him to his listeners as such an authority for many of the show's listeners. What we can identify here is that this role is not simply conferred, but is itself discursively produced both through moments of interaction, such as the metalinguistic commentary in line 13, and also through voicing contrasts, within his own speech between Spanish and Aymara, but also between the guest's Aymara spoken with many hispanicisms and his dehispanicized Aymara.

Contested Representation

Both this program and the station on which it is broadcast were conceived to bring political discussion to the Aymara public within a framework of Aymara cultural affirmation, particularly through the use and promotion of the Aymara language. In a society where Aymara fluency is uneven and often atrophied, the communicative demands of political discussion often bring the conversation into Spanish. Such is the case in the next example. Even while speaking Spanish, the guest advances a thoroughly Aymara-centric discourse both through the topic of his commentary but also through carefully deployed Aymara within his otherwise Spanish. The show's guest outlines the contours of an Aymara subject, but through the figure of an ethnic fraud, all within his own claim to be an authentic, and political, representative of Aymaras.

Language is central to his discourse of Aymara authenticity, but not language qua code, Spanish or Aymara, but instead at the level of metapragmatics. His concern lies with the truth value of talk, not speaking Aymara, per se, but speaking *like* an Aymara, and on behalf of Aymaras. In other words, his concern is with metapragmatic norms and, in particular, one which with an associated local maxim: *Uñjasaw "uñjt" sañax. Janiw uñjkiti jan "uñjt" sañakiti.* "Seeing, 'I've seen' can be said. Not having seen, 'I've seen' cannot be said." Equal parts metalinguistic commentary on the use of the verb *saña* "to say" within the Aymara grammatical category of evidentiality as it is a general call for integrity and truthful conduct, this saying links grammatical form to notions of morality and personhood in a classic language-ideological formulation (Irvine 1989; Silverstein 1979; Woolard 1992; Woolard and Schieffelin 1994).[1]

During the same news cycle, in the lead-up to regional and municipal elections, Flores hosted two candidates, Delfín Pukara and Oscar Chirinos, from a small opposition party, the *Movimiento por la Soberanía* (Movement for Sovereignty, MPS). The party positioned itself as being with the "*proceso de cambio*," an offshoot of the ruling MAS that critiques the MAS with the aim of advancing the revolutionary process. In the excerpt of his participation in Akhulli below, we hear how this party's candidate for the mayorship of El Alto, Oscar Chirinos, considers himself to be a true heir to Evo Morales' revolution. As a political candidate he seeks to represent the public he is addressing on the show, but representation is also at stake in terms of represented speech. In Table 3.6, we see how he thematizes the metapragmatics of linguistic representation itself during the course of the radio interview itself, within a broader warning to the programs' listeners that Morales' inner circle has been taken over by whites, *q'aras*. In his critique he diagrams a figure of Aymara personhood, but inversely, by describing how the ethnic Other, the *q'ara*, has adopted Aymara ways, while violating Aymara metapragmatic norms:

If the arrival of Evo Morales to the presidency was to mark the end of white rule in Bolivia and a return of the Indian to power, what to make of the conspicuous presence of whites (*q'aras*) like Vice President Álvaro García Linera and Sacha Lorenti who form part of Evo Morales' inner circle of political advisors? What to make of the increasing number of *q'aras* who chew coca, eat Aymara food, and wear ponchos and sandals (lines 34 through 38)? These anxieties are articulated with the poetic punch of a politician, delivering his denunciation with parallelisms, repetition, and exquisite metricality.

Table 3.6 *"Q'aras"* and MASistas

(1:04:26)		
1	F: ¿Cuánto por ciento todavía es MASista Oscar Chirinos?	What percentage MASista is Oscar Chirinos still?
2	C: Yo soy fundador del MAS. (.)	I'm a founder of the MAS.
3	Yo he sido fundador del MAS	I've been a founder of the MAS.
4	F: ¿El MAS vive en Oscar Chirinos?	Does the MAS live in Oscar Chirinos?
5	C: Yo he vivido con los principios ideológicos	C: I've lived with the ideological
6	y políticos del Movimiento Al Socialismo	and political principles of the Movement to Socialism
7	pero ese Movimiento Al Socialismo	but that Movement to Socialism á
8	que era de lucha,	that was of struggle,
9	que era de búsqueda de liberación,	that was in search of liberation,
10	que era, por ejemplo, de poder marchar	that was for example able to march
11	desde Caracollo para buscar diferentes actividades.	from Caracollo in order to search different activities.
12	Pero no soy militante de este MAS	But I'm not a militant of this MAS
13	que son de los q'aras,	that [belongs to the] q'aras
14	de Álvaro Garcí::a	to Álvaro García,
15	e de Sacha Llore::nti.	to to Sacha Llore::nti.
16	de éstos no::.	to these ones nooo.
17	Este MAS ya no es del pueblo.	This MAS no longer belongs to the people
18	Este MAS ya es de los q'aras=	This MAS belongs to the q'aras=
19	=de esta derecha	=to this right
20	Por ejemplo alguna vez creo que hemos	For example, once I believe we've
21	discutido contigo, Gabriel, cuando yo	argued with you, Gabriel, when I
22	te decía, por ejemplo, si bien nosotros	was saying to you, for example, if we
23	hemos sido los actores para sacar esa	were the actors to take out that
24	derecha recalcitrante	recalcitrant right wing
25	lamentablemente (.) el MAS de	unfortunately (.) The MAS of

(*continued*)

26	Álvaro García, de Sacha Llorenti	Álvaro García, of Sacha Llorenti
27	está permitiendo el nacimiento de una nueva derecha	is permitting the birth of a new right
28	pero más peligrosa que la anterior.	but more dangerous than one before.
29	La anterior ya era identificado.	The one before was already identified.
30	Conocíamos al Goni. Era q'ara.	We knew Goni. He was a q'ara.
31	Conocíamos a Tuto. Era q'ara.	We knew Tuto. He was a q'ara.
32	Era de la derecha, era bien claro	He of the right, it was quite clear
33	y lo hemos expulsado del país.	and we expelled him from the country.
34	Pero ahora estos? (.)	But now these ones? (.)
35	Pijchean igual que nosotros pueees.	They chew coca just like us.
36	Igual que nosotros comen del *apthapi*.	Just like us they eat *apthapi*.[2]
37	Igual que nosotros se ponen ponchos,	Just like us they wear ponchos,
38	se ponen abarcas.	wear sandals.
39	Y lo peor hablan de nosotros	And the worst is that they talk about us
40	como si ellos hubiesen vivido en el caampo	as if they'd lived in the countryside
41	como si ellos hubiesen participado de	as if they'd participated in
42	diferentes marchas. (.)	different marches.
43	Eso es lo más peligroso.	That's the most dangerous.
44	Si tienen capacidad de mimetizarse	If they have the capacity for mimesis,
45	tienen la capacidad de camuflarse rápidamente	they have the capacity to camouflage rapidly
46	en cada uno de los sectores obviamente	in each one of the sectors obviously
47	nos pueden empezar a someter nuevamente con	they can begin to conquer us anew with
48	nuestra propia ideología.	our own ideology.
49	Eso hay que cuidarse	That is what we have to take care of and
50	por lo tanto nosotros, yo, Oscar Chirinos	that's why we, I, Oscar Chirinos
51	nunca puede ser militante	can never be a militant
52	de ese Movimiento al Socialismo.	of that Movement to Socialism.
53	Sí el Movimiento al Socialismo del pueblo	Yes, the Movement to Socialism of the people
54	que nació para poder defender	that was born in order to defend
55	y buscar la verdadera liberación.	and search for true liberation.

(continued)

56 F: Eso vive todavía en su corazón.	F: That still lives in his heart.
57 C: Así es. Y creo que con esos principios	C: That's how it is. I believe with those principles
58 hemos conformado la, el Movimiento Por	we've shaped the Movement for
59 la Soberanía para poder llevar adelante	Sovereignty in order to be able to advance an
60 una actividad en beneficio de nuestra sociedad.	activity for the benefit of our society.

His denunciation is the one place in this long stretch of Spanish language discourse where we encounter a saliently Aymara word, the epithet *q'ara*. The word is salient for both its emotional charge and because of its very phonological makeup. The ejective post velar stop [q'] is not a sound heard in Spanish, and one that is usually difficult for speakers of Spanish to produce even after much practice. The term itself is not a color term, *janq'u* is Aymara for "white," but instead a semantic extension of the Aymara word for "naked." The epithet remains a historically powerful metaphor. Aymaras account for its meaning by pointing to the early days of colonialism when the Spanish came to the Andes "with nothing" and needed to be provided for by Aymaras. The epithet reverses the eurocentric defamation of American Indians as "naked savages" by characterizing the invading Spanish as such. Within his discourse (see Table 3.7), the epithet becomes almost a homeopathic trace of Aymara venom, just one word, but enough to establish a footing of Aymara opposition to the contemptible, and contemptuous, scheming ethnic fraud.

In lines 26 through 43, Chirinos reaffirms historical enemies and questions the racial allegiances of potential frauds. The ability of whites to engage in mimesis and become "just like us" raises the spectre of their continued dominance within an advancing Indian political sphere. But what's the worst of all? The worst is the violation of a metapragmatic norm concerning the truth-value of talk: "*The worst is they speak as if they've lived in the country. As if they've participated in marches*" (lines 39 through 42).

Chirinos' accusation resonates with the Aymara maxim, *Uñjasaw uñjt sañax. Janiw uñjkiti jan uñjt sañakiti* ("Seeing, 'I've seen' one can say. Not having seen, 'I've seen' cannot be said"). Chirinos' mention of speech and representation, and the expression of personal experience, emerges within a larger poetic structure diagramming the outlines of an Aymara subject, one who chews coca, dresses

Table 3.7 The poetic epithet *q'ara*

12 Pero no soy militante de este MAS	But I'm not a militant of this MAS
13 que son de los q'aras,	that [belongs to the] q'aras
14 de Álvaro Garcí::a	to Álvaro García,
15 de de Sacha Llore::nti.	to to Sacha Llore::nti.
16 de éstos no::.	to these ones nooo.
17 Este MAS ya no es del pueblo.	This MAS no longer belongs to the people
18 Este MAS ya es de los q'aras=	This MAS belongs to the q'aras=
19 =de esta derecha	=to this right
30 Conocíamos al Goni. Era q'ara.	We knew Goni. He was a q'ara.
31 Conocíamos a Tuto. Era q'ara.	We knew Tuto. He was a q'ara.
32 Era de la derecha, era bien claro	He of the right, it was quite clear
33 y lo hemos expulsado del país.	and we expelled him from the country.

with poncho and sandals, has lived in the countryside, and has participated in the movements that brought the MAS to power—and we can infer, would not speak falsely of their experiences.

Chirinos' comments also draw upon a trope that is unfortunately familiar across national contexts—the lying politician. Chirinos and his party, however, were not above engaging in their own acts of semiotic trickery. Chirinos and his party used the same colors as the governing party (blue, black, and white) in their campaign, and, in a strange move, printed counterfeit 200 Bolivian Peso bills on the backs of their flyers (see Figure 3.2). Sitting in the studio during the recording of this interview, I was initially alarmed seeing him handing these to the radio personnel as he entered the studio. Was I becoming witness to a pay-to-play exchange for air time? He also handed me and others in the studio these "bills" and, upon inspection, I realized it was not, in fact, money. Chirinos explained his motivation behind the campaign materials as a way to get the materials in people's hands. His idea was that if anyone were to throw one on the ground, it might be picked up when mistaken for money. He also liked the idea that he would become associated with economic prosperity. If the prospect of campaign literature being wasted as litter worried him, building on the trope of the corrupt politician buying votes did not.

Figure 3.2 A campaign leaflet for Oscar Chirinos with a false 200 Boliviano note from the "National Bank of Fortune" (rather than Bank of Bolivia) on one side. Like an actual 200 Boliviano note, the bill features icons of Aymara nationhood—the ruins of Tiwanaku and the mountain Wayna Potosí.

Chirinos' candidacy ultimately did not resonate with enough of El Alto's electorate. His warnings concerning the MAS failed to dissuade the electorate from voting in the MAS candidate, Edgar Patana. Patana, however, only won but by a margin that felt slim in the city that had been considered a bastion of MAS support. The main challenge to MAS came not from Chirinos, but from a young Aymara woman with rural roots, Soledad "Sol" Chapetón, who would go on to oust him in 2015 (at the time of writing she continues as mayor of El Alto). Chirinos' party did fare well in a few districts of the Aymara heartland, winning the six municipalities of Achacachi, Sorata, Mecapaca, Escoma, Combaya, and Pucarani. In the 2015 elections, the party ran the prominent Aymara nationalist and former head of the CSUTCB Felipe Quispe on its gubernatorial ticket and won fifteen mayoral seats, making it the third largest party in the number of municipalities in the country, although still far behind MAS.

In the course of the interview on *Akhulli Amuyt'awi*, Chirinos spoke to a number of concerns—unemployment, transportation, education, and citizen safety. His main concern was not primarily the ethnic one examined above. His concern with imposters in the ranks, however, revealed something of his own notions of being Aymara, and a particular perspective on the dynamics of cultural shift in this moment of Bolivian society. What we heard in Chirinos' Aymara nationalist critique of MAS was one articulation of a model of Aymara subjectivity, albeit via a negative definition of what a *q'ara* would do to "camouflage" as an Aymara—chew coca "just like us," participate in political militancy, have a rural background, and wear Aymara clothing. In providing the contours of this figure of personhood, the covert *q'ara*, Chirinos made explicit his own semiotic ideology of what it means to be Aymara which grouped together sartorial, behavioral, and even culinary behaviors as an authoritatively Aymara semiotic register. Curiously enough, speaking Aymara did not figure into this framework, and his critique was made in Spanish. Language did figure into his critique at the level of metapragmatics, that is, at the level of the norms governing the conditions and effects of language, how it is one can speak about one's own experiences and those of others.

The adoption and spread of practices like chewing coca beyond Aymara and Quechua communities stem in part from the successes of Indigenous protagonism in the political sphere. The coca leaf is a powerful emblem of Andean indigeneity for many reasons. It is a metonym for larger processes—battles over land, its use, and political control itself. That the foundation for a communicative practice of community deliberation and the raw material for international narcotics trade are one and the same is a strange, tragic accident of history. More than just a model of communication, we can also consider the *akhulli* as a model of democratic conduct, Indigenous autonomy, and Aymara personhood. Where Flores invoked a chronotopic depiction of the initial *akhulli* in a rural *ayllu*, his own show takes the *ayllu* to the airwaves, establishing an Aymara national chronotope convened through the mediatized *akhulli*. In his radio broadcasts, Flores projects "indexical images of speaker actor(s)" (Agha 2005: 39), or figures of personhood, tied to Aymara subjectivity (coca growers, market vendors, farmers, and domestic workers) that are both presupposed but also disseminated as discursive figures from this platform. Register contrasts are central to Flores' establishing of discursive figures representing a commenting Aymara public who, increasingly, speak Spanish rather than Aymara. Flores' codeswitching, the sonic presence of the different voices he animates through this practice, can also be understood as consistent with the dialogic aims of the *akhulli*.

Aymara social historian Silvia Rivera Cusicanqui explains the increasingly quotidian, if not less meaningful, nature of coca consumption in contemporary Bolivia as an assertion of national sovereignty, "Contradictory as it may seem, the allure of indigenous rituals in urban and modern settings is in fact a de-exoticization of the indigenous, and the ritual consumption of coca in public becomes a symbolic assertion of the nation's dignity and sovereignty, crossing class and ethnic borders, and seducing the culturally weak, but politically dominant, mestizo-criollo minority" (Rivera-Cusicanqui 2008: 146). The fears of insidious and persistant *q'ara* political domination expressed by Chirinos above may blind him to such other possible interpretations of the appearance of *q'aras* who chew coca. That these practices have been previously enregistered as Aymara in no way means that this will always be the case. Asif Agha has noted that "registers exist continuously in time only as a function of communicative processes that disseminate awareness of and competence in such registers to *changing* populations" (Agha 2005: 47, emphasis in the original). The CEA's Radio Pacha Qamasa is one point of dissemination, and contestation of awareness of such registers of being Aymara. So, too are electoral campaigns. Yet, as the next chapter on Aymara hip-hop will show, these are certainly not the only ones.

Part Two

Song

The act of singing has a curious status with its relationship to speech and the individuated voice. Singing can be both intimate and public, an individual act or a collective one. It is a practice through which one's voice may be cultivated to achieve recognizable distinctiveness, or, alternatively, join in a chorus of others and seem to dissolve into the collectivity. The dividing line between song and speech or, for that matter, sung verse and poetry is not a universally accepted boundary. With music, like language, we enter into an arena that concerns universal human experience. Music making is as universal among human societies as language is. How, and whether, humans establish a music-language divide, however, are questions for which the ethnographic record demonstrates tremendous diversity (Faudree 2012). Linguistic anthropologist Paja Faudree writes compellingly about recognizing the challenges our own language places on understanding this regimentation when she writes that "music and language are socially determined constructs that arbitrarily divide, in fundamentally cultural ways, a communicative whole … we lack the language to refer easily to this expressive whole without using terms that artificially divide it, thereby reinscribing the divisions they presuppose" (Faudree 2012: 520). The next two chapters take up music-language within Aymara song; in particular, the lyrical element of songs that advance sentiments of Aymara national belonging. Following from the previous two chapters' discussions of the aural dissemination of dehispanicized Aymara over the airwaves, the next two chapters attend to the production and circulation of Aymara nationalist song as an important site to understand the enregisterment of dehispanicized Aymara.

Like self-directed speech or interior dialogue in the absence of others, song and melody can occupy the most private corners of our consciousness. Melodies may play in our minds in the total absence of music, and, even when memory or attention has lost a song's lyrics, a tune may linger on in variations of mental glossolalia. For better or worse, not quite remembering all of a song's lyrics does not always present an obstacle to raising one's voice in song. Singing the US national anthem as a child, I misunderstood the opening lines believing that "dawn's early" was not two words, but one. For years, I sang loudly alongside my classmates at morning assemblies, "Oh say can you see by the dawnserly light?" believing that "dawnserly" was an adjective, albeit a mysterious one, that described a quality of light. This misunderstanding continued for years without provoking any pause. In moments like these, song lyric's semantico-grammatical meaning recedes to varying degrees of non-importance, whether partially (I still understood "dawnserly" grammatically, taking it as an adjective, for example) or completely, such as would be the case with improvised forgotten lyrics, sung glossolalia, vocal "scat" jazz improvisation, or invented "language-like" lyrics, like those of the 1980s Scottish post punk, dream pop band Cocteau Twins. Other elements of a song come to matter more here, the melody, the rhythm, or, in the case of my experiences singing national anthem as a young boy, the act of joining and performing a civic ritual of citizenship.

In many languages, a national anthem is a national *hymn*. This is the case in Spanish, *himno nacional*. The word "anthem" in English shares hymn's etymology, related to choral antiphony, or the singing of psalms in Christian ritual. Where the aim of a hymn is to exalt and express devotion to the divine through the communal act of song, national anthems similarly aim to praise a transcendent value of belonging to a nation. Singing a national anthem is rarely only an act of phonation, and usually also involves coordinated embodied acts of gesture (hands over hearts), and of joint attention, such as gaze directed toward symbols of state like a flag. In many communal acts of devotion to the nation, singing the anthem is not simply the raising of voices, but also the hoisting of a flag, and the coordinating of bodies to act in concert, making the act itself a metonym of the nation.

In his famous treatise on the emergence of modern nation-state and rise of nationalism, *Imagined Communities*, Benedict Anderson (2006) described the affective power of singing a national anthem in chorus as a form of "unisonance" that produces a shared sense of belonging:

> There is a special kind of contemporaneous community which language alone suggests—above all in the form of poetry and songs. Take national anthems, for example, sung on national holidays. No matter how banal the words and mediocre the tunes, there is in this singing an experience of simultaneity. At precisely such moments, people wholly unknown to each other utter the same verses to the same melody. The image: unisonance … How selfless this

unisonance feels! If we are aware that others are singing these songs precisely when and as we are, we have no idea who they may be, or even where, out of earshot, they are singing. Nothing connects us all but imagined sound.

(Anderson 2006: 45)

Anderson's embodied and musical example in this passage stands out as an exception among his other examples of vehicles for nationalist sentiment within his broader analysis. Text, in the narrower definition of the printed word, plays a more central role throughout his account of the rise of nationalism. Print and written language, newspapers and novels, facilitated by technological developments in printing coordinated with the emergence of capitalist production and the consolidation of markets, provide the main analytic focus for Anderson's influential study, rather than the kind of music-language-mediated sociality he describes here. In her ethnography of Mazatec language revival in Mexico, Paja Faudree has argued that singing often plays as consequential a role in the creation and dissemination of texts, and of cultural forms more broadly, as does spoken language or writing (Faudree 2013: 17–18).[1] The sociopolitical and sociolinguistic scenario in which Aymaras live differs from the Mazatec communities studied by Faudree in notable ways, but there are important similarities.[2] Like in the Mazatec case, the Aymara artists in the next chapter cultivate their lyrical prowess in a context where intergenerational language shift to Spanish looms as a threat, perceived and real, for artists and audiences alike. Despite the evident and dramatic differences between the Mazatec and Aymara contexts, however, whether in Mexico or Bolivia, the unisonance of shared song becomes a crucial modality in the generation of "contemporaneous community."

Nations have no monopoly on anthems, and social movements across the globe have famously mobilized song as a way to build solidarity among their ranks (Redmond 2014). Many have characterized the global spread of the hip-hop itself in social movement terms. Others have even characterized the spread of global hip-hop as the emergence of a multiethnic Global Hip Hop Nation (Alim et al 2008: 3). The communities imagined, and felt, through song in this section include the Bolivian nation-state, but even the most nationalist songs discussed in this section are not limited to it. They invoke social groups which extend both beyond Bolivia and collectivities nestled within it. The names and words of Aymara martyrs are quoted in the verses of El Alto rappers. The artists in the next chapter pride themselves for their role as representatives of Bolivia within a global hip-hop scene. Their awareness that they perform on a global stage, that their words are attended to by cosmopolitan, multilingual audiences of hip-hop enthusiasts, at home and abroad, informs the varied ways they address their fans. In Chapter 5, the book's penultimate chapter, we will encounter a new version of an old anthem in which we will hear the echoed name of a political unit from before Spanish invasion, a name from the reign of the Inka, only now sung in a republican military cadence.

The music of Aymaras and Quechuas is well known on the world stage. Music from the Andes has enjoyed prominence within global "World Music" markets for generations now. Many Bolivians express pride when they point out that the hit 1989 song *Chorando se foi (Lambada)* was first composed and written by the Bolivian group Los Kjarkas in 1981. Before them, the folk singers Simon and Garfunkel popularized another traditional Andean melody with their 1970 recording of *El Condor Pasa*.[3] Musicians from Andean countries have found global audiences and opportunities for touring; poncho-clad Andean musicians can be heard singing and playing traditional songs on "pan pipes" (instruments like the *siku* and *zampoña*), on subways of New York and in European city squares among crowds of tourists. The Quechua vocalist Luzmila Carpio has served as important cultural ambassador for Bolivia and Indigenous peoples of the Andes.

There is a large literature on Andean music and its relationship to nationalist projects and to notions of race and indigeneity (Bigenho 2002; Mendoza 2000; Tucker 2013). Michelle Bigenho (2002) has documented how Japanese consumers and practitioners of highland Aymara and Quechua music forged not only musical community, but reimagined notions of ethnicity and race connecting Indigenous Americans with Japan. Through their participation in Andean musical communities, Japanese artists do more than just make music they love, they "produce nostalgia and racialized imaginaries that construe connection to an indigenous world" (Bigenho 2002: 121). Joshua Tucker has explored how the Peruvian music industry transformed Huayno music, making it more respectable to middle class audiences and formative for notions of race and nation (Tucker 2013). The cases in this section do not provide an excursion into the admittedly rich world of traditional or folkloric Andean music; and perhaps the cases examined in the next two chapters may seem to present exceptions within any discussion of Andean music. Indeed, this is the case. This section presents examinations of Aymara nationalism sung within contexts where previously it has been absent or excluded—the city and state officialdom—and in genres of song which have not traditionally been sung in Aymara—hip-hop and the Bolivian national anthem.

The La Paz/El Alto metropolitan region is home to a vibrant hip-hop scene which includes Aymara rappers (Hornberger and Swinehart 2012b; Swinehart 2012c; Swinehart 2019b). Drawing on interviews, ethnographic accounts of performances, and analysis of lyrics, the next chapter examines Aymara hip-hop as an intervention in the sociolinguistic terrain of the city that unsettles prevailing assumptions about the nature of language shift among the children of rural migrants to the city. These artists disseminate models of Aymara subjectivity which overlap with those discussed in earlier chapters, but also diverge in important ways. While lyrically establishing connections between contemporary Aymara struggles with historic ones, these artists also situate Aymaras in relation to African American and Black diasporic freedom struggles both lyrically and through their embrace of transnational hip-hop material culture.

Closing the section is an examination of the translation of the Bolivian national anthem into Aymara and its performance at the commemoration of a 1921 massacre of Aymara peasants by the Bolivian army (Choque Canqui 2010). My analysis in this chapter foregrounds latent tensions within Bolivian plurinationalism through a combined consideration of the indeterminacies of translation alongside an ethnographic account of the anthem's performance at a site of racial state violence. Sung at the site of a massacre, the militaristic lyrics take on uneasy valences and raise questions about how an Aymara nation is situated within the now plurinational republic. Questions of linguistic commensurability confront political projects as the new Aymara anthem translates *la patria* "fatherland" as *Qullasuyu*, a political unit from the era of the Inka Empire, and, in the process, semantically rescales the political aspirations of Aymara nationalism. As a performative, public enactment of citizenship, singing the anthem in the newly official Aymara confronts language ideologies that have long excluded Aymaras as citizens, but also challenges anti-statist Aymara political currents which previously rejected Bolivian nationalism (Alvizuri 2009).

In the case of the national anthem, it may seem clear how we are dealing with a project of "official Aymara" but this is less neatly the case with the hip-hop collectives in the next chapter. How might we think of rappers' relationship to "officialdom" when their social capital may rely in part on projecting a stance of rebellion and even conspicuous positions of social marginality, of being "from the street"? We will see that these artists' performances are semiotically dense, and within these, there is a deployment of the Aymara language that makes it maximally distinct from Spanish. Although unfolding within settings that are radically distinct from those in the opening chapters on radio, there is a similar investment in the foregrounding of the Aymara language, and its intended effect, the aim of sounding maximally Aymara. Writing of the musical and media interventions of Aboriginal Australians, Daniel Fisher (2016) emphasizes the mediatized voice as a sociohistorical achievement.[4] Reminiscent of Aboriginal Australians concerns with "sounding Black" (Fisher 2016), these artists stake out explicit alignment with what they perceive to be US Black expressive culture while attending to the metapragmatics of sounding Aymara.

Perhaps because hip-hop is a genre which famously centers lyricism, with rap being a defining element of the genre, or perhaps also because the genre's meteoric rise and global spread over the last half century has made it emblematic of processes of "globalization," it is a verbal art that has gained considerable attention from sociolinguists over recent decades (Alim et al 2008; Terkourafi 2010). Much of the sociolinguistic literature on global hip-hop has emphasized hybridity and novelty, seeing the linguistic practices of participants in hip-hop scenes as linguistic innovators who disrupt what Alistair Pennycook (2009) has termed "ortholinguistic practices." In some ways, this rings true in the Bolivian cases examined here. These artists are often visibly non-traditional in terms of sartorial self-fashioning and audibly so in terms of musical genre and style. One might expect these artists to rebel against what might be presumed to be notions of standard language. Nevertheless, within the verses of the artists in the next chapter we find a commitment to notions of standard within their lyrical production, motivated in part from a sense of embattlement and a fear of language attrition. The novelty of Indigenous Andeans embracing hip-hop culture has garnered substantial attention, both locally and internationally, in large part because of the complex relationship their music has to "traditional" cultural forms. Similar to the San Carlos Apache rock musicians discussed in the work of David Samuels (2004) or the Navajo country musicians discussed by Kristina Jacobsen (2017), Aymara rappers navigate their own and others' expectations of what it means to be Aymara while they master a musical genre many would presume to belong to "others."

In his work on hip-hop scenes in Delhi, Ethiraj G Dattatreyan writes that ethnographies of hip-hop should aim "to show how global forms, as they travel, reveal a far more complex context for everyday life that is specific to time and place and that evokes particular historical struggles that are intertwined with the story of capital as it continues its adventures through time and space" (Dattatreyan 2020: 97) The next two chapters demonstrate the complex ways in which both historical and contemporary struggles of Aymaras have come to be understood through song, and the role of language within this transmission of historical meaning. What is more, the next chapter in particular also demonstrates how these songs emerge through complex relationships to capital. Hip-hop arrived to Bolivia facilitated by US hegemony, but also by counter-hegemonic movements within the United States. The music made by Nación Rap, Wayna Rap, is not licensed to any corporation, and the lyrics are reproduced here, for example, with permission by the artists themselves, and no corporation. What about the Aymara version of the national anthem? As a text which operates outside of market formulations of production and exchange we could recognize the national anthem's Aymara version as standing outside of commodity relations. Still, the fact of its creation does ultimately emerge from the oppositional relationship to global capital taken up by Bolivian social movements, and the direct protagonism within them. That there is an Aymara version of the Bolivian national anthem is a result of individual translators to be sure. The fact that there are official contexts for singing it, as the one presented in Chapter 5, emerges from the conditions created by the achievements of diverse anti-capitalist struggles of Bolivia's Indigenous and working-class movements, namely, the 2009 constitution. Among these movements, the Aymara struggles for Indigenous autonomy can also be considered a movement for control of the most primary form of capital—land and territory.

Song as music-language occupies a central role within the projects of "contemporaneous community" (Anderson 2006: 45) in the next two chapters. Song as lyric-poetry often demands considerable deliberation on the part of the author. It may not always matter to find the right words for a song, but it often does. The deliberate and concerted attention to lyrical form done in the service of the cultivation of the Aymara language motivated the selection of the cases that follow. By juxtaposing two evidently distinct projects, hip-hop composition and performance on the one hand, and the translation and singing of the national anthem on the other, the hope is to open new vantage points on enregisterment processes underway among contemporary Aymara speakers. By distributing analytic attention across both radio and song and, within this second section of the study, across musically communicative acts as evidently distinctive as hip-hop performances and official state acts of commemoration, we may begin to understand the enregisterment of dehispanicized Aymara more fully, through tracking the production and dissemination of this register within an ethnographically comparative frame.

4

Tupak in Their Veins: Race, Nation, and Memory in Aymara Hip-Hop

On a narrow street leading up from *La Plaza del Estudiante* near the large public university in the center of La Paz, the Universidad Mayor de San Andrés, is a nightclub known for its hip-hop and reggae nights and for its unusually nationalist décor. The venue is fashioned like a mine and can be found thanks to the miner's helmet swinging outside. Patrons descend into a basement with false rock walls for "underground" entertainment. It so happens that it is not the only mine-themed nightclub in this famously mineral-rich country's capital. Standing outside the club's entrance one cold night before a hip-hop show, I spoke with some concertgoers and fans of the large, vibrant hip-hop scene in the greater La Paz/El Alto metropolitan area. One of that night's concertgoers, Javier Gutiérrez Velázquez, expressed his enthusiasm for the local hip-hop scene to me in terms of both affect and history:

> The hip-hop movement in Bolivia and especially in the city of El Alto ... is very Aymara. Very Aymara-tized, but also very aligned with what's gringo, no? With what's from the US and even the European because there's a lot of influence, right? ... and, well, it's beautiful because it unites what is Black with what is Aymara and a hallucinatory mix of Aymara hip-hop comes out that's so "sick." *Muy sick*. You listen to it, to Ukamau and it's like he makes you fly. It's a mix of a Black, Aymara, Bolivian, Latin American, it's incredible, right?

His comment surprised me for many reasons. For one thing, it was unusual how he coupled a term so often denoting whiteness in Latin America—"gringo"—with Blackness, even when addressing me, a person of European descent from the United States. Furthermore, to be "aligned with what's gringo" was an astounding thing for a young Aymara Bolivian to mention favorably. In the thoroughly anti-imperialist milieu of working-class Bolivia, this young man mentioned US and European cultural influence favorably and as an account of how a mixed Black and Aymara musical form emerged.

The mixing of "Black and Aymara" and the adoption of foreign, US and European, influences combined for him to produce an effect he describes as hallucinatory; it made him feel like he could fly. For some, to hallucinate is to leave one's body, or at least the confines of everyday sensation—to fly! To hallucinate is also tripping: to escape the weight of gravity, to leave your context, to become unmoored from the everyday, to be here, but be far away, to be in one's body, but to be in another's. He makes clear in the comment the affective impact of the music is what appeals to him, and central to this is both a simultaneous identification with what's not just familiar, but Aymara, and also with what is not just foreign, but incredible.

Responding to my follow-up question about why he thought it was so unusual to hear music that was both Black and Aymara, he continued on this trip:

> Whether you like it or not, Bolivian land is more Aymara, like, ancestrally. And Blackness (*lo negro*) comes with Spanish colonization, right? Well they bring the Blacks. First they bring them to Potosí, from Potosí they die from the cold, because of the change of climate and all that, and so they bring them to Yungas (*a region with Afro-Bolivian towns*) … Now this mix of music together with Saya (*traditional Afro-Bolivian music*) and all that, they're also bringing Black hip-hop, even Yankee hip-hop, here to Bolivia. And this mix with the people of El Alto who live in the suburbs, you could say in the favelas of El Alto, is a mix more of protest, so we've made hip-hop our own, we've made it our own and in our own style.

That this music's aesthetics tie together intimate knots of language, history, and political economy was not lost on this fan, and it seems, in part, to be what had roped him in. His account of what produces a hybrid musical form like Bolivian hip-hop slips quickly from Spanish colonialism into the arrival of "Yankee" music. In referring to the peripheral neighborhoods of El Alto as "favelas," he also establishes a homology between El Alto and Rio de Janeiro, connecting Aymaras in El Alto not only to US African Americans, and Afro Bolivians in the Yungas, but also to Afro-Brazilians. His response is similarly hallucinatory, reaching back to the seventeenth century to the mining of gold in Potosí and then flying across the continent to the favelas of Rio and north to the United States. Situated as such, he affirms hip-hop's status as a music of protest and as a protest that is "our own and in our style." His connecting of music to trajectories of colonial racialization and movement of peoples underscores connections both historic and ongoing between notions of Blackness and Indigeneity (Gilroy 1993; Solis 2015).

Velázquez's encounter with Aymara hip-hop becomes an occasion to situate Aymaras within a constellation of diasporic Blackness in a way that merits revisiting Stuart Hall's (1993) remarks in his now famous essay "What Is This 'Black' in Black Popular Culture?" on the relationship between popular culture and imaginings of the self:

[Popular Culture] is a theater of popular desires, a theater of popular fantasies.
It is where we discover and play with the identifications of ourselves, where we are imagined, where we are represented, not only to the audiences out there who do not get the message, but to ourselves for the first time.
(Hall 1993: 113)

Rather than an essentialist understanding of race, both Hall and Velázquez invite us to consider the historical, situated, and dynamic character of racial categories themselves. Ukamau's music, for Velázquez, provoked a pan-ethnic identification with African diaspora that situated Aymaras as a node within it.

Velázquez mentions the music of Ukamau, referring to the hip-hop project of the late Abraham Bojórquez, a prominent figure of this scene who died an untimely death in 2009. The full name of Bojórquez's project was Ukamau y Ké, a name that demonstrates one of the linguistic strategies that Aymara rappers use to make rap "their own": the combining of Aymara and Spanish, and, as we will see with Nación Rap below, other languages including French and English. Velázquez himself described Ukhamau's music positively using the English word "sick." Although just one "word," the name *ukhamau* is a composite of three morphemes that together mean "that's how it is." The second part, *y ké*, is an orthographically non-standard rendering of *¿y qué?*, meaning "and what?" in Spanish. The name itself, both in meaning and form, provides an example of both the code mixing and also the oppositional stance of protest to which Velázquez refers in his comments above. The incorporation of Aymara and Quechua in the names of venues and spaces where the hip-hop scene gathers is widespread. Examples include *Wayna Tambo* "youth meeting/resting place" (in both Quechua and Aymara), *Centro Taypi* "Center center" (in Spanish and Aymara, respectively), *Centro Cultural Utasa* "Cultural Center Our Home." In March of 2006, when there was what was perhaps Bolivia's largest national hip-hop festival in the city of El Alto, the festival's name was Aymara—*Qhana Aru Imantata* which might translate to English as "the Hidden, Clear Voice."

Among the rappers Velázquez had come to hear on that night in 2013 was the group *Nación Rap*. This group includes members who had been alongside Bojórquez in the same El Alto hip-hop scene which coalesced during and in the wake of the 2003 Gas War around the youth community center and radio station Wayna Tambo (Hornberger and Swinehart 2012b; Swinehart 2012c). Eber Miranda Quispe, for example, began performing with the group Wayna Rap during this period and then later would help form Nación Rap in 2007. The collective Wayna Rap's name includes the Quechua and Aymara word for "youth" or "young"—*wayna*. They often referred to themselves as "Wayna Rap Clan," a resonant parallelism alluding to a more widely known 1990s US hip-hop collective and inspiration for their own work—Wu Tang Clan. Like Ukamau y Ke and Wayna Rap before them, Nación Rap's lyrical and musical style mixes linguistic codes in ways consistent with Velázquez's description of Bolivian hip-hop more generally. Their lyrics foreground an interplay of linguistic codes with verses in Spanish, Aymara, French, and English. In this regard, Nación Rap is exceptional among these artists, but many artists in this scene mix Aymara and Spanish to some degree, and mix local and global elements in other features of their artistic and everyday semiotic practices. The sonic elements of their musical production include loops from tracks both foreign and domestic, and often the reformatting of Andean music through programs like Fruity Loops Studio. "Andean" here refers to musical practices shared by both Aymaras and Quechuas including the use of percussion and wind instruments ("panpipes") like the *siku* (zampoña), *tharqa* (tarka), *qina* (quena), and *pinkillo* and the use of, often minor, pentatonic scale. This mixing extends to sartorial presentation-of-self in music videos, performances, and daily lives. They set elements of US hip-hop fashion alongside garments that would otherwise be identified as rural and "Indian" in the Bolivian context such as ponchos and *luch'us*, the conical knit hats often worn by Quechua and Aymara men. Across these diverse modalities, they draw on mediatized signs enregistered (Agha 2007) on a global scale to index participation in a Global Hip-hop Nation (Alim, Awad and Pennycook 2008) alongside signs that locally index Quechua and Aymara identity. To the extent that any of these diverse signs are enregistered as indexing "Aymara-ness" or "hip-hop" in stable ways, their participation in and drawing from each of these supposedly separate spheres of life to create a local style resists this very semiotic regimentation, underscoring how such register formations are themselves, living, dynamic categories (cf. Agha 2003).

Global hip-hop has garnered considerable attention from sociolinguists, linguistic anthropologists, and cultural studies scholars, many of whom argue along the lines of Alistair Pennycook (2007), who asserts that "Much of hip-hop challenges ortholinguistic practices and ideologies, relocating language in new ways, both reflecting and producing local language practices" (Pennycook

2007: 112). In the music of Wayna Rap and Nación Rap we certainly hear a relocation of language; Aymara, a language that in Bolivia has indexed the rural and traditional, becomes relocated within a frame, the musical genre of hip-hop, that is widely perceived as urban and cosmopolitan. But what of "ortholinguistic practices"? In Chapter 2, we encountered RSG's regime of *seguimiento,* perhaps as good an example of an "ortholinguistic practice" as could be found. In this chapter, we will find that, while embedded within an otherwise thoroughly hybrid cultural form, these artists' verbal art provides another form of "ortholinguistic practice." Although the composition of their verses are delivered within a co-textual array that diverges radically from the broadcasts of RSG, the deliberate poetic act these artists engage in shares both many of the aims of *seguimiento* at RSG—the elaboration and promotion of the Aymara language—and also a similar result—contributing to the consolidation of a register of Aymara that is maximally distinct from Spanish.

When I spoke with Velázquez outside the club that night, I was not just passing by. I had followed the work of one of Nación Rap's members, Eber Quispe, since 2007 when he was a member of the group Wayna Rap. When he attended university to study linguistics with a specialty in Aymara, he would later form a new group with other linguistics students to form Nación Rap. During my early fieldwork in Bolivia, in 2007, I had reached out to Wayna Rap through the then widely used social media platform MySpace to request both information about upcoming performances and the possibility of interviewing them. "Aymara rappers in El Alto" had some notoriety by this point, and the Aymara language educators I was in touch with, as well as others interested in Aymara language more broadly, had mentioned these artists to me. Responses to, or rather, enthusiasm for this development in Aymara cultural life was uneven. For instance, when discussing the state of Aymara's vitality and the linguistic situation facing urban Aymara youth with a former leader within the *Consejo Educativo Aymara* (Aymara Education Council), I mentioned Wayna Rap as a positive example of Aymara intergenerational linguistic vitality. It seemed to be a very different example for him. Mention of "raperos Aymaras" served as a cue to lament the supposed cultural loss, confusion, and delinquency of younger generations. The educator established a link between hip-hop and what he perceived to be the deterioration of Aymara culture among alteño youth in particular and, more generally, the social conditions in the city. That this music was in any way Aymara was obscured to him by other signs that affirmed his anxieties about his perception that Aymara society was embattled by an ongoing encroachment of foreign influences, and laid siege by profound social problems of poverty and alienation.

Rather than a clear break or departure from Indigenous tradition, other Aymaras recognize the long history of productive engagement and transformation with foreign expressive culture. Aymara sociologist, historian, and activist Silvia Rivera Cusicanqui draws on the Aymara color lexicon to use the term *ch'ixi* [tʃ' εXε] to describe Indigenous Andean appropriation of the foreign in ways that produce novel forms, an Aymara term for the dialectic incorporation of opposites:

> *Ch'ixi* has many connotations: it is a color that is the product of juxtaposition, in small points or spots, of opposed or contrasting colors: black and white, red and green, and so on. It is this heather gray that comes from the imperceptible mixing of black and white, which are confused by perception, without ever being completely mixed. The notion of *ch'ixi*, like many others (*allqa, ayni*), reflects the Aymara idea of something that is and is not at the same time. It is the logic of the included third ... *ch'ixi* combines the Indian world and its opposite without ever mixing them.
>
> (Rivera Cusicanqui 2012: 105)

The artistic practice of these hip-hop artists fits her description of cultural practices that are *ch'ixi* for how they bring together and set in juxtaposition elements of the foreign alongside the local, sounds that are rural alongside others that are urban, within a unified field of performance, creating something new, a "logic of the included third."

Hip-hop musical communities exist across the globe; they incorporate local languages and styles, while drawing on translocal, global elements of hip-hop culture. Global hip-hop is an arena of cultural production which has exemplified the tensions between homogenization and heterogenization within contexts of advanced capitalism, otherwise known as globalization (Appadurai 1996: 33). Global hip-hop has been understood as both a motor and a precipitate of processes of globalization, and an arena of particular interest for scholars of language, music, and popular culture more broadly (Alim et al 2008; Condry 2006; Terkourafi 2010). Scholars of Indigenous hip-hop in North America such as Kyle Mays and Jessica Bisset Perea have noted how hip-hop has served as a means of positive self-expression among Indigenous youth and as a vehicle for countering stereotypes of Indigenous culture as anti-modern (Mays 2018; Perea 2016). In this Bolivian context, we find hip-hop playing a similar role, one where practitioners cultivate the Aymara language in the face of trends toward language of shift to Spanish.

The first hip-hop track released in Latin America is widely recognized to have been "La Cotorra Criolla" (1980). It was performed by the Argentine group Malvaho with lyrics written by Venezuelan humorist Perucho Conde (Biaggini 2020: 33). Rather than a product of an emergent hip-hop scene, this track is best understood as music industry creation. The song was created in a a bid to appeal to a possible market. Taking its inspiration directly from the popularity and success of Sugarhill Gang's 1979 "Rappers Delight," itself widely considered to be hip-hop's inaugural track. "La Cotorra Criolla" and other early instances of Latin American rap, while garning some attention, did not launch anything like a movement per se. What Martín Biaggini writes in his history of Argentinian rap holds similarly true for Bolivia, noting that, "These sporadic musical experiences had no continuity nor direct influence in the development of rap in our country" (Biaggini 2020: 34). There are other parallels between what Biaggini writes about the emergence of a hip-hop scene in Argentina and the development of a local scene in Bolivia, namely, the importance of dance crews to the emergence of a local hip-hop culture. A synergy developed during the 1990s between the formation of dance crews among urban youth in El Alto and La Paz and the increasing circulation of pirated US hip-hop cassette tapes. The circulation of cassette tapes through interpersonal networks combined with hip-hop programs on pirate radio stations contributed to a growing audience and the eventual development of a local scene. The first Bolivian MC to develop a profile in the country was "El Cholo" Marcelo Yáñez in the early 2000s (Ávila et al 2007).

The future members Wayna Rap were among those participating in dance crews and also contributing to the popularization of hip-hop in Bolivia through their running of pirate radio broadcasts during the late '90s and early 2000s. In an interview on the Bolivian television program "Ojo del Alma," founding member of Wayna Rap, Grover Cañaviri, explained their role in making hip-hop part of the city's soundscape and explains how this was also a collective effort in which he and his friends would take up a collection to pay for a slot on one of the pirate radio broadcasters' frequencies:

> You had to pay. For one hour we paid five Bolivianos and we'd do a lot on the weekends, on Saturdays. Ten bolivianos for three hours. Sometimes we'd collect among the groups, we'd pitch in, get like twenty bolivianos, and then we'd record four hours. And you'd hear it on the street. Sometimes if going out on excursions, we had our radio that was called The Gutter Cholos and [it had a jingle] that said, "This is the program The Gutter Cholos" An then when the kids

were listing on their radio to a song and it was already on their stereo, that they had copied it from the radio to casette, and they'd go listening to it like that on the street, and we'd say wow, you heard that on our program.[1]

("Ojo del Alma," August 20, 2011)

Hearing his own voice recorded and then later associated with the circulation and expansion of hip-hop in his city gave Cañaviri confidence in his ability to intervene among his peers to assert pride in being Aymara and speaking the language.

That these artists rap in Aymara flies in the face of the presumption that, once in an urban context, bilingual Aymara youth rush to abandon their heritage language (cf. Guayaga 2000). In this case as elsewhere, multilingual rappers' decisions about the language in which they compose their lyrics are embedded within local social and political contexts (Makoni and Pennycook 2005), particularly the combination of both their own experiences with local sociolinguistic dynamics and also their perceptions of the reality facing rural migrants in their home communities and in the city of El Alto. Specifically, they view language shift away from Aymara to increased Spanish language use as a response to the anti-Indian racism rural migrants face in the city and the broader denigration of Aymara language and culture in Bolivian society. Speaking with me in 2007, Cañaviri and Rolando Franklin Casas Quispe, or "Rolo," identified these dynamics as motivating them to compose Aymara lyrics:

Grover: But we thought it's best [to sing in Aymara] because partly in those towns where the custom of speaking Aymara is getting lost, earlier in the countryside they spoke purely in Aymara but now it's between Aymara and Spanish like that.

Rolo: In the schools too they teach in Spanish and not in Aymara any more.

Grover: And it's getting lost, so we thought, we said, let's rap in Aymara because we believe that it's ours and because also you're going to help another generation.

Rodolfo: One idea is that they feel proud, that they not be embarrassed to speak in Aymara. When they arrive from the countryside, people obligatorily have to learn Spanish and from there they forget their dialect [sic].

Rolo: It's a big shock. Someone that is an Aymara speaker and arrives here to La Paz and everything is in Spanish. It's hard to learn and later it's embarrassing to speak [Aymara] and later when he goes back to his own town he only speaks in Spanish.

Karl: To show off a little too I imagine.

Rolo: Yes of course. We want to divert that a little in order for people to acquire those habits of speaking in Aymara. What better way than hip-hop, let's say that it's a central point? And we don't make commercial hip-hop but rather with the message we try to [persuade others to] value our culture more, our grandparents, good things.

Grover: During adolescence more than anything because everyone looks at you—that one's Aymara. Here there's a little bit of discrimination even among ourselves. We live where one person has their house, and the other person doesn't have anything and so, yes. And if the other speaks Aymara everyone puts him down, with his arrival from the countryside, and he can't even speak Spanish well. Little by little, I was taking nourishment, and I said this has to be done, hip-hop in Aymara, because hip-hop is attitude, it's strength, it's youth energy and I think that when someone is listening, he's going to put on that attitude and that pride, and I don't say in order to fight, but of being oneself, we're continuing to develop ourselves and the times are changing and if we lose our languages, our ancient customs, then I think that we're going to encounter a level where, damn it, and now? What do we do then?

Rolo: lost

Grover: What do we do then? Lost. So, I wouldn't want that to happen, to my children, possibly to my grandchildren and [things like that (lit. 'that wave')].[2]

In this interview, he animated a voice of an unnamed bully who equates speaking Aymara with being an animal. He represents the speech of the detractor as hurling the anti-Indian *t'ara* epithet in a way that aligns it through poetic parallelism with *llama* and *indio*:

Te discriminaban,	They discriminated against you
decían—A! esas ^^llamas,^^	They said, "Ah! Those llamas!"
esas ^^llamas^^ cantan en aymará,	those ^^llamas^^ are singing in Aymara
son unos ^^indios^^,	they're some ^^Indians^^
unos ^^t'aras. ^^	some ^^t'aras^^

T'ara is a Quechua word that means ignorant or unintelligent, but has entered highland Bolivian Spanish as a poetically symmetrical counterpart to the epithet for whites, *q'ara*, that we encountered in the last chapter. It is an insult directed against Indians, whether Quechuas or Aymaras, that builds on the negative stereotype of Indians as uneducated, inarticulate brutes. Calling their peers llamas for speaking Aymara is a painful example of self-loathing, of appropriating a racist discourse in Bolivia that dehumanizes Indians by referring to them as animals. Despite Bolivia being a majority Indian nation, *indio* has often been used as an insult. That such denigration is not only about language, or rural provenance, but also racializing, foregrounding the body and one's skin color was articulated by Casas Quispe in an interview he gave on Bolivian Television in 2011:

> Before it was, it wasn't banned, but it was viewed badly to speak in Aymara. In junior high, with your friends of your own age, you spoke Aymara or you'd say some little word that would just come out and they'd call you an Indian, uff, a hick, this or something else, they judged you a lot. And we saw it as a form of rebellion, as a way to change the situation, like a form of revolution, to be rebels in this aspect. To do hip-hop in Aymara and to say, "I'm Aymara and what? I'm from El Alto. I have brown skin. I'm made of earth."[3]
>
> ("Ojo del Alma")

These artists' concern with combating racism through the embrace of verbal art in the Aymara language is also motivated by the perception that the Aymara language is getting lost, "*se va perdiendo*," a process they connect to both the pejorative associations of Aymara language use (being llamas, *t'aras*) and also to institutional realities like schools excluding Aymara language education. The movement of people between the countryside and the city is a framework that provides one backdrop for these processes. In this stretch of the interview the figure of the returning migrant appears as the harbinger of Aymara language death through his deployment of Spanish as evidence of urbanity and sophistication. It is within this frame that they mention rural youth as their target audience. This is an inversion of how other Aymara and Quechua musicians have approached traditional Andean music within a framework of "world music." Where groups like the *Kjarkas* popularized Indigenous music styles among urban, cosmopolitan audiences and a through a "world music" market, these Aymara youth reformat the urban, cosmopolitan genre of hip-hop with an eye to their more Aymara-dominant rural counterparts (cf. Bigenho 2002).

In 2003, when the cultural center and radio station Wayna Tambo made a call for rappers and hip-hop enthusiasts to attend a series of workshops, Cañaviri, Quispe, and others responded. It was out of these workshops the Wayna Rap collective was formed. Wayna Tambo provided an institutional space for a hip-hop scene to come together, but other events of 2003 forged ties of unity and purpose for not just the El Alto hip-hop community, but entire city of El Alto and Aymara Bolivians more Broadly, namely what became known as the 2003 "Gas War." This uprising in the City of El Alto and the surrounding high plain in October of 2003 demanded the re-nationalization of Bolivia's natural resources, brought down the government of Gonzálo "Goni" Sánchez de Lozada, was a crucial precedent in the subsequent election of Evo Morales in 2006, and a defining moment for the residents of El Alto who lived through it. The events of 2003 proved to shape the perspectives of those who participated in it in profound ways. In Chapter 3, we heard how the leadership of Radio Pacha Qamasa understood this moment as a birth by fire which forged its political identity and relationship to its constituents. The youth of El Alto who lived through this conflict were similarly profoundly marked by this experience. This includes many who were in the El Alto hip-hop scene. Members of Wayna Rap Grover Canaviri, Rolo Quispe, and Eber Miranda Quispe described the Gas War as an awakening for the city of El Alto and as an inspiration for their music in an interview I conducted in 2007:

> Rolando: Two thousand three was the awakening of all the people of El Alto. Each one, everyone, we were, I don't know, depressed, saying—what a shame, our reality is so sad and all that. But that was the instant that all the neighbors, we all united, everyone carried a rock, or was protesting, or escaping (the armed forces) on every corner, each neighbor, each neighborhood council was very organized. The youth came out and everything. There were deaths. The people were going. Even one of our friends died, shot down (to Grover) you saw it (Grover: Yeah) personally. It was a great shame, which was the awakening of the rebellion of the people.
> Grover: October was like the awakening and, well, a lot of neighbors when organizing talked about, because our parents had struggled during the Banzer dictatorship and that whole era, so they had their experiences as young people and commented among themselves that we've always been marginalized. And that was the way they were talking.
> Eber: In 2003 it started a little bit for me. Goni left and all that. I hit the street, checked out everything that was happening, I saw how people had died and that reality I began to tell, to rap that reality.[4]

Grover situates the 2003 uprising of the Gas War within an intergenerational framework, mentioning the ways his parents had fought against the Banzer dictatorship. Speaking to a Finnish radio journalist (in an interview for which I served as interpreter), Miranda Quispe again explained the role of the events of

October 2003 had in both his personal life and, like Grover, places the Gas War within the larger arc of Aymara history, but reaches even further than Grover in recognizing its cultural impact:

> Well, I began in the year 2003 that was the year of the Gas War and all those historic moments of war, of struggle inspired me to do rap ... 2003 had been being constructed since the struggles of Tupak Katari, since the dictatorship, since other struggles, the water war, the war of February [in La Paz] ... and all that weight of so many years and epochs exploded in the year 2003. pow. A big explosion. An explosion of struggle. An ideological struggle. An explosion of culture and music. From there hip-hop was born I think for me. Hip-hop from El Alto. Aymara Hip-hop.[5]
>
> (Interview with Mårten Wallendahl for Finnish Radio, YLE, Radio X3m, July 2011)

The importance of 2003 as a turning point was emphasized by other members of the El Alto hip-hop scene as well. Nina Uma (Elena Amparo Tapia, b. 1976) is a hip-hop performer and radio host who spoke with me in 2011. In her interview with me she emphasized the 2003 uprising and subsequent political developments as the coming forth of a spirit of rebellion and Aymara identity among youth in El Alto. In the following exchange, in response to a question about youth attitudes toward the Aymara language, she pivots to address the changes in fashion in the hip-hop scene and accounts for them by explaining the broader political and social context of Bolivia's recent history. Speaking from the vantage point of 2011, she says that only a decade prior the only young people who would be seen wearing ponchos or *lluch'us* would be foreign tourists or backpackers. Interestingly, she brought up this introduction of traditional clothing within the local hip-hop fashion repertoire when responding to a question about Aymara language use in the course of our interview:

> Karl: Have you seen changes among the youth in El Alto concerning Aymara?
> Nina Uma: Look, I think that right now we have a very interesting Bolivian context that ten years ago didn't exist. Ten years ago, it would be difficult for you to see a young person with a lluch'u in the city. Some gringo, like, "How funny that he's going to wear that! That's what Indians wear." That's how it is. But beginning, principally here in El Alto, beginning in 2003, the rise of Evo Morales to the presidency and all that, there's a search among many generations including in the urban context. They begin to say, "We have someone there. We've done this. We have this power." And furthermore,

when we organize, come together, we can remove a president. To realize that capacity you have as an Aymara, as an Andean, and furthermore to respect what you are, it's difficult now for them to call you "Indian." Now it's, "I'm an Indian and what the fuck does anyone have to say about it." You see? That's how it is.

K: *Ukhamaw y qué*?

NU: You understand. Ukhamaw y qué? That's how it is. And what? Don't you see? That search and that revalorization of all the knowledge that was half hidden before but was present there. Then that's why now that becomes more visible, because many people, let's say it's like they've been losing their fear.[6]

Nina Uma situates the adoption of clothing by urban youth as part of a broader politicization and anti-racist reaffirmation of Aymara identity. She identifies 2003 as an important turning point in this process where people, particularly Aymara people in Bolivia, began to feel powerful.

Rappers like Nina Uma, Cañaviri, and Quispe understand 2003 as a crucial moment for the consolidation of hip-hop culture in El Alto, and also as a moment that was linked to others within a long trajectory of struggles reaching back through the struggles against the dictatorships of their parents' generation, and back to the days of colonialism and the struggle of Tupak Katari. In invoking the name of Tupak, Quispe anchors the moral authority of Aymara hip-hop to a baptismal site (Gal and Irvine 2019: 201) of Aymara resistance. In any Aymara cultural institution—educational, religious, and syndical—somewhere one will encounter the portraits of Tupak Katari and his comrade Bartolina Sisa. Tupak Katari led an insurrection in 1780, laying siege to the city of La Paz, crippling colonial powers for months. A contemporary of George Washington and Toussaint L'Ouverture, Tupak Katari's movement was part of a coordinated pan-Andean insurrection in which Tupak Amaru the Second also played a crucial part. Tupak Katari was publicly executed, torn apart by four horses, the pieces of his mutilated corpse displayed by the colonial powers in towns throughout Upper Peru (now Bolivia), and his heart buried in El Alto (Thomson 2004).

If the institution of Bolivian hip-hop has no walls for hanging portraits of Tupak Katari, Wayna Rap pays tribute to him through their rhymes. The lyrics to their song *Chamakat Sartasiry* ("Coming out from the Darkness"), the song for the video examined above, are as follows:

waranqa waranqa waranqanakawa	There are millions,
waranqa waranqa waranqanakawa	There are millions,
Aymar markaxa	My Aymara nation
wilampi Tupak Katari	with the blood of Tupak Katari,
Uka sutinak pirqan qhillqañani	That name we'll write on the walls
Aymara Qhichwa sart'asiwa	The Aymara, the Quechua rises up
Ch'amampi, ch'amampi	with power, with power
Jutaskiwa	is coming

These lyrics cite Tupak Katari's last words, now famous among Aymaras after having been repeated across generations since his execution by Spanish authorities: *Nayasaparukiw jiwayapxista, waranqa waranqanakaw kutt'anipxani* (You only kill me, but I will return and I will be millions). For these artists and others in Bolivia, the events of 2003 and the years since have been understood as a fulfillment of Tupac's prophecy of the return of the millions.

Members of Wayna Rap credit Miranda Quispe as composing the first track of entirely Aymara language hip-hop, a track written to convey his experience during 2003. In his words, this was his first step in "rapping that reality" (*rapear esa realidad*). The track titled *Ch'ama* (Power) merits particular attention for its historical significance but for other reasons too. *Ch'ama* has lyrics that are more evocative than precise, and could even be called vague. While a song like *Ch'amakat Sartasiry* explicitely makes calls for pan-Indian, or at least Quechua and Aymara unity, *Ch'ama* is less immediately recognizable as "political" in terms of its lyrical content. Yet both the poetic organization of meaning and the sonic organization of the track's production configure meaning in ways that can be understood as politically consequential, and even reminiscent of Tupak Katari's prophetic, final words. In addition to the lyrics' semantic, denotational meaning retrievable in what Miranda Quispe is saying with the lyrics, there are additional layers of semiotic function that also contribute. Namely, both the sonic qualities of production and the metrical organization of structural sense and reference in the lyrics construe texture and outline the contours of performer-audience interactional stance in meaningful ways (Tables 4.1–4.3).

Table 4.1 Lyrics to *Ch'ama*

Ch'ama	(Power)
Wayna Rap, 2003 (Written by Eber Miranda Quispe)	
Jiwañaru	To death
puriñani mä uru.	we'll arrive one day.
Lak'aru	To the earth
puriñani mä uru.	we'll arrive one day.
Saxranaka jutt'apxi.	The evil ones are coming.
Jan axsaramti.	Don't be afraid.
Wali ch'amampi nuwasiñani.	With strength we'll beat them ourselves
Atipañani	We'll win.
Khuchhi saxranakaru jiwayañani.	We'll kill the dirty, evil ones.
Ch'ama	Power
Akankaskiwa	Here it is
Akankaskiwa	Here it is

Table 4.2 Metrical organization of structural sense in *Ch'ama*

1	a	Jiwa-ña-ru die.NOM.DAT to death		
2	b	Puri-ñani Arrive.4FUT FUT we'll arrive	c	mä uru one day one day
3	a	lak'a-ru earth.DAT to the earth		
4	b	puri-ñani Arrive.4FUTFUT we'll arrive	c	mä uru one day one day
5	d	saxra-naka evil.PL the evil ones	e	jut-t'a-px-i come.INST.PL.3s are coming
6	f	jan axsar-am-ti neg.voc fear.IMP2.NEG don't be afraid		

(continued)

7	a	wali ch'ama-mpi good power.COM with strength	b	nuwa-si-ñani beat.REF.4FUTFUT we'll beat them ourselves
8	b	atipa-ñani win.4FUT we'll win		
9	a	khuchhi saxra-naka-ru dirty evil.PL.DAT we'll kill the dirty, evil ones	b	jiwa-ya-ñani dead.CAUS.4FUT
10	d	ch'ama power		
11	e	aka-n-ka-s-k-i-wa here.LOC.V.CONT. DELIM.3s.EVID Here it is.		
12	e	aka-n-ka-s-k-i-wa here.LOC.V.CONT. DELIM.3s.EVID Here it is.		

Table 4.3 Metrical organization of reference in *Ch'ama*

1	Jiwa.ña.ru die.NOM.DAT		to death	
2	Puri.ñani Arrive.4FUT	mä uru one day	we'll arrive one day *i + j*	
3	lak'a.ru earth.DAT		to the earth	
4	puri.ñani Arrive.4FUT	mä uru one day	we'll arrive one day *i + j*	
5	saxra.naka evil.PL	jut.t'a.px.i come.INST.PL.3	the evil ones are coming *k*	
6	jan neg.voc	axsara.am.ti fear.IMP2.NEG	don't be afraid *j*	
7	wali ch'ama.mpi good power.COM	nuwa.si.ñani beat.REFL. 4FUT	with strength *l*	
8	atipa.ñani win.4FUT		we'll win *i + j*	
9	khuchhi saxra.naka.ru pig/dirty evil. PL.DAT	jiwa.ya.ñani dead.CAUS.4FUTFUT	we'll kill the dirty, evil ones *i + j*	

10	ch'ama	power
	power	l
11	aka.n.ka.s.k.i.wa	here it is
	here.LOC.V.CONT.	l
	DELIM.3s.EVID	
12	aka.n.ka.s.k.i.wa	here it is
	here.LOC.V.CONT.	l
	DELIM.3s.EVID	

The first verse provides a frame for subsequent verses. These opening lines set a somber tone through an assertion of a grim truth—everyone dies. Rather than a generic truth, however, these lines also build urgency and specificity through verbal inflection by grounding this truth to the participants in the act of performing and hearing this song. These lines specify *who* dies one day, not just everyone, but *we* do, both the performing MC and the listening audience:

1	*Jiwañaru*	To death
2	*Puriñani mä uru.*	we'll arrive one day
3	*Lak'aru*	to the earth
4	*puriñani mä uru.*	we'll arrive one day

In lines 2 and 4, the verb *puriña* (to arrive) is inflected in the inclusive "we." Like many Indigenous languages of the Americas, Aymara has a greater level of specificity with regard to participant roles within the verb complex than Indo-European languages, through grammatically distinguishing between an exclusive we (+speaker, –addressee) and an inclusive we (+speaker, +addressee). The verbal inflection in lines 2 and 4 is inclusive, *puriñani*, emphasizing that *you* (the audience) and *I* (the MC) share a common fate.

Against this backdrop, the second line of the second verse *jan axsaramti* (don't be afraid) introduces an element of fear, recognizing the possibility of facing the *saxranaka* (the evil ones) alone. The sequential placement of this imperative advances a developing theme within the verse—the unity between the performer and his audience. The reflexive "*si*" in *nuwasiñani* (line 7) may also underscore that this is collaboration—we'll beat them *ourselves*.

The final verse consists of the lexeme *ch'ama* "power" in nominal case and the deictic *aka* "here" verbalized into the third-person present tense—*akankaskiwa* "it's here"—with the only other nominal subject together with third-person present tense appearing in line 5: *saxranaka jutt'apxi* "the evil ones are coming." These lines' parallelism set "power, here it is" in opposition to "the evil ones are coming."

But what is *power* and where is *here*? The way that the denotational text of the verse diagrams the interactional text, the relation between the rapper and his audience, helps to answer these questions. "Here" is anchored in mutual orientation between the MC and his audience. The morphological richness of the Aymara language provides additional layers of semiotic function in the final two lines. These lines are not only *akankaski* but *akankaskiwa*. The final morpheme "-wa" is an evidential marker of first-hand, experiential knowledge, indexically invoking the speaker's presence (Adelaar 2004; Hardman 2001). So, *here* is wherever the speaker and addressee are united—whether at a hip-hop show, a demonstration, listening on the radio, or performing for friends.

Ch'ama is a short verse that can be easily learned and repeated. In the recording, it is repeated multiple times; as the song advances, additional layers of Quispe's voice rapping are layered over the initial loop. The result of this aspect of the song's production is something between a round and complete cacophony. Richard Bauman and Charles Briggs (1990) have said that "Performance provides a frame that invites critical reflection on communicative processes. A given performance is tied to a number of speech events that precede and succeed it (past performances, readings of texts, negotiations, rehearsals, gossip, reports, critiques, challenges, subsequent performances and the like)" (60–1). This recording models the rhyme's future repetition and, in a way, provides instructions on how to use it—the internal organization models the repetition and amplification of many voices joining together. Where *Chamakat Sartasiry* re-entextualizes Tupak Katari's famous last words, *Ch'ama* provides a sonic model of Tupak's return of the millions, and the reason for their union—the defeat of a common enemy.

In his next project, *Nación Rap*, Eber and his collaborators took lyrical multilingualism to a new level by not only rapping in Spanish and Aymara, but also including verses in French and English. Having met as students in the school of languages and linguistics at the public university in La Paz, the members of *Nación Rap* established a linguistic and lyrical division of labor among themselves. As an example, we can listen to their homage to the coca leaf, *Mama Koka*, a track on the group's first album released in 2011, *La palabra es un arma* ("The Word is a Weapon"). This is also the track for their first professionally produced music video. The song itself is a homage to a prominent element of Andean culture, the coca leaf. Coca is both sacred and quotidian, used in religious ceremonies and divination, but also consumed widely and daily throughout the Andes as a stimulant. Coca is chewed to endure a long day's work or simply brewed to make tea. While its legal production and consumption in Bolivia is widespread, its illegal commercial uses are infamous. The illegal extraction and refinement of its alkaloids for the production of cocaine justified decades-long campaigns by the US and Bolivian governments for its eradication. The struggle against these campaigns became the primary vehicle through which Bolivia's first Indigenous president, Evo Morales, rose to political prominence as a leader of the Coca Growers Union. More broadly, the conflict over coca made it a metonym for Indigenous cultural resilience and Bolivian national sovereignty (Spedding 2004). In this song, the rappers defend the dignity of coca, announce their allegiance to coca in an idiom of religious veneration, and celebrate the friendly and familial sociality it facilitates, as well as its role in ritual divination by Aymara shamans, or *yatiris*:

Mama Koka lyrics (English translated on right column where not in English, French in *italics*, Aymara underlined.)

Eber:
Esta canción va dedicada
para la hoja sagrada milenaria,
Inal Mama
Ésto es Nación Rap. Vamos

This song is dedicated
to the millenarian sacred leaf,
Inal Mama
This is Nación Rap. Let's go.

Santi:
Directly from the ancestral drug store

David: (French)
Coca ce n'est pas cocaína
coca ce n'est pas cocaína

Coca isn't cocaine
Coca isn't cocaine

Eber: (Spanish)
Akhullicando pijchando
Aguantando en el trabajo
surgiendo desde abajo

Chewing coca, chewing coca
Getting through work
surging from below

Female voice Refrain: (Spanish)
hojita verde de la coca
humito blanco del cigarro
adivíname la suerte

Little green coca leaf
white cigar smoke
tell me my future

Santi: (English)
Directly from the ancestral drug store

It's coming delivered to us and more	
You will understand, everybody can,	
It will not be the same con la coca	(It will not be the same) with coca
Sagrada jalla coca de mis tías	Sacred jalla coca of my aunts
De la canción de la compañera Doña Jota	Of the song of our compañera Mrs. J.
Y ese ritmo de la coca	and that rhythm of the coca
Y sigue el rito for your mama	And that rhythm follows (for your mama)
Medicinal extraction de Pachamama	(Medicinal extraction) of Mother Earth
Hoja milenaria no se compara	Millenarian leaf has no comparison
No, no se compara	No, there's no comparison
Nación Rap	Rap Nation
En esta vida, en la que naces un día	In this life, in which you're born one day
Frenar así te toca	It's your turn to stop
Frente a estos narco-cocas	before these narco-cocas
Que destruyen vidas	who destroy lives
Ya no más	No more!
With a little bit of coca	
my Bolivia dale más	(my Bolivia) gives more
(Refrain, same as above)x2	

David:

Coca ce n'est pas cocaína, (x4)	Coca isn't cocaine (x4)
Coca es la hoja sagrada de Bolivia	Coca is the sacred leaf of Bolivia
Pijchando, cantando	Chewing coca, singing
Vamos a mostrar	We're going to show
la historia milenaria	The millenarian history
de la hoja boliviana	of the Bolivian leaf
(Aymara)	
<u>Inal Mama satawa</u>	Inal Mama (she) is called
<u>Inal Mama pijchawa</u>	Inal Mama is chewed
<u>Jay ukhamawa</u>	Yes that's how it is
Con su lejía	With her *lejía*[7]
Con mucha energía	with a lot of energy
Vamos a poner un poco de alegría	We're going to put a little bit of happiness

Con un cumpa lo voy a disfrutar	With a buddy I'm going to enjoy
Con un cumpa lo voy a pijchar	With a buddy I'm going to chew
Yendo del este al oeste	Going from the east to the west
Dónde sea, cuándo sea, cómo sea	Wherever, whenever, however
Yo lo voy a disfrutar	I'm going to enjoy it

(Refrain) x2

Eber:

Akhullicando pijchando	Chewing coca, chewing coca
Aguantando en el trabajo	Getting through work
surgiendo desde abajo	surging from below
siempre pa' adelante carajo	always forward damn it
suerte, vida, o muerte	luck, life, or death
mañana ¿qué será?	Tomorrow what will be
contigo soportando	with you putting up
hambre y pena	with hunger and shame
contigo compartiendo tristezas y alegrías	with you sharing sorrows and joys
venga alcohol, coca, y lejías	come alcohol, coca, and lejía
Sí léeme la suerte <u>Tata Yatiri</u>	Yes, read my fortune Tata Yatiri
en estas hojitas pa dónde mi camino	in these little leaves to where my road
pa dónde mi destino	to where my destiny

<u>Munat Inal mamita</u>	Dear Inal Mamita
<u>jumampi saraskä</u>	with you I will go
<u>Munat Inal mamita</u>	Dear Inal Mamita
<u>Jumampi sarnaqä</u>	with you I will go all over

Quédate conmigo	Stay with me
Guía mi camino	Guide my way
Guía mi destino	Guide my destiny
En esta vida tan jodida	In this life so fucked

(Refrain)

The very topic of the song is one particular Aymara cultural practice, and one that is shared by other Bolivians, chewing coca. The way in which coca is celebrated here is particularly Aymara, however, in how coca is venerated as sacred, as Inal Mama, and as a divination tool used by shamans, *yatiris*. As mentioned above, the insistence that "coca is not cocaine" became not just a description of fact, but a political stance of opposition to international efforts to eradicate the coca leaf and coca production. This stance came to feature prominently within Bolivian nationalist discourses opposed to US encroachment on Bolivian national sovereignty, a position which dovetailed with the defense of Indigenous cultural practices more broadly. The idea that coca is a medicinal gift of Mother Earth, or *Pachamama*, is a prominent message.

The Indigenous element of the lyrical content extends beyond the lyrics' topic to their linguistic form. Aymara rhymes are included alongside Spanish, French, and English. The longest verses are in Spanish and English, interspersed with the affirmation in French that "coca ce n'est pas cocaína (Coca is not cocaine)." The Aymara interludes are brief, introducing the ritual name of coca's spirit, *Inal Mama*: *Inal mama satawa*—"(she) is called Inal Mama"—and declaring the artists' commitment to her—*Munat Inal mamita, jumampi saraskä, munat Inal mamita jumampi sarnaqä* "Beloved Inal mamita, with you I will go. Beloved Inal mamita, with you I will go all over."

The music sampled for track comes from the popular 1987 song *Hoja verde de la coca* "Green coca leaf" by Peruvian Andean fusion "ethnorock" musician Miki González. The track prominently features the native Andean lute, the charango, and intermittent female vocals. Nación Rap's Eber Miranda Quispe described his own practice of searching for inspiration and samples from diverse genres as in line with the practice of "the greats" of hip-hop:

> I think, the same bases of hip-hop we hear now like 2Pac, Eminem, Wu-Tang Clan or of Cypress were born in those djs search for those, those loops, those pieces of music on vinyl, you understand they were born from hip-hop itself, you understand? And that's the same process that, will be here too, right? And sometimes rappers don't realize, I think what's lacking is to investigate a little the musical base. From where has it come from? From the god of the Americans, from the African American, from jazz, from other genres of, from the diverse genres the DJs have taken. I've made some loops of music that's from Proyección, That's a national group then too, eh, I look for little pieces that have the "beat." The tempo from then I adapt it, I mix it with something. Then it's the same process, just that it's different genres. And, yes, some say, "How can you mix that, how?" But alright, I think that's why music is music, isn't it? It born of the mix. Many genres have been born from the mix. If it's not mixed, new genres aren't born. If it wouldn't be mixed it would be static. It would be, i think boring. That's the dynamic music has then, no?
>
> (Eber Quispe, September 13, 2013, translation by author)

Quispe's approach to sampling echoes the practices of early US hip-hop artists from what Kemberly McLeod and Peter DiCola have called "the golden age of hip-hop sampling" (McLeod and DiCola 2011: 19). Nación Rap is one example and Mama Koka one song, but the Andean hip-hop repertoire is filled with examples of Indigenous sonic elements intermingling with samples of 1990s US hip-hop and digitally composed beats. For Quispe this is both a feature of hip-hop musical practice but also, crucially, a feature of music more universally. In his account of the kind of mixing that produced a track like *Mama Koka*, he also reveals his admiration for the "god of the Americans, the African American," a comment that resonates with the concert goer's comment at the opening of this essay.

The embrace of African American cultural forms, however they are understood from an Andean perspective, is notable in a context thoroughly permeated with racial ideologies of what Ecuadoran-Mexican philosopher Bolívar Echeverría has called "civilizatory whiteness," where, even without large populations of European descendants, such as is the case in Bolivia, a logic demanding allegiance to a eurocentric civilizatory order in which white supremacy prevails (Echeverría 2010). When asked by local media who their inspirations are, the artists of Nación Rap name Tupak Katari, the eighteenth-century leader of an Aymara revolt, but also Malcolm X and Martin Luther King Jr. This embrace of figures from US African American history as part of their own lineage may seem surprising, but represents an extension of earlier Aymara nationalist impulses to look to the Black diaspora as a source of anti-colonial inspiration. The mid-twentieth-century Aymara thinker Fausto Reinaga (1906–94), for example, introduced Bolivian readers to thinkers from the Black radical tradition such as Stokely Carmichael and Frantz Fanon in the 1970s (Reinaga 1970) through works of his like *La Revolución India* (The Indian Revolution), which includes long quotations of both of these thinkers. The lyrics of these artists' music integrate Aymara and Bolivian nationalist currents within a cosmopolitan framework that is multilingual and anchored to a genre that for them is squarely rooted in African American protest.

The pan-ethnic solidarity and anti-essentialism that is evident in this music simultaneously reproduce a separation between linguistic codes that is rarely found outside of contexts of performance. In their everyday, these artists speak Bolivian Spanish as marked by anglicisms like *MC, homie, bro,* and *flow* as by stretches of Aymara. In El Alto, in this Bolivian Aymara context, this repertoire increasingly includes the use of a dehispanicized register of Aymara that operates as an indexical icon, or emblem, of Aymara authenticity or "realness." Ultimately, how notions of race are structured in Bolivian society cannot be separated from questions of how ongoing processes of Aymara's enregisterment unfold, and how these competing models come to coexist with each other across the diverse social domains of this society marked by wide-scale multilingualism and a resurgence of Indigenous political power.

The hip-hop scene in El Alto consolidated and emerged from a particular historical moment for Aymara people and the Bolivian nation, the wake of the 2003 Gas War and subsequent years of Indigenous resurgence. When Miranda Quispe composed *Ch'ama* the fear and trauma of death was real for both him and his audiences. Like much effective protest music, however, his verses were also highly extractable from this context and transportable to other situations where calls for strength in unity against an advancing foe could be in order. Like many works of protest music emerging from moments of social upheaval, it draws on themes of solidarity in the face of adversaries, strength of numbers, reassurance, and courage in the face of repression and violence, but it is also vague enough to be re-entextualized across social contexts. Later songs composed by Nación Rap like *Mama Koka* take up themes that are less vague and take up themes of Aymara cultural sovereignty and resilience, many with short, catchy Aymara verses that, in a context of language shift, feel almost pedagogical in their replicability among bilingual audiences.

Such an operation, of replication and decontextualization, presupposes a command of the Aymara language that only a fraction of their audiences share. We might also reflect on these artists' own relationship to the lyrics of the artists whose work they admire and emulate. In one of my encounters with Rolo and Eber, they asked me to explain the lyrics to songs by US hip-hop artists. In a notable moment of translation, we listened to Wu Tang Clan's "The Mystery of Chessboxing." The opening verse of this track features U God (Lamont Jody Hawkins) mentioning Bolivia, when he says, "Raw, I'm a give it to ya with no trivia. Raw like cocaine straight from Bolivia." The name of their country was called out by U God and this much they understood. Listening to the track together, when the "hoo-ha, hoo-ha" back-up chant began, Eber laughed, joined the chant, and transformed it to the Aymara command, *Jutam! Jutam!* (Come! Come!) combining with a "come closer" gesture. "See? They know Aymara."

When a grammatical system is washed out of referential meaning, what of its poetics remain? An "unintelligible" language can still hold symbolic value as a recognizable, audible icon, if not as a decodable grammatical system. Lyrics, like all linguistic signs, are never encountered in isolation from a broader surround. These verses are heard also as part of and alongside other aspects of music and its performance. Even as an impenetrable code, the Aymara language in this musical context figures into a larger diagram of a hip-hop subjectivity legible by the other globally recognized signs of hip-hop—clothing, embodied stance and gesture, and the sonic quality of recordings (beat and rhythm)—examined above. The cadence of the voice, whether accessible as a denotational code, or "language," is another material (if sonic) sign within the larger diagram of social personhood communicated by these performers. When denotationally opaque their language moves from being a symbolic system to an emblem, a Peircean indexical icon, not just of indigeneity generally, but one enregistered with a composite of diverse qualia. There is a rhematization of the language into the sound and stance of a politically combative, contemporary, and Indigenous subject operating within the transnational terrain of global hip-hop. Their music remains intelligible to audiences beyond El Alto and the Bolivian high plain in ways similar to how hip-hop was meaningful to them when they first began listening to US artists. Just because they did not speak English does not mean they did not understand the music. When Tupac Shakur insisted, "Holla if ya hear me!" they might not have spoken English, but they answered.

5

Singing the National Anthem in Jesús de Machaca

The preamble to Bolivia's 2009 constitution outlines the nation's long history of Indigenous struggles. It places struggles of the past together with the uprisings of the early twenty-first century, mentioned by name (the Water War, the October War), situating them within a unified history of social struggle that has culminated in a constitution that aims to "construct a new state":

> The Bolivian people, of plural composition, from the depth of history, inspired by the struggles of the past, in anticolonial indigenous uprising, in independence, in the popular struggles of liberation, in the indigenous, social, and union marches, in the water war and the October war, in the struggles for land and territory, and with the memory of our martyrs, we construct a new state.[1]
>
> (Preamble to the Bolivian Constitution, 2009)

This chapter examines Bolivian plurinationality from the vantage point of an act of state commemoration of "struggles for land and territory" carried out to invoke "the memory of our martyrs." But within a plurinational state, to whom does this "our" refer? One answer is clear, that as a document for all Bolivians, it refers to all of the citizenry. But what of the martyrs from these "struggles for land and territory" who died at the hands of the Bolivian army? The emblems of the state mobilized in this context make both visible and audible the tensions between the old state and the new while simultaneously obfuscating them. In raising the flag or raising one's voice to sing the national anthem, performative acts of citizenship enact belonging to a nation that is one and plural, both the Bolivian and the Aymara nation. Following the passage of the 2009 constitution, Bolivia has two flags, the republican tricolor and the rainbow-checkered *wiphala*. The national anthem may now be sung not only in Spanish, but also in Aymara, with lyrics that carry dual indexicality arising from more than just the fact of being sung in a new linguistic code. In this chapter, I examine the translation of the Bolivian national anthem into Aymara and consider an instance of its performance in which linguistic indeterminacy dovetails with indeterminacies of nationhood, highlighting latent tensions within the project of constructing a plurinational republic.

Historian and co-founder of the Bolivian Communist Party (PCB), Jorge Alejandro Ovando Sanz was perhaps among the first to articulate a formulation of Bolivia as plurinational. Although calling Bolivia multinational, rather than plurinational, in his 1961 treatise *On the National and Colonial Problem of Bolivia*, he stands out as a thinker who advanced an early formulation of Bolivia as a plurinational society. In this work, he characterized Bolivia comprising multiple nations situated within relations of domination, both within and beyond its borders. From today's perspective, it is interesting to note that he did not refer to the Bolivian nation as an inclusive entity that contained others, but rather characterized the Bolivian nation as a dominant and distinct nation that subjugated oppressed Indigenous nationalities within its territory:

> Bolivia is, then, a multinational State, formed by one nation alone, the Bolivian nation; five principle nationalities, various small nationalities and numerous tribes and ethnographic groups. The characteristic and antagonistic trait of this multinational State is that the number of inhabitants of the oppressed nationalities, tribes and ethnographic groups is infinitely superior to the number of members of the Bolivian nation. The result of this is that the Bolivian nation, being a minority, subjects and oppresses the majority formed by the indigenous nationalities. But this oppression, apparently inconceivable, is explained entirely because the Bolivian nation has in its hands the state apparatus, that, in turn, is subject to and controlled by the yankee imperialists.[2]
>
> (Jorge Alejandro Ovando Sanz, 1961 [1984: 104–5, translation by author])

For Ovando Sanz, "the Bolivian nation" was one among others, rather a superordinate category encompassing those within it. For Ovando Sanz, the Bolivian nation was the urban, Spanish-speaking minority of the population. The colonial problem, for him, was not the long reach of legacies of the Spanish colony, as articulated later by Rivera-Cusicanqui (1984), but the ongoing political and economic domination of Bolivia by the United States, and Bolivia's subordinated status as an exporter of raw materials for a US-dominated global capitalism. Writing in the wake of the agrarian reform of 1953 and the immediate wake of the Cuban Revolution and global decolonization movements, Ovando Sanz was critical of assimilationist efforts at subordinating Indigenous nations to a Bolivian nationalism dominated by a pro-US Bolivian bourgeoisie.

Decades later, a political proclamation made by the katarista leadership of the CSUTCB would resonate with Ovando Sanz's formulations, although articulating a distinctly Aymara nationalist politics. They called for the transformation of the state to recognize both the plurinational character of Bolivian society and also the forms of Indigenous self-governance operative within it.

> We do not want bandages nor partial reforms, we want a definitive liberation and the construction of a plurinational society that, maintaining the unity of a state, combines and develops the diversity of the Aymara, Quechua, Tupí-Guaraní, Ayoreo, and all other nations which constitute it. There cannot be a true liberation if the plurinational diversity of our nation and the diverse forms of self-government of our peoples are not respected.[3]—Second Congress of the Unified Syndical Confederation of Rural Workers of Bolivia (CSUTCB), 1983
> (cited in Albó 2008: 40, translation by author)

Many of the delegates to the constituent assembly who participated in the constitution's re-rewriting, including members of the Movement to Socialism (MAS), can trace complex political genealogies that combine both Indianist and Marxist lineages. For many in Bolivia's social movements, including participants in the constituent assembly, there would be no apparent contradiction to recognize both of these texts as influential and formative political reference points in their thinking about the character of their nation. The notion of Bolivia as plurinational arrived to the halls of the constituent assembly from a variety of political currents, in other words. More than simply another version of "e pluribus unum" or a recognition of Bolivia's multiculturalism, the new constitution recognized Indigenous nations within a framework of a Plurinational Republic and the opening articles of the constitution affirm the plurality of the state itself. The second article states, "Given the precolonial existence of nations and indigenous peasant first nations and their ancestral dominion over their territories, they are guaranteed their free self-determination in the framework of the unity of the State, that consists in their right to autonomy, to self-government, to their culture, to the recognition of their institutions and to the consolidation of their territorial units, according to this constitution and the law."[4] Article 30 of the constitution defines "a nation" in the following way: "Every human collectivity that shares a cultural identity, language, historical tradition, institutions, territory and worldview (*cosmovisión*) whose existence is prior to the Spanish colonial invasion is a Peasant Indigenous First Nation (*pueblo indígena originario campesino*) and a nation."[5] Nation is used interchangeably and alongside "*pueblos indígena originario campesinos*" which I am translating as Peasant Indigenous First Nations.

Drawing closely from the 2007 UN Declaration on the Rights of Indigenous Peoples, the twenty-ninth article of the new constitution recognizes Indigenous Autonomy as "*self-governance through the free determination of Indigenous nations and Indigenous Peasant First Nations who share a territory, culture, history, language, and legal, political, social, and economic organization or institutions*."[6] Shortly following the ratification of the new constitution, in August of 2009, the Ministry of Autonomy passed Supreme Decree 231 that finalized the Law 4021 of the Transitory Electoral Regime, signaling municipalities that wanted to establish Indigenous Autonomy could conduct referenda during the elections of December of that year. Eighteen municipalities began the process and twelve completed the process to carry out elections. These referenda resulted in the establishing of eleven Autonomous Indigenous Municipalities: Mojocoya, Tarabuco, and Huacaya (Chuqisaca); Charazani, Chayanta, and Jesús de Machaca (La Paz); Salinas de García Mendoza, Pampa Aullagas, Chipaya, and Totora (Oruro); and Charagua (Santa Cruz).

The demand to rewrite the constitution through a constituent assembly had long been a rallying cry of Bolivian social movements. For many Indigenous communities, a participatory constituent assembly charged with rewriting the constitution was seen as a crucial vehicle for securing political autonomy and self-determination. The promise of a constituent assembly to rewrite the country's founding charter was among Morales's leading campaigning points in the lead-up to his election and subsequently a top priority and early achievement of his government. To make such demands across social movements, from the conflicts over the privatization of water in 2000 in Cochabamba, or during the Gas War, discussed in Chapter 3, provides examples of modes of political participation that Nancy Postero terms "postmulticultural citizenship" (2006: 2) in which large parts of the Bolivian public, the Indigenous social movements in particular, have been "demanding radical changes in the traditional relationship between state and civil society, calling for an end to the structured inequalities that mark Bolivian Society" (Postero 2006: 2).

New Emblems of the State

The constitution included measures to publicly mark the state as newly refounded. The new constitution expanded, rather than replaced, what had been the national symbols. The emblems that would now represent Bolivia would also include symbols representative of Indigenous plurinationality alongside those that had up until 2009 stood for the Republican State. The tricolor flag of red, yellow, and green that had been the sole national flag until 2009 now came to fly as co-official alongside the multicolored *wiphala* following the passage of the new constitution. Meaning "flag" in both the Aymara and Quechua languages, the word *wiphala* came to denote the checkered multicolored flag used by Indigenous movements in Bolivia since the 1970s. A square flag made up of forty-nine squares of the seven colors of the rainbow set out in a diagonal configuration, the *wiphala*'s multicolored patchwork color scheme visually diagrams the very notion of plurinationalism. Although some argue for the flag's roots in the Inka Empire (Limber 2015), historian of Aymara social movements and social thought Verushka Alvizuri identifies Constantino Lima of the *Movimiento Indianista Tupak Katari* (MITKA) and Germán Choque of the *Movimiento Universitario Julián Apaza* (MUJA) as the figures who initially introduced and popularized its use (Alvizuri 2009: 276–83). The *wiphala*'s subsequent adoption and use of the katarista leadership of the CSUTCB during the 1970s and the 1980s led to its ubiquity in social movements since (Albó 2008: 38). Article 5 of the constitution recognizes no longer just Spanish, but also Aymara, Quechua, Guarani, and thirty-three Amazonian Indigenous languages. Article 5 of the constitution also encourages the use of minimally two languages at both the federal and municipal levels, Spanish and an Indigenous language appropriate for the region. The constitution names "*el himno Boliviano*" as the national anthem, although the language of the anthem is not specified. The original lyrics are those written in Spanish by José Ignacio Sanjinés in 1845. While there are not yet versions of the Bolivian national anthem in all of Bolivia's national languages, there are now lyrics in the Aymara, Bésiro-Chiquitano, Guaraní, Guarayu, Moxeño, and Quechua languages.

In the broader Latin American context, Bolivia is not alone when it comes to the inclusion of Indigenous languages within the operations of officialdom. Most Latin American nations have either rewritten their constitutions or carried out major constitutional reforms in recent decades (Uprimny 2011). Across the hemisphere these initiatives involve diverse degrees of recognition of and participation by Indigenous nations. Ecuador, for example, since the rewriting of its constitution in 2008 is also officially a plurinational republic, recognizes Kichwa as a language of intercultural communication, and has a Kichwa version of the Ecuadoran national anthem.[7] Venezuela's redrafting of its constitution through a constituent assembly and its approval through referendum in 1999 served as an important precursor to the Bolivian process. Venezuela counts a much lower proportion of its citizens as Indigenous than do Bolivia and Ecuador and, unlike in these countries, the recognition of Indigenous peoples and of the multicultural character of Venezuelan society has been external to the constitutional process. Still, the recognition of Indigenous peoples has featured prominently in the political transformations underway in contemporary Venezuela. Linguistic anthropologist Juan Rodríguez (2020) has discussed how cultivating new associations with symbols of the state has been central to the socialist project of the Venezuelan government during the last two decades in what he calls the re-grounding of signs of Venezuelan nationhood. Discussing performances of the Venezuelan anthem in the Warao language, Rodríguez points out that "New translated texts such as the national anthem come now to stand to us [Venezuelans] for a transformed nation-state (as semiotic object) demanding its citizens to be reacquainted with the new relations (the new semiotic ground) between the socialist nation-state and its signs" (Rodríguez 2020: 92). Translated versions of the anthem and their performances not only recast the state in new ways for its citizens, but also recast non-Indigenous Venezuelans' views of Indigenous peoples like the Warao. Namely, the Warao translation of the anthem was scrubbed of all traces of Warao bilingualism in such a way to invite essentialist performances. "Essentialism requires purism, and in turn, purist versions of texts help produce semiotic grounds for essentialist interpretations" (Rodríguez 2020: 91).

Further north in Mexico, following the passage of the 2003 General Law on Indigenous Languages, the Mexican national anthem was translated into a number of Indigenous Mexican languages. Chatina linguistic anthropologist Emiliana Cruz contrasts her community's experience with that of the Warao translation of their national anthem in Venezuela as described by Rodríguez (2020). "The translation of the national anthem of Venezuela into the Warao language was supposed to be a form of patrimony that belonged to non-indigenous citizens as well as indigenous ones, whereas the Chatino translation of the Mexican anthem of San Juan Quiahije was more highly Chatino specific and not meant to be performed by people who are not from this municipality nor Chatinos" (Cruz 2020: 4). Cruz notes that the translation of the Mexican anthem into the Chatino language introduced unexpected and unintended resonances with local politics and histories. Cruz points out that the verses in the anthem that mention protecting land from invaders take on a new meaning when translated into Chatino of San Juan Quiahije. Rather than evoking scenes of the distant Mexican Revolution, these lines resonated with an immediate context in which land disputes with neighboring communities are ongoing and often violent (Cruz 2020: 35–6). The latent indeterminacy of spatial and referential deixis increases with the translation of the anthem from Spanish to Chatino. Once sung in Chatino, "this land" may shift from broadly Mexican to specifically Chatino territory, and recalibrate who the "we" of the heroic anthem includes. Translation introduces other levels of indeterminacy, not only spatial and referential, but political ones, both historic and ongoing.

Lyrical Indeterminacy

Themes of protecting land from invaders are recurrent throughout national anthems in Latin America (Castany 2011). The Bolivian anthem is no exception. The opening stanza declares the land itself free from a state of former bondage, "the land is free at last, its servile state has finally ceased," while the final stanza warns that, "If a foreigner may, some day attempt to subjugate Bolivia, let him prepare for a fatal destiny" (See Table 5.1). When the verse was written in 1845, the War of Independence from Spain would have been a conflict of still recent, living memory. Bolivia's anthem, however, was composed to commemorate a different conflict: the 1841 Battle of Ingavi. This was a border war fought with Peru in the wake of the Peru-Bolivia Confederation's dissolution. The anthem was adopted on the anniversary of the battle in 1845 and was composed by Leopoldo Benedetto Vincenti with lyrics by José Ignacio de Sanjinés. Like other national anthems, its lyrics reflect themes of war's end, liberation, and freedom. Consider the first verse and chorus:

Bolivianos: el hado propicio	Bolivians, a propitious fate
coronó nuestros votos y anhelo,	has crowned our vows and longings!
es ya libre, ya libre este suelo,	This land is free, free at last.
ya cesó su servil condición.	Its servile state has now finally ceased.
Al estruendo marcial que ayer fuera	The military turmoil of yesterday
y al clamor de la guerra horroroso	and the horrible clamor of war
siguen hoy, en contraste armonioso,	continue today in harmonious contrast,
dulces himnos de paz y de unión.	Sweet hymns of peace and union
Coro	**Chorus**
De la patria el alto nombre	The lofty name of our fatherland
en glorioso esplendor conservemos	in glorious splendor let us conserve
y en sus aras de nuevo juremos	and on its altars once again swear
¡Morir antes que esclavos vivir! (3x)	To die before living as slaves! *(3x)*

This first verse and the chorus provide the source material for the Aymara, Quechua, and Moxeño translations of the national anthem. The original Spanish language anthem has four verses (see Appendix), while the Quechua, Guarani, and Moxeño versions have a more truncated format of one two-stanza verse followed by the chorus. There is more than one Aymara language version of the anthem in circulation, one with two verses and a chorus and another, similar to the other Indigenous language versions, with only one verse followed by the chorus. The quatrain stanzas of the original Spanish follow an enclosed ABBC rhyme scheme, while the Indigenous language versions present rhyme only within the chorus. Why does the Spanish version have more verses than the Indigenous ones? We might see it as another instance where, despite good intentions, the Indians are given yet again less. Translations are not easily done, and despite the official nature of the hymn, there is not an official translation. The most widely circulated and the version in the discussion below was made by the Aymara educators Basilio Mamani and Alfredo Mita.

The anthem begins with a vocative address to fellow citizens in Spanish, *Bolivianos!* Yet in both the Quechua and Aymara versions, this is the only time the name "Bolivia" is uttered, and the only instance of Spanish. Nowhere else in either the Aymara or Quechua versions of the anthem does the phonologically assimilated *Wuliwya* of vernacular Aymara and Quechua appear (both languages lack the voiced bilabial plosive /b/ and tend to replace it in loanwords with the voiced labio-velar approximant /w/). This contrasts with the Guarani version, where we hear the phonologically assimilated name with a pre-nasalized initial consonant: *Mborivia*. In fact, following the Spanish call to citizens that opens the anthem, the rest of the verse is in a neatly dehispanicized Aymara. Like the Warao Venezuelan anthems discussed by Rodríguez (2016, 2020), aside from the opening call to attention, all traces of Aymara bilingualism are scrubbed from the Aymara version of the anthem.

Perhaps the most salient, rousing lines of the anthem come at the close of the chorus, ¡*Morir antes que esclavos vivir!* "To die before living as slaves!" Aymara intellectual Esteban Ticona Alejo testifies that during the Gas War of 2003 when news of President Goni Sánchez de Lozada fleeing the country arrived to the demonstrations in La Paz, crowds broke out singing this final line from the chorus the national anthem (Ticona Alejo 2005: 193). This line's translation into Aymara, however, does not mention slavery, but instead suffering. This provoked a disapproving evaluation from at least one Aymara schoolteacher I spoke with who told me he did not appreciate the implication of this line. He insisted that a song meant to arouse national pride should convey a message of perseverance and bravery, and that this was lost in the translation. "Aymaras are not afraid of suffering!" He went on to emphasize that he felt the point should be to struggle against indignity and humiliation. Pride and dignity was at stake, not comfort. This is unlikely the intention of this line, but resulted in at least one unsympathetic interpretation.

There are other points of semantic stickiness within the translation. In one of the Aymara versions, we find a conspicuous slippage in the translation of a key term of national belonging. "Bolivians" remains untranslated from Spanish, but *la patria* "homeland" is translated into Aymara as *Qullasuyu* in the first line of the chorus

Taq'itaki	Chorus
***Qullasuyu** jach'a sutipa,*	***Qullasuyu**, her great name*
qhapax suma k'axañapa imañani.	*Her shining wealth we'll guard*
Sutiparu wastat surañani,	*To her name again we salute*
¡Jiwañan janirar t'aq'iskasin! (3x)	*We will die before suffering (3x)*

This semantic slippage moves away from the language of nation as patriarchal kinship (*la patria*) and toward the language of Andean antiquity. *Qullasuyu* was the political division of the Inka Empire in which most of the contemporary Bolivia sits. This is not a neologism, but an archaicism and one from times of the Inka Empire. The Inka Empire was called *Tawantinsuyu* in Quechua, "the country of four countries united." Quechua, like Aymara, is an agglutinative language. The name for the Inka Empire in Quechua was composed of the three morphemes: *tawa* "four"; *-ntin-* "composite," "separable units joined"; *suyu* "country." *Qullasuyu* as a historic territory overlaps with highland Bolivia, but was not limited to it, reaching as far north as the Inka capital of what is today Cusco, Peru, and south into contemporary Chile and Argentina. From the perspective of broader Bolivia, and particularly lowland Bolivia, *Qullasuyu* is crucially not coterminous with the contemporary Bolivian state. The Inka polity did not extend into the Amazonian north of Bolivia, nor reach as far east as the contemporary eastern limits of Bolivia, nor as far into the southeastern Chaco region of Guaraní and Ayoreo lands.

In contrast to the archaicisms encountered in Chapter 2 at Radio San Gabriel, *Qullasuyu* is not a term remote to contemporary discourse. Although evocative of the language of the sixteenth century, this is not an obscure "rescued" archaicism from a colonial era source, although it seems similar to this. With the rise of Indianist political discourse during the 1960s and since, Indianist formations have taken up Qullasuyu as the goal of their political projects. Following the philosophy of Aymara intellectual Fausto Reinaga, the "reestablishment of Qullasuyu" defined, and for some continues to define, a political horizon for Indianist and katarista movements beyond the contemporary nation-state, not coterminous with it (Albro 2010: 76). In the new national anthem, however, the Bolivian nation-state becomes synonymous with *Qullasuyu*. Whether this represents semantic expansion, reduction, or perhaps even historical erasure remains a question for Aymaras to decide. The indeterminacy and potentially contentious or even anti-state valence of *Qullasuyu* might explain why it is absent in other translations. A translation produced by the educational service *Recursos Educativos Multimedia Educabol* opts instead to translate *la patria* as *markasäna* "our country's" (see Aymara 2 in Table 5.1).

Still, we could also consider the inclusion of *Qullasuyu* as consistent with another practice common in many national anthems across Latin America, the use of archaicisms. Latin American national anthems often employ archaicisms to sound as if they come from a deep past and to insist on the eternal nature of both the nation and its heroes (Castany 2011). In the Spanish lyric, this effect is produced both lexically through words such as *loor* "praise," and also grammatically. In the fourth stanza, we encounter the subjunctive future conditional inflection of the verbs *poder* and *intentar* (*Si un extranjero poder algún día/sojuzgar a Bolivia intentare* … "If a foreigner ever tries one day/ attempts to subjugate Bolivia") which, although still a grammatical feature of the closely related Portuguese, is a verbal inflection not in use in any variety of contemporary spoken Spanish (Castany 2011: 60).

The second Aymara version from *Multimedia Educabol* also includes two verses rather than just the one, namely, the second verse of the original which heralds "*loor eterno a los bravos guerreros cuyo heroico valor y firmeza conquistaron las glorias que empieza hoy Bolivia a gozar*" ("eternal praise to the brave warriors whose heroic valor and firmness conquered the freedom and glories that now a happy Bolivia begins to enjoy") (Table 5.1). The verbal deixis of the Aymara lines diagram more explicitly the participation roles than does the Spanish line that opens with the bare noun phrase "loor eterno" ("eternal praise"). Where the suggestion in the original Spanish remains implicit that, through the very act of singing, "loor eterno" is conferred "a los bravos guerreros" ("to the brave warriors"), this Aymara translation includes an inflected verb "*wakt'aña*," which is translated into Spanish as "tocar el turno" or "to have a turn" with a verbal inflection that specifies a third-person agent (*jupax*) and fourth-person patient (inclusive "us"/*jiwasarux*) ending "-istu." This dative construction of *wakt'istu* "being our turn" (Spanish: "nos toca") suggests an obligation both upon those singing and also to those listening by way of the inclusive "we/us" inflection. The obligation is to confer eternal praise (*wiñay q'uchuñaw*) upon those people who died (*jiwir jaqinakaru*) for our country (*markaslayku*):

Wiñay	q'uchuñaw	wakt'istu	markaslayku	jiwir	jaqinakaru
Eternal	praise	Confer a turn.3S4O	country.4pos. because	dead	people.DAT
"It's our turn to give eternal praise to those who died for our country."					

Jupanakaw	markas	ut'ayapxi	jichhurun	kusisit	jakañani
3S.PL.EVID	country.4POS	construct.3PL	today	happy	Live.4FUT
"They built our country so that today we can live happily."					

Perhaps *Qullasuyu* sung in the context of the national album could also be heard in a register divorced from any katarista overtones, within an indigenist, rather than an indianist, register, invoking the Inka past in a way analogous to the presence of images of Tiwanaku on Bolivian currency (Fig. 3.2). In fact, the absence of any mention of pre-Colombian antiquity could be considered conspicuously absent from the original version of the Bolivian national anthem, particularly when contrasted with the opening lines to the anthem of neighboring Peru:

Gloria enhiesta en milenios de historia	Glory erected in millennia of history
fue moldeando el sentir nacional	molded the national sentiment
y fue el grito de Túpac Amaru	and it was the yell of Túpac Amaru
el que alerta, el que exige	which alerts, which demands
y el que impele, hacia la libertad.	and which impels, towards liberty.
Y el criollo y el indio se estrechan	And the creole and the Indian embrace
anhelantes de un único ideal	yearning for a single ideal

Even if not indigenist in the same key as earlier elite projects (cf. De la Cadena 2000), to be able to hear the call for *Qullasuyu* outside of a framework of katarista political discourse and instead as part of an official standard dehispanicized register of Aymara suggests the shifting trajectories of enregisterment of this term and the dynamic nature of Bolivia's *proceso de cambio*. The more this version of the national anthem is sung, not only divorced from katarista political projects but within a performative act of civic allegiance, the more any incommensurability between the historic Inka polity and the contemporary Bolivian state will be suppressed (Fig. 5.1). Now, to sing the anthem in Aymara praises both the martyrs of the Bolivian nation and the glory of the Inka past.

Figure 5.1 "The Fatherland/Qullasuyu's great name": "Patria" translated as "Qullasuyu" (screengrab from Recursos Educativos Multimedia Educabol). https://www.youtube.com/watch?v=VQMhCP-2OD4 (accessed December 25, 2022).

As in the case of the Mexican anthem translated into the Chatino language mentioned above (Cruz 2020), the anthem's themes of conflict, violence, and liberation take on different valences than those suggested in the original version. When sung with an Aymara lyric at the site of an act of Bolivian state violence against Aymaras who fought to reclaim lands usurped by white ranchers, the anthem resonates with a history distinct from the republican history of its original composition. What is more, the new lyrics reflect, but do not resolve, tensions between Aymara nationalist politics of refusal and the plurinational politics of the new Bolivian state.

Commemorating the Martyrs of Jesús de Machaca

Considering the national anthem from Jesús de Machaca might be considered particularly appropriate considering that it is located in the province of Ingavi, the site of the battle that the national anthem commemorates. When I traveled to Jesús de Machaca in March of 2010, it was to attend a march and public ceremony commemorating a historic event, but not the events of 1845. This was instead a march commemorating a historic moment in the history of Aymara struggles for territory and autonomy: the 1921 Jesús de Machaca Uprising. During the uprising of 1921, *machaqueños* imprisoned the mayor, lynched a corrupt priest, and forcibly evicted white cattle ranchers from what had previously been communal Aymara lands. Decades earlier, in 1874, the Bolivian state had passed the Ley de Exvinculación de Tierras which amounted to a massive land grab of Aymara held lands by white ranchers (Ovando Sanz's "Bolivian nation"). In the words of Aymara historian Silvia Rivera-Cusicanqui, this law "formalized, after the fact, an aggressive recolonization of indigenous territories throughout the country, resulting in a massive expansion of large estates through the expropriation of communal lands" (Rivera-Cusicanqui 2012: 100). After decades of white landowners' usurpation of communal Aymara lands, a change in the federal government led Aymaras to believe that they would have the support of the central government to reclaim their lost territories. They were wrong. The state responded by sending in troops to burn the homes of the "lawless Aymaras" and arrest and execute those identified as the community's leaders—Faustino Llanki, along with his father, Marcelino Llanki.

These men were visible to the state in their role as *caciques apoderados* who had been advocating in courts for their communities' land tenure in the face of encroaching cattle ranchers, using titles to lands granted to them during the colonial period (Choque and Quispe 2010). The events of 1921 are commemorated both as an uprising and a tragic massacre, remembering ancestors as victims but also protagonists. It is a day of remembrance for the Aymara peasants who died at the hands of the Bolivian army, but also in memory of Aymara leaders who defended their land against whites who did not respect Aymara titles to it. Faustino and Marcelino Llanki pursued legal means to their ends, but paid with their lives for those who pursued extra-legal, if legitimate, channels for their grievances.

The former director of Radio Pacha Qamasa, Franz Laime, who has family ties to this region had provided me with the names and contact information for both family members and elected leaders within the *Cabildo de Ayllus y Comunidades Originarias de Jesús de Machaqa* (CACOJMA) to whom he encouraged me to introduce myself in order to attend. I made the two-hour trip from El Alto by bus together with two members of *Nación Rap*, Eber Quispe and David Acarapi. Joining us on the bus were many others from El Alto who were also planning on attending the day's events. As the bus approached Jesús de Machaca, a sign for the community announced the public status of this community within Aymara history: *Jesús de Machaca—Marca Rebelde*, "rebel country."

When we arrived at the small church of Qalla Arriba a few miles outside of Jesús de Machaca, hundreds had already gathered and were seated in groups around long rows of textiles with cooked potatoes, corn, and cheese. This is the Aymara heartland just south of Lake Titicaca, only separated from the ruins of Tiwanaku by a low mountain range. Jesús de Machaca is considered by many as a heart of Aymara territory, not only because of questions of territory (Fig. 1.2), nor because of proximity to Tiwanaku, but because of the history of events like the one that is commemorated on this day. Many of those gathered are farmers who work on the lands visible spreading out across the stark, open surrounding landscape. Many more have family connections to these lands, and, like those who came in with us by bus, have also traveled in from the city of El Alto. The men wear the red ponchos typical of the region, while the women don the black head coverings and dress also typical of Aymara women of this region. Local accounts explain this black dress as a testament to *machaqueñas* historic opposition to Spanish rule, explaining that the black is worn as a gesture of mourning dating to the death of the last Inka (LaBarre 1948: 88). Whether or not this account is true, it speaks to Jesús de Machaca's status as *marca rebelde*, the valorization of a long-standing commitment to Indigenous autonomy, a particular position that the communities of this region hold within Aymara narratives of resistance.

Following words from the parish priest and community leaders, those in attendance marched to the central plaza of the regional center of Jesús de Machaca to attend an *acto cívico*, a civic act, a public commemoration of the uprising and massacre. If the tone of the march and the following event is somber, there is also a sense of reverence, and also pride and vindication. The commemoration of 2010 was taking place only one year after the ratification of the new constitution, which, in turn, opened the way for a referendum for Jesús de Machaca to establish itself among the first autonomous Indigenous municipalities. The referendum passed and the residents of Jesús de Machaca were in their first years moving toward autonomy and self-governance. The struggle for land, which had left martyrs in its wake, martyrs commemorated on the day of this march, was understood by many present as having been won in their securing the recognition and exercise of their autonomy.

By the time the marchers arrive and assemble in the plaza, so have others, a group of men in suits, uniformed students from local schools, and a high school band. The sound system in the plaza's central gazebo pipes up, and an MC greets those assembled in rapid-fire Aymara, with the clear elocution of a radio announcer. He tells the crowd the event is beginning and greets "the *pobladores*," the residents of Jesús de Machaca. He announces the reason for the gathering:

Aka marzo phaxsita 1921 [mil novecientos veintiuno] *maranxa jichhurkamaxa niyawa makipawaykaraki kimsaqallq tunk llatunkani maranxa* ochenta y nueve aniversario de la fiesta libertaria sublimación y massacre de *Jesús de Machaca uka amtapxañani* ...

"This month of March, in the year 1921 until today it will approach eighty ninth year eighty nine anniversary of the 'fiesta libertaria' the uprising and massacre of Jesús de Machaca that we will remember ... "

(Aymara with Spanish)

He continues in Aymara, greeting those who have arrived marching from Qalla Arriba, the political representatives, the *mallkus*, and then the elderly, and the students who have arrived. The MC then convenes those about to perform the civic ritual to their appropriate places: the director of the band to his place, a member of the Bartolina Sisa women's organization to the flagpole. He instructs the assembled choir, the marchers, and attendees to take of their hats and tells them how they are to sing the Bolivian national anthem. There will be two rounds of the anthem, first in Aymara and then in Spanish. The MC's welcoming of the congregated public and his confirming of places and roles in the civic ritual, and his explanation of how and when, and in which language the national anthem will be sung is delivered in Aymara.

His voice is loud and clear, not only thanks to the amplification. He delivers these instructions with the cadence and timbre of someone who has done this before. Perhaps he has worked in radio and media, or is simply a good MC, but unlike the Aymara of radio announcer from Radio San Gabriel (Chapter 2), this is not a dehispanicized Aymara free of loanwords (*invit'arakiñaniwa* "let's also invite") or even Spanish (*hermana* "sister," *sombrero* "hat"). Perhaps in a more pedagogical mode reminiscent of the speech of the more bilingual speech of a bilingual teacher, like Radio Pacha Qamasa's Gabriel Bonifacio (Chapter 3), there are moments in which the MC models modes of translation. When he says the year of the uprising in Spanish, he follows this announcing that this marks 89 years since the massacre, says "eighty nine" first in Aymara, immediately followed by the Spanish (*kimsaqallq tunk llatunkani maranxa* ochenta y nueve). As the moment for opening the event nears, his language shifts from Aymara to Spanish. He does not repeat the metalinguistic explanation concerning the singing of the anthem in both the Aymara and Spanish languages. In shifting to Spanish, there is a move away from explanation and a shift toward directives. The directives arrive first with the formulaic speech of an MC (querida concurrencia, "dear audience") but quickly there is another shift, to a military register (*Todos a mis órdenes* "Everyone at my command") delivering an authoritative bit of Spanish, authoritative because the call to "attention!" sounds reminiscent of the bark of a military officer. While the MC's speech is overwhelmingly in Aymara, the final instructions to prepare to sing, and the call to "attention!" are delivered with the bark of a military drill, and are delivered in Spanish:

> *Qallt'apxañaniwa kunatixa aka <u>programa especial</u> wakt'ayataki ukarjama nayririnxa utjapxistuwa <u>Himno Nacional Coro General</u> invit'añaniwa kawkiritixa <u>profesor de música del colegio</u> [Name] nayraqatxa q'uchupxañaniwa aymara aruta uk'amarakiwa <u>Himno Nacional castellano</u>*

> *Waliki jawillt'añani kawkhankaskisa <u>hermana de Bartolina Sisa</u> jupawa eeee ... wiphala jiykat'arakinisa ukhampansti invit'arakiñaniw kawkhirinakatix aksatuqinkaptan taqiniw <u>sombreros</u> asaqt'asipxañani Bolivia markasana q'uchupa q'uchuñtaki qhawqhanxaña tuqinxa Aymara aruta Castellano aruta q'ucht'apxarakini. Ukhamaxa <u>professor de música, Así, bien, querida concurrencia, vamos a pedir a todos a quitarse los sombreros. Todos a mis órdenes. Atención, firme, estandartes, banderas, wiphalas, mande al hombro mar</u> ... (music)*

> Let's all begin this <u>special program</u> has been prepared. First there'll be the <u>National Anthem, General Choir</u> who will be <u>the highschool professor of music</u> [Name] first we'll sing in the Aymara language and then also like that <u>Spanish National Anthem</u>

> Alright let's welcome, where's the <u>sister from Bartolina Sisa</u> she eeee.. is going to raise the *wiphala* and then let's invite everyone in this place we'll take off our hats to sing the Bolivian national anthem where we'll sing in Aymara language and Spanish language too. Like that <u>the music professor, so, well, dear audience, we'll ask everyone to take of their hats, everyone at my orders, Attention, steady, banners, flags, shoulders to the sea ...</u>

(Aymara with <u>Spanish</u>)

As the music starts, a man and woman, each of them in traditional dress, approach the flag poles on either side of the bust of Faustino Llanki and proceed to raise the national flags (Figure 5.2). The man raises the republican tricolor and the woman raises the *wiphala*. The gendered division of labor in the raising of the two flags fulfills a normative discourse of *chachawarmi* "man-woman" of gender parity and complementarity in political participation in Indigenous Andean communities (De la Cadena 1995). The particularly gendered way in which the division of labor in the raising of the flags unfolds, or unfurls as it were, becomes another instance of practices in which women take on roles or practices which are taken to be more Indian (Canessa 2008; De La Cadena 1995; Narayanan

Figure 5.2 Bolivia's two national flags raised at the commemoration of the 1921 Rebellion.

2022; Swinehart 2018). The hoisting of the newly official *wiphala* is done by the woman, while the red, yellow, and green tricolor flag is raised by the man.

The crowd proceeds to sing the national anthem in Aymara and then in Spanish. The crowd's singing, however, is hardly a rousing rendition. Many in attendance seem not to know the lyrics. Event organizers seem to have anticipated the possibility of the participants' lack of familiarity with the anthem's Aymara lyrics and had distributed small half sheets with text during the lead-up to the raising of the flags. Attendees struggle with the small pieces of paper and mumble their way through the verses. The singing of the anthem closes with the MC leading an Andean (both Quechua and Aymara) call-and-response cheer—Jallalla!—praising the leaders of the 1921 uprising, Faustino and Marcelino Llanki, followed by parallel cheers for the authorities of Jesús de Machaca.

MC:	*Jallalla* Marcelino Llanki!
Crowd:	*Jallalla*
MC:	*Jallalla* Faustino Llanki!
Crowd:	*Jallalla!*
MC:	*Jallalla Cabildo de autoridades de Jesús de Machaca!*
	[Council of authorities of Jesús de Machaca]
Crowd:	*Jallalla!*

With this closing the MC establishes a poetic equivalency between the present, current authorities, the Cabildo de autoridades, surrounding him and their predecessors, Marcelino and Faustino Llanki. Emphasizing parallels between the past and the present becomes a recurrent motif in the course of the program. The first of the speakers approaches the microphone and begins the speeches for the day. His opening words toggle between the present and the past and connect the uprising of 1921 to the struggles of the contemporary moment through formulations of "like now ... there was" (*jichhurjamaw ... utjawayatayna*):

> *Anchhita urasana jiwasanka jikxatasiwaytanwa jach'a <u>histórico</u> Jesús de Machaca. Uka taypina jiqxatasiwaytana ukhamakipansti, munata jilatanaka kullakanaka, jichhurjamawa mä ch'axwawixa utjawayatayna aka <u>juridicción</u> Jesús de Machaca ...*
>
> Right now in this time we find ourselves here in great historic Jesús de Machaca. Right in the middle here, dear brothers and sisters, then, like now there was a great rebellion in this jurisdiction of Jesús de Machaca

The historical uprising of 1921 and the social movements of the twenty-first century are both referred to with the same Aymara term for uprising, or conflict more generally, *ch'axwawi*. This is also the term that is mobilized in both of the Aymara versions of the national anthem for the lines referring to war (*estruendo marcial, clamor de la guerra*). The anthem's Spanish lyric contrasts, however, with the Spanish words used by the MC and others to describe the 1921 uprising: *sublevación* "uprising, revolt" and even *fiesta libertaria* "liberatory party." What was lost in translation, the military overtones of the original Spanish lyric, becomes a more indeterminate *ch'axwawi* that can accommodate now a popular uprising of farmers reclaiming their lands.

The speaker addresses the students in attendance and speaks with passion about the importance of education. He characterizes the students' pursuit of an education as a culmination of the history of the Aymara social movement, that the struggle for education is a continuation of the struggle of their ancestors. The idea that the assembled students' diligent pursuit of education and eventual careers, or even that this solemn commemoration, carried out with military discipline and order, is equivalent to the *ch'axwawi* "uprising" of a century ago could seem strangely incongruous to an outside observer. For those present, however, the uprisings that lead to the securing of their recently won autonomy are fresh in their memory. Their martyrs are not only historical figures from 1921, but family members and friends lost to state violence in the uprisings of the last decade.

Qullasuyu jach'a sutipa "Qullasuyu her great name"

What sense can be made of the unevenness or even lackluster singing of the national anthem? This commemorative ceremony took place only one year after the passing of the new constitution, afterall, and to sing the national anthem in Aymara was still a novel act in itself; and at a more fundamental level, the very lyrics themselves were new. For many in attendance, the number of times they had sung these words may have been few, and none of them would have had childhoods in which they rehearsed these words daily in school. Even as of 2013 the provocatively Aymara future Vice President and at that time Foreign Minister David Choquehuanca admitted to not having mastered the Aymara lyrics to the national anthem (Rojas 2013):

> The other day I felt an emotion, I was happy because I have not yet sung the national anthem in Aymara, I still speak Aymara, but they have called me to reflection. In this ministry we have had the first cohort, the professional diplomats have been brought here the initiative of some authorities of consular management and have implemented an Aymara course, because the Constitution says we have to talk … Years are going by here and we have implemented and I am happy, it has also surprised me and I felt bad when we are here diplomats speaking in Aymara, we did a promotion here and everyone is working in Aymara, speaking words of gratitude in Aymara, everything was Aymara. And then we sang the national anthem, I thought then that we were going to sing in Spanish, when they sang in Aymara I remained silent.[8]

The headline of the news article in which this quote appears, "Chancellor reveals he does not know how to sing the national anthem in Aymara," suggests a journalistic "gotcha moment," but Choquehuanca's could be better described as a "humble brag," or an act of self-deprecation that ultimately reflects favorably on the speaker. Choquehuanca admits to not knowing the lyrics to the national anthem within a context of outlining the advances that he and his administration have achieved within the federal government in ensuring that Aymara is used as a professional language within the ministries. He admits to not knowing the lyrics to the national anthem while suggesting that very soon he will and that you, dear reader, should too.

Conclusion

The uprising of 1921 was a violent contestation of sovereignty, between the will and rights of Aymara authority on one side, and, on the other, the will of white landowners and the Republican state that mobilized the national army on their behalf. This is a clear illustration of the scenario described by Ovando Sanz (1961) at this chapter's opening, of the Bolivian nation subjugating the Aymara nation through the brutal deployment of the state apparatus. Commemorating this massacre within a frame of Bolivian patriotism raises questions about how these Aymara Bolivians, citizens of a now plurinational state, reconcile the historical tensions articulated by Ovando Sanz, the CSUTCB, and many others. The *acto cívico* sets new symbols of the state alongside those of the ancient regime. In doing so, the commemoration provides a moment that illuminates how the Aymara nation is becoming situated within the now Plurinational Republic. It raises the question, although admittedly one that might not be fully answered here, of whether the Bolivian state becoming more Aymara, more broadly Indian, or whether Aymaras are becoming more assimilated into existing state discourses.

Rather than simply stark tension, the performance of the *acto cívico* at the commemoration of the 1921 massacre presents an integration of two frameworks, with a nearly complete incorporation into the existing norms and protocols of state commemoration. In his discussion of Char Peery's (2012) historical examination of the standardization of the Navajo language in the 1930s, Asif Agha described "assimilation by analogy" as a process calibrating external and internal norms of institutional conduct. "If a Standard Navajo imports analogous criteria for discursive conduct into tribal government and education, such criteria facilitate the calibration of distinct spheres of local conduct with each other, and of local politics with national politics" (Agha 2012: 99). This process was not lost on many Navajos who viewed language standardization as assimilationist, while it was viewed as apolitical by settler linguists. We encounter a similar discursive calibration within this *acto cívico*, where the *wiphala* and the Aymara language become analogues to the republican tricolor and Spanish, and, paradoxically, the commemoration of a massacre of Aymaras by the Bolivian military is carried out through a discursive register of military command.

Linguistic anthropological work on narrative has emphasized that "Remembering is not the negative of forgetting. Remembering is a form of forgetting" (Haviland 2005). What is true for narrated selves may also be true of narrations of state and nation. An oft-cited passage of the French historian Ernest Renan's 1884 essay on nationalism, *Qu'est-ce qu'une nation?*, suggests precisely this, "the essence of a nation is that all its individuals have many things in common and also that they have forgotten many things."[9] Writing of the South African national anthem, Shana Redmond (2014) points out that, while "performing the unity of a sovereign and distinguishable nation … the anthem's performance also reads as an effort to reinforce the compatibility of two competing political systems through a coerced forgetfulness," one that is "reliant on a national amnesia that forgives and, devastatingly, forgets the recent history of radical exclusion and violence that organized their twentieth century" (Redmond 2014: 286). The dynamics of racialized violence and state transformation resonate across the distant but, perhaps deceptively, parallel histories of South Africa and Bolivia, both countries whose Indigenous majorities suffered under systems of violent white supremacy. In Jesús de Machaca we find a kind of remembering, a kind of forgetting, the soldiers praised in the national anthem could be the same ones who murdered Aymara villagers in 1921, or who shot demonstrators in 2003, and again only some years later, during the coup of 2019. But when singing of those who fought and died so that *jichhurun kusisit jakañani* "today we will live happily," they are singing instead for their martyrs (*jiwir jaqinakäru*), not their assassins.

Table 5.1 Spanish and Aymara versions of the Bolivian National Anthem with English

Bolivian national anthem

Spanish	Aymara 1	Aymara 2	English
¡Bolivianos!¡El hado propicio	Bolivianos samiw yanapistu	Bolivian jaqinakatakixa	Bolivians, a propitious fate
coronó nuestros votos y anhelo!	jiwasan munañasax phuqasiwa	Phuqhasiw jiwasan suyt'ataru	has crowned our vows and longings!
Es ya libre, ya libre este suelo,	Uraqisax qhispiyataw, qhispiyataw	Qhisphiyataw qhisphiyataw markasaxa	This land is free, free at last.
ya cesó su servil condición.	pakuñas, mit'añas tukusitaw.	T'aqisit jakañax tukusxiw.	Its servile state has now finally ceased.
Al estruendo marcial que ayer fuera	Nayrapacha chàxwawin sarnaqata	Chàxwañanakana sarnakaña	The martial turmoil of yesterday,
y al clamor de la guerra, horroroso,	axsarqañ chhixtaw nuwasiñana	Nuwasiñas warariñas tukusxiwa,	and the horrible clamor of war,
siguen hoy, en contraste armonioso,	Jichast mä chuymak saskakiwa	Uka chàxwañanakata mistusiña,	continue today in harmonious contrast,
dulces himnos de paz y de unión.	muxsa mayacht'ir q'uchuwina.	Jichhürux kusisit q'uchuñan	by sweet hymns of peace and unity.
CORO	TAQI'TAKI	TAQI'TAKI	CHORUS
De la Patria el alto nombre	Qullasuyu jach'a sutipa,	Markasäna, suma sutipa,	The lofty name of our fatherland
en glorioso esplendor conservemos	qhapax suma kàxañapa imañani.	Jach'ar aptasa suma arsuñäni,	in glorious splendor let us conserve.
Y, en sus aras, de nuevo juremos:	Sutiparu wastat surañani,	Markasatxa sayt'asipxañäni:	And, on its altars, once again swear:
¡Morir antes que esclavos vivir!	¡Jiwañan janirkuch t‹aq›iskasin!	Jiwañan janïr t'aqiskasïn!	To die before we would live as slaves!
¡Morir antes que esclavos vivir!	¡Jiwañan janirkuch t'aq'iskasin!	Jiwañan janïr t'aqiskasïn!	To die before we would live as slaves!
¡Morir antes que esclavos vivir!	¡Jiwañan janirkuch t‹aq›iskasin	Jiwañan janïr t'aqiskasïn!	To die before we would live as slaves!

(*continued*)

Bolivian national anthem

Spanish	Aymara 1	Aymara 2	English
II	--	II	II
Loor eterno a los bravos guerreros,		Wiñay q'uchuñaw wakt'istu,	Eternal praise to the brave warriors,
cuyo heroico valor y firmeza		Markaslayku jiwir jaqinakäru:	whose heroic valor and firmness
conquistaron las glorias que empieza hoy Bolivia feliz a gozar.		Jupanakaw markas ut'ayapxi,	conquered the freedom and glories that now a happy Bolivia begins to enjoy!
Que sus nombres, el mármol y el bronce, a remotas edades trasmitan		Jichhurun kusisit jakañani. Sutinakpax qilqantatawa, Uka pachtapachaw jiwasax yatipxtana,	Let their names, in marble and bronze, transmit their glory to remote ages.
y, en sonoros cantares, repitan:		Wali ch'amamp arsuñasawa:	And in resounding songs let them repeat:
¡Libertad, Libertad, Libertad!...		Qhisphiyataw, qhisphiyataw, qhisphiyataw!	Freedom! Freedom! Freedom!
CORO			CHORUS
III		--	III
Aquí alzó la justicia, su trono		--	Here has Justice erected its throne
que la vil opresión desconoce,			which vile oppression ignores
y, en su timbre glorioso, legóse a			and, on its glorious laurel it bequeathed us

(*continued*)

Bolivian national anthem

Spanish	Aymara 1	Aymara 2	English
Libertad, libertad, libertad.			Freedom, freedom, freedom
Esta tierra inocente y hermosa,			This innocent and beautiful land,
que ha debido a Bolívar su nombre,			which owes its name to Bolívar,
es la Patria feliz donde el hombre			is the happy homeland where mankind
goza el bien de la dicha y la paz.			enjoys the benefits of bliss and peace.
CORO			CHORUS
IV			IV
Si extranjero poder, algún día,			If a foreigner may, some day
sojuzgar a Bolivia intentare,			attempt to subjugate Bolivia,
al destino fatal se prepare			let him prepare for a fatal destiny,
que amenaza a soberbio agresor.			which menaces such superb aggressor.
Que los hijos del grande Bolívar			For the sons of the mighty Bolívar
han ya, mil y mil veces, jurado			have sworn, thousands upon thousands of times:
morir antes que ver humillado,			to die rather than see humiliated
de la Patria el augusto pendón.			the country's majestic banner.
CORO			CHORUS

Lyrics for Aymara 1 by Basilio Mamani and Alfredo Mita.
Lyrics for Aymara 2 retrieved from Recursos Educativos Multimedia Educabol
https://www.youtube.com/watch?v=VQMhCP-2OD4 (accessed December 25, 2022).

6

Conclusion

In 2013, a right-wing senator from the Amazonian department of Beni in the north of the country tweeted her opposition to the state-sponsored celebrations of *Machax Mara*, the Aymara New Year. Also celebrated as the *Fiesta de San Juan*, this is now also a state-sponsored celebration observed in a neo-traditionalist mode of welcoming the first rays of the sunrise following the southern hemispheric winter solstice, discussed in Chapter 2. "I dream of a Bolivia free of satanic indigenous rituals, the city is not for Indians, let them go to the *altiplano* or the *chaco*."[1] Designating Aymara cultural practices as both satanic and incompatible with urban life, her comment echoed earlier proclamations from a long history of elite Bolivians characterizing Indigenous Bolivians as anti-modern problem populations while simultaneously fantasizing of their disappearance.

A little more than a century earlier, in its report on the 1900 census, Bolivia's National Office on Immigration, Statistics, and Geographical Propaganda published a report with a prognosis of the inevitable eradication of the "indigenous race":

> At present, the proportion of the indigenous race, including the savages,
> is the same now as it was fifty-four years ago, in circumstances in which
> the white race and the half-breeds have increased considerably. Thus, in a
> short time, following the progressive laws of statistics, we shall find that the
> indigenous race, if it has not been completely wiped off the face of the planet
> will at least be reduced to a minimal expression.
>
> (cited in Thomson et al. 2018; 251)

The statement's declarations about "the white race" and "half-breeds" within a teleological scientific discourse of the "laws of statistics" betray the extent to which Bolivian elites at the time were as swayed by eugenics as their counterparts throughout the hemisphere. Local history also provides an answer to where such a hope among white government officials might emerge. Bolivia in 1900 had just come out of two years of civil war, a conflict in which armed Aymara peasants under the leadership of Pablo Zárate Willka played a decisive role, something that raised concerns about their numbers, social power, and the possibilities of Indian insurrection (Mendieta 2010).

While the senator's comment was motivated more by evangelical Christianity rather than early twentieth-century eugenics, a menacing tone of genocide resonates between the two proclamations. Both also represent a variety of racial revanchism corresponding to the fears of each era's elites. While in 1900 the victories of Zárate Willka's Aymara troops were a fearful memory for Bolivian elites, more than a century later, the senator's concern arose not from a fear of the possibility of Indian insurrection, but from a realization that she was living in the wake of one. Her comment expressed opposition not just against cultural practices she deemed "satanic," but from a sense that Indigenous political hegemony was establishing itself as a fact in the country's political terrain.

Six years after this tweet, this senator, Jeanine Áñez, would come to be illegally installed as the interim president during a short-lived, but violent military coup that began on November 10, 2019. The coup forced President Morales, whom right-wing politicians like Áñez referred to contemptuously as *el indio*, to flee the country, something that certainly must have felt, for her, like a step toward realizing her dream. During the initial days of the coup, videos circulated on social media and in the news of police lowering the *wiphala* from public buildings and cutting it off of their uniforms (San José 2019). Demonstrations were attacked by police in Sacaba, Cochabamba, and in the Senkata neighborhood of El Alto, leaving eleven dead there.

"The city is not for Indians" makes explicit the racialization of space central to the ideologies and practices of Indigenous exclusion from political life and full citizenship that has dominated Bolivia's republican history. For much of the twentieth century, Indians were barred from many urban public spaces, perhaps most symbolically, the Plaza Murillo, the seat of the federal government. During a coup, control of a city is posed in stark terms. Blockades, checkpoints, tear gas, and bullets demarcate space through the crudest and cruelest means. This control also did not last. Elections were eventually held in October of 2020, in which MAS regained control of the presidency and a majority in the legislature. Jeanine Áñez was found guilty of acting against the country's constitution and is serving a ten-year prison sentence.

Despite early twentieth-century eugenicist predictions and the best efforts of Jeanine Áñez and others like her, Aymaras not only remain, but thrive where before they have been excluded. Hardly living confined to a "minimal expression" and certainly not "wiped off the face of the earth," Aymaras are among the most populous nations in the Plurinational Republic of Bolivia, and comprise the overwhelming majority of the country's second largest and fastest growing city, El Alto. To the extent to which an Aymara nation exists within plurinational Bolivia, it is a complex one, as complex as any other. The Aymara nation of plurinational Bolivia is filled with as many varied communities, and as fraught with as many competing interests and contending aspirations as any other.

My aim with the preceding chapters has been to account for at least some of these dynamics. Recall the anonymous educator in Chapter 4 who was dismayed by the very existence of Aymara hip-hop. More than just a question of musical taste, his objections concerned what he perceived as violations of the integrity of Aymara culture. The rappers were not just any youth, but they represented the future of the Aymara nation, one, he worried, that was becoming too oriented to a US-dominated culture. The rappers themselves account for their own activity in terms of seeing that their culture is not lost. The educator's notion of Aymara culture was informed by essentialist frameworks that were also invoked by others throughout the course of the book. In different ways, most of these figures were individuals influenced in some way by katarista, Aymara nationalist politics. One was the radio director who objected to the Christian proselytizing of RSG and explained the politics of resource extractivism in terms of Aymara agricultural practice (*pirwa*). A more straightforward essentialism was delivered by the political candidate who expressed his distrust of non-Aymaras engaging what he deemed to be essentially Aymara practices. This came out most clearly in his full-throated accusations that *q'aras* (whites) were masquerading as Aymaras. Worse than simply being frauds, his accusation was that they were usurpers who were taking power away from Indians in a moment that was meant to be one of political ascendency for them, or rather, him. Whether in music, economic development, or governance, all of these actors drew on frameworks that evaluated cultural expressions along axes of differentiation between what could count, or not, as adequately Aymara.

Whether rappers, school teachers, or politicians, we can also note that nearly all of the actors we encountered in the previous chapters were squarely urban Aymaras, yet all of them invoked rural life in some way as the authorizing scene of Aymara cultural practices, linguistic or otherwise. Again, the former director of Radio Pacha Qamasa, who, in his explanation of the country's political scenario and the failures of previous governments to care for the country's natural resources, chose the Aymara agricultural practice of *pirwa* (grain and potato storage) as his explanatory metaphor. He holds advanced degrees, but the knowledge base that he uses to authenticate himself in his conversation with a foreign researcher comes from the domain of the agricultural practices of the rural *altiplano*. In addition to serving as a source for explanatory metaphors, we also saw how the authority of the countryside impacted the life trajectory positively for a young woman with professional aspirations. This was the case for Celia Colque, the member of the Aymara Language Department at Radio San Gabriel, who leveraged her rural provenance to outcompete linguists and graduates of communication programs in an Aymara language competition. The linguistic skills that she had developed growing up within an Aymara-dominant rural community facilitated her ability to secure steady employment at RSG. All of them would, of course, certainly find Jeanine Áñez's remarks concerning Indians in the city repugnant. These moves of authentication are ones that advance Aymara perspectives and clearly run counter to the senator's views and larger political project. Still, we can also recognize that the right-wing senator's views represent a different mode of privileging the rural countryside as an Indian social space, albeit within a denigrating and unabashedly anti-Indian discourse. The senator's remarks stood in continuity with the practices of racist exclusion that have aimed at limiting Indians to the countryside, at best, and, at worst, hoped for their eventual eradication as a presence in national life at all.

The individuals we encountered in the previous chapters were not simply urban in a general sense, but specifically denizens of El Alto and La Paz, perhaps the most densely Indigenous urban region of the Americas. This is also the case for Celia Colque, even with her rural background. She is urban, but recently so, as a migrant from the countryside. The reality of a dynamic exchange and shared existence between the countryside and the city was evident not only in her biography, but also in the experiences of the people who have appeared in the previous chapters. Many of the participants in the march in Jesús de Machaca discussed in the previous chapter had come in that day from El Alto. They are among the many *alteños* who maintain strong ties with their relations in the countryside while making their living in the city. These "strong ties" are certainly affective, but they are also more than that, including responsibilities, whether participating in community events, like the commemoration discussed in the last chapter, or participating in the agricultural cycle, planting potatoes, participating in harvest, and contributing to community projects. Nearly all of the participants in the hip-hop scene discussed in Chapter 4 are the children of migrants from the countryside. In this way, the previous chapters also illuminate urban Aymara perspectives on the dynamics of Indigenous rural-urban migration. These accounts invite reflection on the challenge posed by Dene philosopher Glenn Coulthard as one of his five theses on decolonization and Indigenous resurgence, "Disposession and Indigenous Sovereignty in the City," in which he argues that "the efficacy of Indigenous resurgence hinges on its ability to address the interrelated systems of dispossession that shape Indigenous peoples' experiences in *both* urban and land-based settings" (Coulthard 2014: 173–6). A similar concern is made by the Bolivian intellectual Silvia Rivera Cusicanqui (2012), who insists on the need to grapple with the reality of urban indigeneity. In her view, essentialist framings of Aymara, and more broadly Indigenous, identities that confine notions of authenticity exclusively to the rural are problematic not only because they are inaccurate, erasing whole domains of life from view, but also for how they limit the scope of political possibility and social transformation. To understand only Jesús de Machaca as truly Aymara, but never fully El Alto or La Paz, would "deny the ethnicity of the multicolored [*abigarradas*] and acculturated populations—the settlement areas, mining centers, indigenous commercial networks in the internal and black markets, the cities" (Rivera Cusicanqui 2012: 99).

The potential for a certain paradox seems to arise when urban Aymaras replicate, even if only partially, a conception of authenticity anchored to rural life, one that has been identified in other contexts of Indigenous language and cultural revitalization. Elsewhere, researchers and practitioners have documented how proficiency in an Indigenous language may strengthen community members' links to global networks in which linguistic skill in the Indigenous language becomes a valued commodity. Recognition of linguistic skill, subsequent professionalization, and participation in global networks may in turn increasingly pull individuals further from their communities, undermining the very authenticity that gave them access to these networks and upward mobility in the first place (Moore, Pietikäinen, and Blommaert 2010; Povinelli 2002). The irony being that the scenarios in which speakers are valued for their authenticity and commitment to traditional practices or lifeways are also contexts that ultimately orient them toward horizons beyond their communities, making them increasingly cosmopolitan and potentially more divorced from lifeways more widely regarded as traditional. We could ask whether this could describe the experience of the Aymara rappers finding opportunities to tour Europe and South America. We could also ask if this would have been the case for the radio broadcasters who found that professionalization and upward mobility introduced them to and integrated them within larger global networks of media professionals. Here, it is worthwhile to recall the experience of Gabriel Flores at Radio Pacha Qamasa who, following his travel abroad during his education in Spain, only felt more Aymara, not less, and he returned better positioned to engage with his communities as both an educator and media professional. These experiences underscore that the effect of being more integrated into global networks does not automatically result in a feeling of alienation from one's own community, much less come to be perceived as resulting in some sort of bind or dilemma (cf. Ottoson 2010).[2] In the end, as Silvia Rivera Cusicanqui (2012) has pointed out, these are not completely new dynamics either, as Aymaras and other Indigenous peoples of the Americas have had *ch'ixi* engagements with the broader world now for centuries. These dilemmas may not be dilemmas at all, and, to the extent that they count as such, are certainly ones these diverse Aymaras are well equipped to handle.

To provide ethnographically rich accounts of how models of Aymara personhood are tied up within the linguistic practices of a large and diverse population is inherently challenging. This study took comparative views from distinct sectors of Aymara life in the hope that such an approach would respect the complexity of the dynamics at play. Admittedly, such an approach provides necessarily and inevitably partial views. Inevitably partial, in the sense that I, of course, can make no claim to account for all the ways that Aymaras are being Aymara. Instead, the aim was to offer views from vantage points from which those involved take the Aymara language as a deliberate object of attention. While this was straightforwardly and intentionally a multisited ethnography of contemporary Aymara life in the more traditional social-scientific sense of fieldwork sites, there is another sense in which this study operated from one site—dehispanicized Aymara. Looking out and listening from this vantage point, from the perspective of the semiotic construct of a putatively pure Aymara language, the previous chapters have presented us with a diverse set of actors who orient to it as an object of shared attention and activity.[3]

To hear how the register of dehispanicized Aymara was produced, reproduced, and disseminated as an oral, spoken phenomenon motivated the decision to organize this study around radio and song. The first case was a prominent institution long recognized as a language authority throughout Aymara territory, Radio San Gabriel. This institution's investment in dehispanicized Aymara was such that it served as the focus of a sustained metadiscursive intervention, such a focused intervention, in fact, that it served as the *raison d'être* for an entire organizational unit within the radio's administrative structure, the Aymara Language Department. At Radio San Gabriel, the intense protocol of *seguimiento* targeted the hispanicism, Spanish loanwords, which were treated as lexical invaders of Aymara territory. As indexical traces of the historical process of colonialism, the hispanicism became a metonym for colonialism, and its replacement an act of decolonization. What was at a stake was not simply one word or another, but nothing less than the righting of historic wrongs, the reestablishment of Aymara autonomy in the wake of centuries of colonial domination. That the tools for this process—sixteenth-century Jesuit dictionaries—were themselves products of the colonial enterprise did not provoke any sense of irony, but instead a sense that these objects mediated the voices of sixteenth-century Aymaras, bringing them into the twenty-first century.

On the talk-show *Akhulli Amuyt'awi* on the radio station of the rural teacher's union, this register of dehispanicized Aymara came to serve as the linguistic backdrop for the show. The host's voice was distinctive, not only as an aesthetically pleasing "radio voice," which his certainly was, but it was also a voice that commanded this register in a way that contrasted to many, in fact most, of the guests who came to speak on the program. Speaking in dehispanicized Aymara established a normative baseline against which other voices became distinctive, and potentially evaluated. The voice commanding this register was the voice of authority in the context of the program, the voice that both commanded the program's direction and also provided evaluative commentary along the way.

The dehispanicized Aymara spoken by the host of *Akhulli Amuyt'awi* was used within a show that was, in fact, mostly in Spanish. The host, however, opened and closed in Aymara, intervening with evaluations, transitions, and summaries in Aymara throughout. In this way, the Aymara language operated as a matrix language in which Spanish is embedded, not unlike in Flores' earlier voicing of the Aymara public. At Radio San Gabriel, although broadcast nearly entirely in dehispanicized Aymara, situated Spanish as the matrix language for the ledgers of *seguimiento*, and for the title of the program itself, *Lengua Aymara*. There were European sources lurking in the etyma of the neologisms for the days of the week. In this way, the two programs, *Akhulli Amuyt'awi* and *Lengua Aymara*, present inverse patterns of use for Aymara and Spanish.

Among the rappers of Chapter 4, composing and performing Aymara for their peers and the broader public was understood as a political intervention in and of itself, both by the performers and for their listening audiences, whether or not they themselves were Aymara speakers. In this case, the language itself moved beyond being narrowly a denotational code to standing in as a diacritic emblem of Aymara authenticity. In contrast to the code mixing typical of Aymara-Spanish bilinguals, the Aymara verses within these artists' songs were maximally distinct from Spanish verses, but also French and English ones, a move which situated the Aymara language as a language among languages, one worthy of artistic cultivation and the world stage.

In rural Jesús de Machaca, we heard the Aymara language now operating within a mode of state officialdom. Dehispanicized Aymara arrived on a small slip of paper and again in the raised, and sometimes mumbled, voices of attendees and officials. The lyrics to the newly translated national anthem allowed attendees of an act of civic commemoration to perform citizenship in a novel way, not only by virtue of singing in Aymara, but in an official Aymara in which citizens sing praise to Bolivia, Qullasuyu, and Bolivia as Qullasuyu. The semantic shift of the historic name for a territory within the Inka Empire suggests a contemporary shift in the political valence of the name, from anti-state katarista politics to a language of state officialdom. When we anticipate the anthem's subsequent performances at future civic rituals, whether ones of grand pomp and circumstance or simply more routine early morning public school assemblies, we can recognize the dynamic nature of the term's ongoing and future enregisterment.

Of the four cases, it is within the institution with the most clearly articulated political orientation, the radio of the rural teachers, where we find the most fluid and communicatively flexible linguistic practices. Both the rappers and the language planners at Radio San Gabriel maintained with great fidelity the distinctiveness of Aymara and Spanish as separate linguistic codes. The Aymara translations of the national anthem began with one lone Spanish word, a vocative address interpellating citizens as *Bolivianos*! They were otherwise free of any hispanicism or loanwords, leaving no other traces of bilingualism. In contrast, the host at Radio Pacha Qamasa engaged in none of the monitoring of these boundaries in the speech of others, while maintaining the baseline of his own speech within this register. Perhaps this greater linguistic flexibility relative to the program at Radio San Gabriel is simply reflective of the largely unscripted and dialogic nature of a program like *Akhulli Amuyt'awi* that features interviews and listener calls. The other cases all involve different degrees of scripted language, whether a small half sheet distributed at a civic event, a script approved by the Aymara Language Department, or a verse written in a notebook, revised and edited before trying it out with friends. The communicative demands of a call-in talk show do not always allow for such a rehearsing of form and require more flexibility and openness to varied forms of linguistic participation. Where there were possibilities for deliberate speech, however, the use of dehispanicized Aymara was preferred and served as the voice of the institution. Dehispanicized Aymara remained the linguistic backdrop against which guests' voices, and the animated voices of the public, could be heard and evaluated.

Even as we recognize that Aymara served as a language of authority at Radio Pacha Qamasa, characterizing Spanish as simply the language of the "Other" would be inaccurate, even when Spanish was often described in these terms by both Flores and nationalist politicians like Chirinos. While language can become a convenient shorthand for ethnicity for those who engage in these characterizations, the slippage from language to person obscures other realities. Such a characterization, of Spanish being the language of the *q'aras*, does not match up with the model of ethnic membership we heard voiced on the program. When Flores voiced the Aymara public in his opening monologues, this public was speaking in Spanish. Furthermore, to focus narrowly on Aymara qua language obscures the importance placed upon the metapragmatic protocols of communicative conduct that were typified as essentially Aymara. This typification came both in the naming of the program after the *akhulli* speech genre and then again through the commentary of one of the show's guests. One of the visiting politician's main critiques of his opponents was that they violated an Aymara metapragmatic norm of speaking as if they had seen, and lived through, things that they had not. The mark of being truly Aymara certainly concerned speech and communication, but in speaking like an Aymara, not in Aymara qua linguistic code.

Narrative threads of lived experience and historical memory became woven together at multiple points across these accounts. Historical time and life trajectory converged in the accounts of the members of Wayna Rap when they spoke of their experiences during and reflections on the Gas War of 2003. Both Grover Cañaviri and Eber Miranda Quispe understood their participation in terms of legacy, kinship, and Aymara liberation struggles. They explained the struggles, the hardships, and also the victories of the Gas War in terms of it being "their turn." Their parents had struggled against the Banzer dictatorship, just as others had before them, and just as Tupak Katari had before them. With this discussion they introduce another sense of *pachakuti*, not the overturning of time, but its return. They articulate their participation in the 2003 Gas War not only as participating in a historical continuity with an Aymara legacy of struggle, but also in terms of simultaneity and homology—they are fighting the battles that their parents and ancestors had fought, and reaffirm their connection to them as both kin and nation, as Aymaras. In addition to their individual experiences of participation in the long history of Aymara national struggles, the rappers discussed in Chapter 4 build a collective sense of Aymara national belonging through their lyrical interventions, whether in verses that reanimate the words of Tupak Katari or by asserting the dignity of the coca leaf. As these verses become available and replicable, whether via YouTube or in the mouths of their fans and peers joining in song, they maintain and expand the Aymara language's presence within the urban spaces of El Alto and beyond.

The indeterminacy of language revealed the possibility of semantic slippages in a civic commemoration of a historic massacre, accommodating new framings of history within the Bolivian national anthem. The soldiers praised in the original anthem would have been the perpetrators of a massacre a century ago, remembered today by the descendants of their victims. Now, in the Plurinational Republic and sung in Aymara, the fatherland is Qullasuyu and the anthem can be sung as a hymn to martyrs fallen in a long struggle for Aymara territory and Indigenous autonomy and sung as a vindication of this struggle in now autonomous Aymara land. Still, the performance itself is inaugurated by and carried out in a military register that draws from the protocols of military pomp and circumstance, protocols of the military from whose ranks officers would soon collaborate with Jeanine Áñez against the new plurinational constitution. If the residents of Jesús de Machaca sang the new Aymara verses with halting imprecision in 2010, perhaps this simply reflects the trajectory of their own autonomy. It comes with fits and starts, and might not sound exactly as intended on the first round. Given the reliably and wonderfully contentious nature of politics, particularly politics at their most democratic, participatory, and deliberative, we might not expect, nor even hope that *machaqueños* and their fellow Bolivians will ever achieve the "sweet hymns of peace and harmony," promised by in the verse. Still, we may at least hope that martyrdom may remain confined to the past, both in hymn and memory.

Jallalla Bolivia Markaxa.
Jallalla Aymar Markaxa.
Jallalla

Notes

Chapter 1

1. Aymara shares this status with Southern Quechua, also widely spoken in Bolivia and Peru, along with Nahuatl and Yucatec Mayan in Mexico and Guaraní in Paraguay.
2. According to Bolivia's 2012 census, Quechuas and Aymaras of the highland west of Bolivia together comprise nearly a third of the nation's population (INE 2012). The 2012 census asked whether citizens identified as members of a *Nación y Pueblo Indígena Originario Campesino Mayoritaria* (NyPIOC) or "Majoritarian Indigenous Peasant First Nation and People," a category many criticized as confusing for not being sufficiently recognized among the population, something which may have resulted in lowered self-reporting. In the resulting census, 1,598,807 responded as Aymara and 1,837,105 responded as Aymara. The total population in the census was 10,059,856. This situation is paralleled in the Americas only by Guatemala, where nearly half of the population is Maya.
3. *Estamos obligados a comunicarnos, a pesar de toda la conflictividad con que actuamos los seres humanos, que, además, afrontamos y solucionamos con la comunicación.*
4. *Entre los sufijos que contiene la palabra a la que nos referimos están los significados y sentidos de la comprensión mutua, cortesía, el tiempo, obligación, diálogo, etcétera. Esta palabra contiene estos y otros significados que resulta reflejar una riqueza lingüística. En otras palabras, es toda una filosofía.*
5. *Pareciera que algún constructor de edificios hubiese edificado esta palabra muy cuidadosamente, poniendo primero el cimiento, que en lingüística llamamos raíz, y sobre eso hubiera colocado meticulosamente los ladrillos, hasta culminar de manera óptima la construcción que es y con el sufijo—wa, que en el estudio de la gramática aymara denominamos sufijo oracional y, además, sufijo de conocimiento personal.*
6. A note on the term "Indian" and terminology more generally: In Bolivia, the word *indio* "Indian" is both a generic exonym used by non-Native Bolivians as well as a term used by many Quechuas and Aymaras as a pan-ethnic term of solidarity and political identity. In the mouths of non-Native Bolivians, the term has often also been used as a term of contempt. The embrace of *indio* by some Quechuas and Aymaras came partly as a response to their classification by the state under the class-based category of *campesino* ("farmer") in the wake of the 1952 revolution,

rejecting the *campesino* category as a form of erasure (see Reinaga 1970). In this spirit, I use Indian when it is used as a relevantly a pan-ethnic term denoting Indigenous peoples of the Americas. I use the terms Indigenous and Native interchangeably and capitalized. Although "Andean," "Indigenous Andean," and "Native Andean" are often used to refer to the many shared cultural practices of both Quechuas and Aymaras, these obscure other peoples of the Andean high plain and valleys. I avoid these more vague terms and have used "Quechua and Aymara" when referring to practices shared by both groups and to use Aymara when referring to people and practices specific to Aymaras. These decisions have been informed by Younging's (2018) *Elements of Indigenous Style*.

7   So-called "savages" of the Americas, the Abenaki, Iroquois, "Peruvians," and other American Others, loomed prominently in the imaginations and writings of sixteenth century and subsequent enlightenment thinkers. This engagement with "savages," the influence of Indigenous thinkers and of the critiques they made of European societies has been underappreciated in what David Graeber and David Wengrow have termed the-myth-of-the-myth of the noble savage (Graeber and Wengrow 2021: 27–77). Engagements of diverse sorts with Indigenous Americans, whether via Jesuit interlocutors or Indigenous Americans themselves, introduced debates about equality and freedom into European discourse that are now considered so central to Enlightenment thinking. How else would have the question of social inequality ever occurred to Jean Jacques Rousseau, when "the closest he'd likely ever come to experiencing social equality was someone doling out equal slices of cake at a dinner party (Graeber and Wengrow 2021: 28)"? While radically diverse in all ways including forms of political organization, many societies of the Americas were characterized both by more freedom relative to Europe and also rich traditions of deliberative debate and political oratory.

8   *Pongos* were Quechua and Aymara servants for white landowners in the era before the 1952 revolution and *pongeaje* a status of servitude. The term *pongo* has Quechua and Aymara etymology, from *punku* "door" in both languages, suggesting the location of where an attendant would be ready to take orders from a master.

9   Paja Faudree's 2013 ethnography of the diverse contexts of Mazatec literacy in Oaxaca convinced me of the value of such a comparative multi-sited linguistic ethnography.

10 See Gal and Irvine 2019, p. 167, for more on this conception of semiotic constructs as sites of ideological work.

11 Viewed in this way, *q'ara* is one of many Aymara loanwords in highland Bolivian Spanish. It is notable that many of these include the ejective consonants distinctive of Aymara and Quechua: *k'aj* "a drink (beer or alcohol)"; *t'isi* "booger"; *ch'alla* "celebrate/inaugurate with confetti and toasts of alcohol." The salience of these ejective consonants in this situation of language contact is reminiscent of the salience of non-pulmonic consonants/clicks in southern Africa in the encounter between Khoi-San and Nguni languages as described by Irvine and Gal (2000).

An important contrast, however, is that where clicks were acquired into a respect register (*hlonipha*), the same cannot be said in the Andean context.
12 "Personally, I don't consider myself *q'ara* (culturally stripped and usurped by others), because I recognize my fully double origin, Aymara and European, and because I live from my own efforts" (Rivera Cusicanqui 2012: 105).
13 An interesting point of comparison to *q'ara* is the Inuit term *qallunaat*. Inuit humorist Zebedee Nungak explains in his 2008 collaboration with Canadian filmmaker Mark Sandiford, *Qallunaat! Why White people are Funny*, that the Inuit term for whites, *qallunaat*, refers not to color but to a demeaner and an outlook on life, a lack of curiosity and humility Inuits recognized in the arrogant behavior of settlers. The epigraph of Minnie Aodla Freeman, author of the 1978 *Life among the Qallunaat*, gives the following definition for the term, "Qallunaaq (singular), qallunaat (plural): literally 'people who pamper their eyebrows' possibly an abbreviation of qallunaaraaluit: powerful, avaricious, of materialistic habit, people who tamper with nature" (Freeman 1978: 1, cited in Mongibello 2018: 95–6).
14 This is a historically interesting example of what Asif Agha describes as the speech chain of a baptismal naming event (Agha 2007: 66–7).
15 These include rituals such as the *rutucha*, the first cutting of an infant's hair and the burning of *q'uwa*, the blessing of businesses and homes on the first Friday of the month. The leaf is used by *yatiris* "wise ones" who drop the leaves a cloth, for acts of divination. For them and others, the leaf embodies an animate, sacred, and female power with both agency and a name, *Inal Mama*.
16 We could note how this contrasts with the self-absorbed, if still chatty, communicative conduct stereotypically associated with cocaine in societies where it is consumed.

Part One

1 *Achachila* is translated here as "ancestor," but is used both as a kinship term for a grandfather and also for sacred beings in the landscape such as mountains and hills. I thank an anonymous reviewer for suggesting this translation.
2 See Swinehart 2018 for a fuller discussion of the term *chola* and for the significance of the *chola* as a figure of personhood in contemporary Bolivia.

Chapter 2

1 *La motivación principal de los padres Maryknoll para su trabajo entre los indos era, obviamente, la evangelización de una población que a pesar de cinco siglos de cristianización seguía siendo pagana y lejos todavía de una fe cristiana monoteísta. Fue esta situación lo que los indujo a pensar en la necesidad de castellanizarlos, a*

través de la alfabetización, como medio indispensable para la evangelización: recibir la palabra de dios.

2. *Había una convocatoria aquí en la radio misma, lo han publicado, entonces yo he escuchado un ratito, o sea, un medio día un programa de felicitaciones, Aruntawi, en ese programa he escuchado. Y yo, yo me he dicho ¿Por qué no puedo ir? Convocatoria lo decía que tienen que saber leer y escribir Aymara, traducción, y también tienes que saber a escribir a máquina. Entonces, ¿Por qué no puedo ir? He venido un día lunes directo y dieron el examen, entonces para la competencia. He venido y allí estábamos, treinta éramos y estaban de la UMSA también, determinada comunicación había de lingüística de la UMSA. Y también de otras radios han venido también. Cuando hemos venido nos han dado una hoja en castellano estaba escrita y nosotros eso tenemos que leer en Aymara, hablar en Aymara directo. En una hoja estaba dada y esto directo teníamos que hablar en Aymara—traducción. Y otro cuántas palabras puedes escribir en un minuto, y luego locución, cómo hablabas en Aymara … todo eso, si podemos hablar en radio me han preguntado y luego de eso … los que manejan este radio, los jefes, el personal, ellos han decidido.*

3. The conventions for transcription are as follows: *italics* for Aymara and Spanish. In bilingual discourse, Spanish is in <u>*underlined italics*</u>. English glosses are in "single quotes." For purposes of this chapter's focus (and in this chapter only) neologisms are **bold** and the boundaries of prosodic contours are marked with ^^ ….^^.

4. *Han llegado a la radio, no han pensado a estudiar lingüística pero la necesidad misma, mi pueblo me pide y me dice que aclare esto—¿De dónde viene? … Sabemos hablar pero todavía no comprendemos. Esas cosas me han reflexionado. Allí me he metido en la casa de lingüística en la Universidad Mayor de San Andrés. Inclusive semi presenciales, sábados y domingos, sábados y viernes por las tardes estudiamos. … Me dedico a esto, a estudiar.*

5. *Entonces, cada uno trae su texto con referente a la lingüística. Pese que en la radio, la radio es muy grande y su biblioteca también pero no tenemos aún todos estos textos. … Entonces este es un tipo de ayni que hacemos nosotros. No decir—Tengo en mi casa pero ¿por qué voy a traer? No. Es que la gente, la población misma con una palabrita, nos animan, nos fortalecen. Es por eso que estamos acá.*

6. *Todos los indios de esta provincia y ciudad hablan la lengua general que se llama aymara, aunque también muchos de ellos hablan y entienden la lengua quechua, que es la lengua general del Inga.*

7. Hilarión: *Más en la radio es siempre incursión del préstamo. Yo mismo a veces, no me doy cuenta, pero sale—has dicho esto. Ellos también están en la misma situación. Entonces escuchan la radio nos salta cuál es la palabra castellana que se preste. Los nombres no hay problema pero hay palabras habiendo y se presta. Esto es el problema. Por ejemplo, dicen minutos* minutus. *Dicen* Chika urutxa tunka minutunakampixiw. *Pero en Aymara ya tenemos* q'ata. Chika urutxa tunka

q'atanakampixiw y la gente entiende, no es que no entiende ... Habla mi mamá, habla mi familia, usa esas palabras. Entonces no podemos seguir *minutus, minutus.*

8   *Kasta, kasta* es préstamo, de castellano viene. *May maya* en Aymara tiene que decir. *Phasillakiwa* de "fácil es." Pero aquí *yachaykiwa* en Aymara. El léxico aymara y la aberración que ha cometido, entonces el responsable está consciente, y firma. Así, todos los que tienen programa.

9   *Día y sus partes*: Vide: *Partes del tiempo, donde se hallaran los nombres de las horas, casi correspondientes a las nuestras.*

10 *Llamayu* is similar to the Spanish *mayo* "May" and its Aymarized vernacular form *mayu* is incidental. The source domain for this neologism is the highland agricultural cycle, however, referring to the Aymara word form for the harvest of potatoes (and other tubors) during this time of year. Its use to denote a month, rather than the harvest itself, is novel.

11 The difference between the spelling of *illapa uru* in Table 2.1 and Hilarión's pronunciation is an example of the gap between the Aymara orthographic norm and pronunciation with vowel elision: the second *a* is replaced with a lengthened initial *u* in *uru*: *illapa uru illapüru.*

12 UNESCO designates Aymara as a "vulnerable" language. More critically endangered languages of the highland region include Chipaya and Callawaya.

13 A recurring comment I heard from Bolivian Aymaras contrasted the future of the Aymara to the fate of the *pieles rojos* or "redskins" (their words) and the false notion that there remain almost no Indigenous peoples in the United States.

14 Despite claims to the contrary (e.g., Wardaugh 2010: 26), Aymara and Quechua are not mutually intelligible nor understood as distinct languages merely due to the ideological commitments of their speakers.

Chapter 3

1   This call to truth in speech is more commonly delivered with a Quechua saying attributed to the days of the Inka Empire: *Ama llulla, ama suwa, ama qhilla,* "don't lie, don't steal, don't be lazy." This saying is found throughout elementary schools and, since 2009, even enshrined in the 2009 constitution. It was comically reinterpreted in Rodrigo Bellott's 2007 Bolivian comedy *¿Quién Mató a la Llamita Blanca?* to comment on the preferred destination for corrupt politicians: *Ama llulla, ama suwa, y si no, a Miami,* "Don't lie, don't steal, and if you do, to Miami!"

2   *Apthapi* is a potluck-style meal of boiled tubers, vegetables, hard boiled eggs, grilled and dried meats, and whatever contributions participants bring. This is a traditional way of sharing and enjoying food in Aymara community and family celebrations.

Part Two

1. This recognition motivated inclusion of song within early linguistic anthropological studies, Eduard Sapir's study of Paiute song being one example (Sapir 1910).
2. The clearest and obvious differences between the Mazatec and Aymara contexts concern the sheer size of population relative to the broader national context and their position vis-à-vis the national government. Although the ways in which Aymaras are marginalized in their society would be familiar to Indigenous Mexicans, the Aymara constitute a large majority in the region surrounding their nation's capital and have played a determining role in pivotal moments in the nation's politics, historically and today.
3. *El Condor Pasa* is an example of a widely popular Andean song, although not an example of a Bolivian song. This song was composed by the Peruvian Daniel Alomía Robles in 1913.
4. "As a historically emergent product of intertwined histories of media production, political action and musical sociality the voice here is neither simply transparent nor inert, a 'thing' around which people gather" (Fisher 2016).

Chapter 4

1. *Se tenía que pagar. Por una hora pagamos cinco Bolivianos y hacíamos bastante los fines de semana, los días sábados. unos diez bolivianos tres horas. a veces juntábamos entre los grupos, digamos hacíamos una vaca, como unos veinte bolivianos, entonces grabamos cuatro horas. Y en la calle así escuchabas. A veces si iba de excursiones y teníamos nuestra radio que que se llamaba Los Cholos de la Alcantarilla que [tenía un jingle] que decía—Este es el programa de los cholos del alcantaría—por decirte. Y entonces cuando los changos iban escuchando en su radio una canción y ya estaba en su estereo que ellos ya habían copiado de la radio en casette, e iban escuchando así en la calle ya, digamos y nosotros, wow, en nuestro programa lo has escuchado.*
2. Grover: *Pero nosotros pensamos es lo mejor [cantar en aymara] porque parte en esos pueblos donde vaya perdiendo los costumbres de hablar en aymará, más antes en el campo hablaban puramente en aymará pero ahora entre aymará y español así.*
Rolo: *Los colegios también te enseñan español si ya no aymara.*
Grover: *Y se va perdiendo, entonces nosotros pensamos, dijimos, haremos rap en aymará porque creemos que es de nosotros porque también vas a ayudar a otra generación.*
Rodolfo: *Una idea es que se sientan orgullosos, que no les de vergüenza hablar en aymará. Cuando llegan del campo, gente ya tiene que obligadamente aprender español y de allí se olvidan de su dialecto.*

Rolo: *Es un choque bien grande. Alguien que sea aymara parlante y que llega aquí a La Paz y todo es en español. Y le cuesta aprender y luego le da vergüenza hablar, y luego cuando va a su mismo pueblo habla español no más.*
Karl: *Para presumir un poco también me imagino.*
Rolo: *Sí claro. Nosotros queremos que divertir eso un poco para que la gente adquiera esos hábitos de hablar en aymará. ¿Qué manera mejor que el hip-hop digamos que es un punto central? Y no hacemos hip-hop comercial más bien con el mensaje tratamos de valorizen más nuestra cultura, a nuestros abuelos, las cosas buenas.*
Grover: *En la adolescencia más que todo porque todos te miraban—ese es aymará. Aquí hay un cacho discriminación entre nosotros mismos. Vivimos donde uno tiene su casa, y el otro no tiene nada entonces sí. Y si el otro habla aymará todos lo desprecian, con la llegada del campo, y ni siquiera puede hablar bien castellano. Yo fui poco a poco me fui alimentando, y dije esto tiene que hacer en aymará un hip-hop porque el hip-hop es actitud, es fuerza, es energía de los jóvenes y yo pienso que cuando uno esté escuchando, va a poner ese actitud, y ese orgullo, y yo no digo para pelear, de sentirse, vamos desarrollándonos y los tiempos se van cambiando y si perdemos nuestros idiomas, nuestras antiguas costumbres, entonces yo pienso que nos vamos a encontrar en un nivel dónde, pucha, y ahora? ¿Qué hacemos así?*
Rolo: *perdidos*
Grover: *¿Qué hacemos así? Perdidos. Entonces yo no quisiera que pase esto, con mis hijos, tal vez con mis nietos y esa honda.*

3 *Antes era, no era prohibido sino mal visto hablar en Aymara. En el colegio con los amigos de la misma edad. Hablabas en Aymara o decías alguna palabrita que te salía y te decían indio, uta, campesino, que esto que el otro, te juzgaban mucho. Y nosotros hemos visto como una forma de rebeldía, como una forma de cambiar la situación, como una forma de revolución, que sean rebeldes en ese aspecto. Hacer hip-hop en Aymara y decir—soy Aymara ¿y qué? Soy de El Alto. Soy de piel morena. Soy de barro.*

4 Rolando: *El dos mil tres ha sido el despertar de todos los Alteños. Cada quien, todos estábamos no sé deprimidos diciendo—qué pena, qué triste nuestra realidad y todo esto. Pero ése ha sido el instante en qué todos los vecinos, todos nos hemos unido, cada quien cargaba una piedra, sino protestando, sino huyéndonos, en cada esquina, cada vecino, cada junta vecinal se organizaba así bien. Los jóvenes salían y todo eso. Ha habido muertos. La gente iba. Incluso ha muerto uno de nuestros amigos, baleado (a Grover) tú has visto (G: Sí) personalmente. Ha sido una gran pena, el cual ha sido el despertar de la rebeldía de todo el pueblo.*
Grover: *Octubre ha sido como el despertar y pues muchos vecinos cuando se organizaban hablaban de que, porque también nuestros papás habían luchado en la dictadura de Banzer y toda esa época entonces tenían sus experiencias como jóvenes y comentaban entre ellos y decían siempre hemos sido marginados. Ya esa onda así hablaban.*

Eber: En el 2003 se ha iniciado un poco para mí. Se ha ido Goni y esa onda. Salí a la calle, chequeaba todo lo que pasaba, y allí chequeaba como la gente ha muerto y esa realidad he empezado a contar, a rapear esa realidad.

5 *Bueno, yo empecé el año 2003 que fue el año de la Guerra del Gas y todos esos momentos históricos de guerra, de lucha me inspiraron para hacer el rap ... el 2003 se ha ido construyendo desde antes con las luchas de Tupak Katari, desde la dictadura, desde otras luchas, la Guerra del Agua, la Guerra de Febrero [en La Paz] ... toda esa carga de tantos años y época reventó el año 2003—¡Pau!—una explosión de lucha, explosión ideológica, explosión de cultura y música. De ahí nació el hip-hop yo pienso para mí. El hip-hop de El Alto.*

6 *Karl: ¿Has visto cambios entre los jóvenes alteños ante el aymara?*
Nina Uma: Mira, yo creo que ahoritita tenemos un contexto boliviano bien interesante que hace diez años no había. hace diez años difícilmente vas a ver a un joven con un lluch'u en la ciudad, algún gringuito—Aaa! ¡Qué chistoso que va a poner eso!—Es así. Pero a partir de, principalmente aquí en El Alto a partir de 2003, la subida de Evo Morales a la presidencia y todo eso, hay un tema de búsqueda de varias, digamos, de varias generaciones, incluso de este contexto urbano, comienzan a decir—Tenemos alguien allí. Nosotros hemos hecho esto. Tenemos este poder.— Además de que cuando nos organizamos, nos reunimos, podemos sacar un presidente, darse cuenta de esa capacidad que ienes, como aymara, como andino, y admás haciendo respetar lo que tú eres que difícilmente ahora que te digan indio. Ahora, soy indio y ¿qué putas dice alguien (se ríe)? ¿No ve? Es así.
K: Ukhamaw ¿y qué?
NU: Entiendes. Ukhamaw ¿y qué? Así es ¿y qué? ¿No ve? Entonces esta búsqueda y una revalorización de todas los saberes que antes estaban medio escondidos pero estaban allí presentes. Entonces por eso ahora se visibiliza más esto porque muchas personas digamos como que han ido perdiendo el miedo.

7 *Lejía* is an alkaline element such as baking soda or sweet potato ash that is introduced in the mouth while chewing coca that aids in extracting more of the leaf's alkaloids.

Chapter 5

1 *"El pueblo boliviano, de composición plural, desde la profundidad de la historia, inspirado en las luchas del pasado, en la sublevación indígena anticolonial, en la independencia, en las luchas populares de liberación, en las marchas indígenas, sociales y sindicales, en las guerras del agua y de octubre, en las luchas por la tierra y territorio, y con la memoria de nuestros mártires, construimos un nuevo Estado."*

2 "*Bolivia es, pues, un Estado multinacional, formado por una sola nación boliviana; cinco nacionalidades principales, varias nacionalidades pequeñas y numerosas tribus y grupos etnográficos. El rasgo característico y antagónico de este Estado multinacional es que el número de habitants de las nacionalidades oprimidas, tribus y grupos etnográficos es infinitamente superior al número de miembros de la nación boliviana. De deonde resulta que la nación boliviana, siendo una minoría, sojuzga y oprime a la mayoría formada por las nacionalidades indígenas. Pero esta opresión, aparentemente inconcebible, se explica enteramente porque la nación boliviana tiene en sus manos el aparato estatal, que, a su vez, se halla supeditado y controlado por los imperialistas yanquis*" (Ovando Sanz 1084: 104–05).

3 "*No queremos parches ni reformas parciales, queremos una liberación definitive y la construcción de una Sociedad plurinacional que, manteniendo la unidad de un Estado combine y desarrolle la diversidad de las naciones aymara, quechua, tupí-guaraní, ayoreode y de todas las que lo integran. No puede haber una verdadera liberación si no se respeta la diversidad plurinacional de nuestro país y las diversas formas de autogobierno de nuestros pueblos*" (CSUTCB, cited in Albó 2008: 9).

4 "*Dada la existencia precolonial de las naciones y pueblos indígena originario campesinos y su dominio ancestral sobre sus territorios, se garantiza su libre determinación en el marco de la unidad del Estado, que consiste en su derecho a la autonomía, al autogobierno, a su cultura, al reconocimiento de sus instituciones y a la consolidación de sus entidades territoriales, conforme a esta Constitución y la ley.*"

5 "*Es nación y pueblo indígena originario campesino toda la colectividad humana que comparta identidad cultural, idioma, tradición histórica, instituciones, territorialidad y cosmovisión, cuya existencia es anterior a la invasión colonial española.*" Article 30 CPE.

6 "*La autonomía indígena originaria campesina consiste en el autogobierno como ejercicio de la libre determinación de las naciones y los pueblos indígena originario campesinos, cuya población comparte territorio, cultura, historia, lenguas, y organización o instituciones jurídicas, políticas, sociales y económicas propias.*" Article 29 CPE.

7 Political scientists Jason Tockman and John Cameron describe the range of meanings of "the plurinational" in Bolivia, and elsewhere in Latin America, as "a continuum ranging from theoretical perspectives based on deep forms of nonliberal and noncapitalist decolonization to more practical, policy oriented conceptions aimed at constructing particular elements of plurinationalism" (2014: 46).

8 "*El otro día yo he sentido una emoción, me he alegrado porque yo mismo no sé cantar el Himno Nacional en aymara, yo hablo aymara todavía, pero me han llamado a la reflexión. En este Ministerio hemos tenido la primera promoción, los diplomáticos de carrera han tomado aquí la iniciativa de algunas autoridades de la gestión consular y*

han implementado un curso de aymara, porque la Constitución dice que tenemos que hablar… Ya están pasando los años y aquí hemos implementado y yo me he alegrado, también me he sorprendido y me he sentido mal cuando aquí los diplomáticos hablando en aymara, hemos hechos una promoción aquí y todos estaban dirigiendo en aymara, el que hablaba las palabras de agradecimiento en aymara, todo era aymara. Y luego han cantado el himno nacional, yo pensé pues que vamos a cantar en castellano, cuando ya han cantado en aymara yo me he quedado callado."

9 "l'essence d'une nation est que tous les individus aient beaucoup de choses en commun, et aussi que tous aient oublié bien des choses" (Renan 1884; Anderson 2006: 158).

Chapter 6

1. https://www.eldiario.es/internacional/racistas-presidenta-autoproclamada-bolivia-aferrado_1_1158194.html (accessed December 18, 2022).
2. The experiences Flores and the Aymara rappers recall what is described by Åse Ottoson in her account of Aboriginal Australian musicians: "By performing this music across the desert region and beyond, the men not only come to represent their particular people and places, they also become more knowledgeable of other blackfella as well as whitefella people, places and ways of living. In the process, many of them become more aware of their own cultural distinctiveness and more conscious of the many social problems of their own 'mob'" (Ottoson 2010: 296).
3. See Gal and Irvine 2019, p. 167, for more on this conception of semiotic constructs as sites of ideological work.

References

Adelaar, Willem and Pieter Muysken. 2004. *Languages of the Andes*. Cambridge: Cambridge University Press.
Agha, Asif. 2003. "Social Life of Cultural Value." *Language & Communication* 23(3–4): 231–73.
Agha, Asif. 2005. "Voice, Footing, Enregisterment." *Journal of Linguistic Anthropology* 15(1): 38–59.
Agha, Asif. 2007. *Language and Social Relations*. Cambridge: Cambridge University Press.
Agha, Asif. 2011. "Meet Mediatization." *Language & Communication* 31: 163–70.
Agha, Asif. 2012. "Mediatized Projects at State Peripheries." *Language & Communication* 32(2): 98–101.
Albó, Xavier. 1974. *Idiomas, radios y esculas en Bolivia*. La Paz: CIPCA.
Albó, Xavier. 1977. *El futuro de los idiomas oprimidos en los Andes*. Lima: Centro de Investigación de Lingüística Aplicada.
Albó, Xavier. 2006. "El Alto, el vorágine de una ciudad única." *Journal of Latin American and Caribbean Anthropology* 11(2): 329–50.
Albó, Xavier. 2008. *Movimientos y poder indígena en Bolivia, Ecuador y Perú*. La Paz: CIPCA.
Albro, Robert. 2010. "Confounding Cultural Citizenship with Constitutional Reform." *Latin American Perspectives* 37(3): 71–90.
Alim, H. Samy, Awad Ibrahim, and Alastair Pennycook. 2008. *Global Linguistic Flows: Hip-hop Cultures, Youth Identities, and the Politics of Language*. New York: Routledge.
Alvizuri, Verushka. 2009. *La construcción de la Aymaridad: la etnicidad en Bolivia (1952–2006)*. Santa Cruz: Editorial.
Anderson, Benedict. 2006. *Imagined Communities: A Reflection on the Origin and Spread of Nationalism*. New York: Verso.
Appadurai, Arjun. 1996. *Modernity at Large: Cultural Dimensions of Globalization*. Minneapolis: University of Minnesota Press.
Archondo, Rafael. 1991. *Compadres al micrófono: La resurrección metropolitana del ayllu*. La Paz: Hisbol.
Arguedas, Alcides. 1979 (1909). *Pueblo Enfermo*. La Paz: Ediciones Isla.
Ari, Waskar. 2014. *Earth Politics: Religion, Decolonization, and Bolivia's Indigenous Intellectuals*. Durham: Duke University Press.
Aristotle. 1996. *Poetics*. New York: Penguin.

Arnold, Denise and Juan de Dios Yapita. 2005. *El rincón de las cabezas: luchas textuales en los Andes*. La Paz: Editorial.

Ávila, Jiovanny Samanaud, Cleverth Cárdenas Plaza, and Patricia Prieto. 2007. *Jóvenes y política en El Alto*. La Paz: PIEB.

Babel, Anna. 2019. *Between the Andes and the Amazon: Language and Social Meaning in Bolivia*. Tucson: University of Arizona Press.

Bauman, Richard and Charles Briggs. 1990. "Poetics and Performance as Critical Perspectives on Language and Social Life." *Annual Review of Anthropology* 19: 58–88.

Bauman, Richard and Charles Briggs. 2000. "Language Philosophy as Language Ideology: John Locke and Johann Gottfried Herder." In Paul Kroskrity (Ed.), *Regimes of Language: Ideologies, Polities, and Identities*. pp. 139–204. Santa Fe: School of American Research Press.

Bauman, Richard and Charles Briggs. 2003. *Voices of Modernity: Language Ideologies and the Politics of Inequality*. Cambridge: Cambridge University Press.

Bell, Alan. 1984. "Language Style as Audience Design." *Language in Society* 13(2): 145–204.

Bertonio, Ludivico. 2006 (1612). *Vocabvulario de la lengua Aymara*. Arequipa: Ediciones El Lector.

Bessa Freire, João Ribamar, and Maria Carlota Rosa. 2000. *Línguas Gerais: Política lingüística e cataquese na América do Sul no período colonial*. Rio de Janeiro: Editorial da Universidade Estadual do Rio de Janeiro.

Biaggini, Martín A. 2020. *Rap de Acá: la historia del rap en Argentina*. Buenos Aires: Editorial Leviatán.

Bigenho, Michelle. 2002. *Sounding Indigenous: Authenticity in Bolivian Music Performance*. New York: Palgrave.

Bigenho, Michelle. 2005. "Making Music Safe for the Nation: Folklore Pioneers in Bolivian Indigenism." In Andrew Canessa (Ed.), *Natives Making Nation: Gender, Indigeneity, and the State in the Andes*. pp. 60–80. Tucson: University of Arizona Press.

Bjork-James, Carwil. 2020. *The Sovereign Street*. Tucson: University of Arizona Press.

Bourdieu, Pierre. 1991. *Language and Symbolic Power*. Cambridge, MA: Harvard University Press.

Briggs, Charles L. 1996. "The Politics of Discursive Authority in Research on the 'Invention of Tradition.'" *Cultural Anthropology* 11(4): 435–69.

Briggs, Lucy T. 1976. The Dialectal Variation in the Aymara Language of Bolivia and Peru. Ph.D. Dissertation, University of Florida.

Cameron, Deborah. 1995. *Verbal Hygiene*. London: Routledge.

Canagarajah, Suresh. 2005. *Reclaiming the Local in Language Policy*. London: Routledge.

Canessa, Andrew. 2000. *Minas, Mote y Muñecas: identidades e indigeneidades en Larecaja*. La Paz: Mamahuaco Press.

Canessa, Andrew. 2008. "Sex and the Citizen: Barbies and Beauty Queens in the Age of Evo Morales." *Journal of Latin American Cultural Studies* 17(1): 41–64.

Castany Prado, Bernat. 2011. "Una estilística de los himnos nacionales de hispanoamérica." In Bernat Castany Prado et al. (Eds.), *Tierras Prometidas: De la colonia a la independencia* [Promised Lands: From the Colony to Independence]. pp. 49–69. Valladolid: Ediciones Universidad Valladolid de Este.

Ccama, Hipólito P. 2006. *Educación a distancia y EIB*. La Paz: Editoriales Plural/PROEIB-Andes.

Cerrón Palomino, Rodolfo. 1994. *Quechumara: Estructuras paralelas de las lenguas quechua y aimara*. La Paz: CIPCA.

Choque, Roberto. 1994. "La problemática de la educación indigenal." *Revista del Instituto de Estudios Andinos y Amazónicos* 5: 9–34.

Choque Canqui, Roberto and Cristina Quisbert Quispe. 2010. *Líderes Indígenas Aymaras: Lucha por la defensa de tierras comunitarias de origen* [Indigenous Aymara Leaders: The Struggle for the Defense of Indigenous Community Lands]. La Paz: Unidad de Investigaciones Históricas, UNIH-Pakaxa.

Colin, Benjamin. 2019. "Afeni Shakur, Black Party Panther Leader, Mother of Tupac, Fought to Liberate African-Americans." *Black News*, May 6, 2019. Accessed online, December 28, 2022: https://www.blackstarnews.com/us-politics/justice/afeni-shakur-black-panther-party-leader-mother-of-tupac-fought-to.

Condry, Ian. 2006. *Hip-Hop Japan: Rap and the Paths of Cultural Globalization*. Durham: Duke University Press.

Coronel-Molina, Serafín. 2008. "Language Ideologies of the High Academy of the Quechua Language in Cuzco, Peru." *Latin American and Caribbean Ethnic Studies* 3(3): 319–40.

Coulthard, Glen. 2014. *Red Skins, White Masks: Rejecting the Colonial Politics of Recognition*. Minneapolis: University of Minnesota Press.

Craig, Douglas. 2005. *Fireside Politics: Radio and Political Culture in the United States, 1920–1940*. Baltimore: Johns Hopkins University Press.

Cruz, Emiliana Cruz. 2020. "Indigenous Identity and the Mexican Educational System: The Case of the Translation of the Mexican National Anthem." *Cuadernos de Lingüística de El Colegio de México* 7(155): 1–52.

Cummins, James. 1994. "Semilingualism." In Ronald E. Asher (Ed.), *Encyclopedia of Language and Linguistics* (2nd Ed.). Oxford: Oxford University Press.

Dangl, Benjamin. 2006. Rapping in Aymara: Bolivian Hip-Hop Helps the Struggle. Blog. Accessed, April 22, 2012.

Dattatreyan, Ethiraj G. 2020. *The Globally Familiar: Digital Hip Hop, Masculinity, and Urban Space in Delhi*. Durham: Duke University Press.

Davis, Jenny. 2018. *Talking Indian: Identity and Language Revitalization in the Chickasaw Renaissance*. Tucson: University of Arizona Press.

De Korne, Haley. 2021. *Language Activism: Imaginaries and Strategies of Minority Language Equality*. Berlin: De Gruyter.

De la Cadena, Marisol. 1995. "'Women Are More Indian': Ethnicity and Gender in a Community Near Cuzco." In Brooke Larson, Olivia Harris, and Enrique Tandeter

(Eds.), *Ethnicity, Markets, and Migration in the Andes: At the Crossroads of History and Anthropology*. pp. 329–47. Durham: Duke University Press.

De la Cadena, Marisol. 2000. *Indigenous Mestizos: The Politics of Race and Culture in Cuzco, Pero, 1919-1991*. Durham: Duke University Press.

Dunkerley, James. 1984. *Rebellion in the Veins: Political Struggle in Bolivia 1952–1982*. London: Verso.

Echeverría, Bolívar. 2010. *Modernidad y Blanquitud*. Cd. México: Ediciones Era.

Ennis, Georgia. 2019. "Multimodal Chronotopes: Embodying Ancestral Time on Quichua Morning Radio." *Signs and Society* 7(1): 6–37.

Faudree, Paja. 2012. "Music, Language, and Texts: Sound and Semiotic Anthropology." *Annual Reviews in Anthropology* 41: 519–36.

Faudree, Paja. 2013. *Singing for the Dead: The Politics of Indigenous Revival in Mexico*. Durham: Duke University Press.

Ferguson, Charles A. 1968. "Language Development." In Joshua Fishman, Charles A. Ferguson, and Jyotirinda DasGupta (Eds.), *Language Problems of Developing Nations*. pp. 27–35. New York: Wiley.

Fisher, Daniel. 2016. *The Voice and Its Doubles: Media and Music in Northern Australia*. Durham: Duke University Press.

Fishman, Joshua. 1991. *Reversing Language Shift: Theory and the Practice of Assistance to Threatened Languages*. Clevedon: Multilingual Matters.

Fishman, Joshua. 1997. *In Praise of the Beloved Language*. Berlin: Mouton de Gruyter.

Forero, Juan. 2005. "El Alto Journal: Young Bolivians Adopt U.S. Pose, Hip-Hop and All." *New York Times*. May 26, 2005.

Foucault, Michel. 1988. "Technologies of the Self." In Luther H. Martin, Huck Gutman, and Patrick Hutton (Eds.), *Technologies of the Self*. pp. 16–49. Amherst: University of Massachusetts Press.

Freeman, Minnie Aodla. 1978. *Life among the Qallunaat*. Edmonton: Hurting Publishers.

Fujita, Mamoru. 2011. "Las radionovelas entre la oralidad y la escritura." Paper presented at the Reunión Anual de Etnología (RAE) XXV, August 22-6, 2011, La Paz. Accessed online, April 26, 2023: https://www.academia.edu/2223116/Las_radionovelas_aymaras_entre_la_oralidad_y_la_escritura.

Gal, Susan. 2006. "Contradictions of Standard Language: Implications for the Study of Practices and Publics." *Social Anthropology* 14(2): 163–81.

Gal, Susan. 2013. "Tastes of Talk: Qualia and the Moral Flavor of Signs." *Anthropological Theory* 31: 31–48.

Gal, Susan and Judith Irvine. 2019. *Signs of Difference: Language and Ideology in Social Life*. Cambridge: Cambridge University Press.

Gianotten, Vera. 2006. *CIPCA y poder campesino indígena: 35 años de historia*. La Paz: CIPCA (Cuadernos de investigación 66).

Gilroy, Paul. 1993. *The Black Atlantic: Modernity and Double Consciousness*. Cambridge, MA: Harvard University Press.

Goffman, Erving. 1981. *Forms of Talk*. New York: Harper & Row.
Graber, Kathryn. 2020. *Mixed Messages: Mediating Native Belonging in Asian Russia*. Ithaca: Cornell University Press.
Graeber, David and David Wengrow. 2021. *The Dawn of Everything: A New History of Humanity*. New York: Macmillan Publishers.
Grebe, Ronald L. and Utta von Gleich (Eds.). 2001. *Democratizar la palabra: Las lenguas indígenas en los medios de comunicación de Bolivia*. Hamburg: Goethe Institut.
Guayaga, Germán. 2000. *Ser joven el El Alto: Rupturas y continuidades en la tradición cultural*. La Paz: PIEB.
Gustafson, Brett. 2009. *New Languages of the State: Indigenous Resurgence and the Politics of Knowledge in Bolivia*. Durham: Duke University Press.
Gutiérrez, Raquel. 2014. *Rhythms of the Pachakuti: Indigenous Uprising and State Power in Bolivia*. Raleigh: Duke University Press.
Habermas, Jurgen. 1989. *The Structural Transformation of the Public Sphere*. Cambridge, MA: MIT Press.
Hale, Charles R. 2006. *Más que un Indio (More than an Indian): Racial Ambivalence and Neoliberal Multiculturalism in Guatelmala*. Santa Fe: School of American Research Press.
Hall, Stuart. 1993. "What Is This 'Black' in Black Popular Culture?" *Social Justice* 20(1–2): 104–14.
Hanks, William. 2010. *Converting Words: Maya in the Age of the Cross*. Berkeley: University of California Press.
Hansegård, Nils. 1968. *Tvåspråkighet eller halvspråkighet?* Stockholm: Aldus/bonier.
Hardman, Martha J. 2001. *Aymara*. Lincom Series in Native American Linguistics 35. Munich: Lincom.
Harrison, David. 2007. *When Languages Die: The Extinction of the World's Languages and the Erosion of Human Knowledge*. Oxford: Oxford University Press.
Haviland, John B. 2005. "'Whorish Old Man' and 'One (Animal) Gentleman': The Intertextual Construction of Enemies and Selves." *Journal of Linguistic Anthropology* 15(1): 81–94.
Heath, Shirley Brice. 1972. *Telling Tongues: Language Policy in Mexico, Colony to Nation*. New York: Teachers College Press.
Himpele, Jeff. 2002. "Arrival Scenes: Complicity and Media Ethnography in the Bolivian Public Sphere." In Faye Ginsburg, Lila Abu Lughod, and Brian Larkin (Eds.), *Media Worlds: Anthropology on New Terrain*. pp. 301–16. Berkeley: University of California Press.
Himpele, Jeff. 2004. "Packaging Indigenous Media: An Interview with Ivan Sanjines and Jesus Tapia." *American Anthropologist* 106(2): 354–63.
Himpele, Jeff D. 2007. *Circuits of Culture: Media, Politics and Indigenous Identity in the Andes*. Minneapolis: University of Minnesota Press.

Hines, Sarah. 2021. *Water for All: Community, Property, and Revolution in Modern Bolivia*. Berkeley: University of California Press.

Hjalvard, Stig. 2008. "The Mediatization of Society: A Theory of the Media as Agents of Social and Cultural Change." *Nordicom Review* 29(2): 105–34.

Hornberger, Nancy. 1994. "Literacy and Language Planning." *Language & Education* 8: 75–86.

Hornberger, Nancy and Francis Hult. 2008. "Ecological Language Education Policy." In Bernard Spolsky and Francis Hult (Eds.), *Handbook of Educational Linguistics*. pp. 280–96. Malden: Wiley-Blackwell.

Hornberger, Nancy and Karl Swinehart. 2012a. "Not Just 'situaciones de la vida': Professionalization and Indigenous Languages in the Andes." *International Multilingual Research Journal* 6(2): 35–49.

Hornberger, Nancy and Karl Swinehart. 2012b. "Intercultural Bilingual Education and Andean Hip-Hop in the Andes: Transnational Sites for Indigenous Language and Identity." *Language in Society* 41(4): 499–525.

Hornberger, Nancy and Kendall King. 1998. "Authenticity and Unification in Quechua Language Planning." *Language, Culture, and Curriculum* 11(3): 390–410.

Hoye, Jacob and Karolyn Ali (Eds.). 2003. *Tupac: Resurrection 1971–1996/Original Concept by Afeni Shakur*. New York: Atria Books.

Huayhua, Margarita. 2018. "Labeling and Linguistic Discrimination." In Linda Seligmann and Kathleen Fine-Dare (Eds.), *The Andean World*. pp. 418–35. New York: Routledge.

Hurtado, Javier. 1987. *Historia de la Radio difusora "San Gabriel" la época Maryknoll*. La Paz: Mimeo.

Hylton, Forrest and Sinclair Thomson. 2007. *Revolutionary Horizons: Past and Present in Bolivian Politics*. New York: Verso.

Hymes, Dell. 2003. *Now I Only Know So Far: Essays in Ethnopoetics*. Lincoln: University of Nebraska Press.

Hymes, Dell. 2004. *In Vain I Tried to Tell You: Essays in Native American Ethnopoetics*. Lincoln: University of Nebraska Press.

Inoue, Miyako. 2011. "Stenography and Ventriloquism in the Late Nineteenth Century Japan." *Language & Communication* 31(3): 181–91.

Instituto Nacional de Estadística (INE). 2001. *Bolivia: Características de la población*. La Paz: INE.

Instituto Nacional de Estadística (INE). 2012. *Bolivia Características de la Población*. La Paz: INE.

Irvine, Judith. 1989. "When Talk Isn't Cheap: Language and Political Economy." *American Ethnologist* 16(2): 248–67.

Irvine, Judith and Susan Gal. 2000. "Language Ideology and Linguistic Differentiation." In Paul Krosrkity (Ed.), *Regimes of Language: Ideologies, Polities, Identities*. pp. 35–84. Santa Fe: School of American Research Press.

Jacobsen, Kristina M. 2017. *The Sound of Navajo Country: Music, Language, and Diné Belonging*. Chapel Hill: University of North Carolina Press.

Jaffe, Alexandra. 1999. *Ideologies in Action: Language Politics on Corsica*. Berlin: Mouton de Gruyter.

Jakobson, Roman. 1960. "Closing Statement: Linguistics and Poetics." In Thomas Sebeok (Ed.), *Style in Language*. pp. 350–77. New York: Wiley.

Jernudd, Björn 1989. "The Texture of Language Purism: An Introduction." In Björn Jernudd and Michael J. Shapiro (Eds.), *The Politics of Language Purism*. pp. 1–19. Berlin: Mouton de Gruyter.

Katriel, Tamar. 2004. *Dialogic Moments: From Soul Talks to Talk Radio in Israeli Culture*. Detroit: Wayne State University Press.

Keane, Webb. 2003. "Semiotics and the Social Analysis of Material Things." *Language & Communication* 23: 409–25.

Kroskrity, Paul. 2000. *Regimes of Language: Ideologies, Polities, and Identities*. Santa Fe: School of American Research Press.

La Barre, Weston. 1948. *The Aymara of the Lake Titicaca Plateau*. Berkeley: American Anthropological Association Larkin, Brian.

Laime, Teófilo and Virginal Mamani. 2008. *Aru imara, aru jayma, descolonización y comunarización lingüística: modelos cooperativos para la reforma de escritura en lenguas andinas*. La Paz: Creart Impresores.

Larkin, Brian. 2008. *Signal and Noise: Media, Infrastructure, and Urban Culture in Nigeria*. Durham: Duke University Press.

Limber, Franco. 2015. *Breve Historia Real de la Wiphala*. La Paz: Jichha.

López, Luís Enrique. 2005. *Resquicios y boquerones: la educación intercultural bilingüe en Bolivia*. La Paz: Editoriales Plural.

López, Luís Enrique. 2007. *Diversidad y ecología lingüística en Bolivia* [Diversity and Linguistic Ecology in Bolivia]. La Paz: Editores Plural.

Machaca, Guido. 2007. *La participación social en la educación en el contexto de la implementación de la EIB: estudio de caso en las comunidades de Itanambiikua y Tomoroco*. Cochabamba: PROEIB-Andes.

Macusaya, Carlos. 2018. "Pachamamadas: aparencia y dominación." Accessed online, May 24, 2023: http://carlosmacusaya.blogspot.com/2018/07/pachamamadas-apariencia-y-dominacion.html.

Makoni, Sinfree and Alistair Pennycook. 2005. "Disinventing and (Re)constituting Languages." *Critical Inquiry in Language Studies* 2(3): 137–56.

Mannheim, Bruce. 1984. "Una nación acorralada: Southern Peruvian Quechua Language and Politics in Historical Perspective." *Language in Society* 13: 291–309.

Mannheim, Bruce and Van Vleet Krista. 1998. "The Dialogics of Southern Quechua Narrative." *American Anthropologist* 100(2): 326–46.

Mays, Kyle. 2018. *Hip-Hop Beats, Indigenous Rhymes: Modernity and Hip-Hop in Indigenous North America*. Albany: SUNY University Press.

McLeod, Kembrew and Peter Dicola. 2011. *Creative License: The Law and Culture of Digital Sampling*. Durham: Duke University Press.

Meek, Barbra and Jacqueline Messing. 2007. "Framing Indigenous Languages as Secondary to Matrix Languages." *Anthropology & Education Quarterly* 38(2): 99–118.

Mendieta, Pilar. 2010. *Pablo Zárate Willka y la rebellion indígena de 1899 en Bolivia*. La Paz: Institute Français d'Études Andines (IFEA).

Mendoza, Zoila. 2000. "Performing Decency: Performing Race in Andean 'Mestizo' Ritual Dance." In Ronald Radano and Philip V. Bohlman (Eds.), *Music and the Racial Imagination*. pp. 231–270. Chicago: University of Chicago Press.

Mongibello, Anna. 2018. "Qallunaat: Inuit (Re)naming White Folks." In Mirko Casagranda (Ed.), *Names and Naming in the Postcolonial English-Speaking World*. pp. 91–100. Trento: Tangram Edizioni Scientifiche.

Moore, Robert E., Sari Pietikäinen, and Jan Blommaert. 2010. "Counting the Losses: Numbers as the Language of Language Endangerment." *Sociolinguistic Studies* 4(1): 1–26.

Muehlmann, Shaylih. 2012. "Von Humboldt's Parrot and the Countdown of Last Speakers in the Colorado Delta." *Language & Communication* 32(2): 160–8.

Narayanan, Sandya. 2022. "'Ni Paisana, ni Jacinta': Language and the Scaling of Indigenous Feminity in Peru." *Signs and Society* 10(3): 314–33.

Neustupny, Jiri V. 1989. "Language Purism as a Type of Language Correction." In Björn Jernudd and Michael J. Shapiro (Eds.), *The Politics of Language Purism*. pp. 211–31. Berlin: Mouton de Gruyter.

O'Connor, Alan. 2004. *Community Radio Stations in Bolivia: The Miners' Radio Stations*. Lewiston, NY: Edwin Mellen Press.

O'Connor, Alan. 2006. *Voice of the Mountains: Radio and Anthropology*. Lanham: University Press of America.

Olivera, Oscar and Tom Lewis. 2004. *Cochabamba! Water Wars in Bolivia*. Cambridge: South End Press.

Orta, Andrew. 2004. *Catechizing Culture: Missionaries, Aymara, and the "New Evangelization."* New York: Columbia University Press.

Ottoson, Åse. 2010. "Aboriginal Music and Passion: Interculturality and Difference in Australian Desert Towns." *Ethnos* 75(3): 275–300.

Ovando Sanz, Jorge Alejandro. 1984 (1961). *Sobre el Problema nacional y colonial de Bolivia* [On the National and Colonial Problem of Bolivia]. La Paz: Libreria Editorial Juventud.

Peery, Char. 2012. "New Deal Navajo Linguistics: Language Ideology and Political Transformation." *Language and Communication* 32(2): 114–23.

Pennycook, Alistair. 2007. "Language, Localization, and the Real: Hip-Hop and the Global Spread of Authenticity." *Journal of Language, Identity, and Education* 6(2): 101–15.

Perea, Jessica B. 2016. "Indigenous Pop: Native American Music from Jazz to Hip-Hop." *American Indian Culture and Research Journal* 40(3): 144–8.

Pérez, Elizardo. 1992. Warisata: La Escuela-Ayllu. La Paz: HISBOL/CERES.

Postero, Nancy. 2006. *Now We Are Citizens, Indigenous Politics in Post-Multicultural Bolivia*. Stanford, CA: Stanford University Press.

Povinelli, Elizabeth. 2002. *The Cunning of Recognition: Indigenous Alterities and the Making of Australian Multiculturalism*. Durham: Duke University Press.

Quisbert, Cristóbal Coronel. 2003. *En un estado de coma: Radio Illimani 1950–1964*. La Paz: Universidad Andina Simón Bolívar.

Radio San Gabriel (RSG). 2005. *Radio San Gabriel: Bodas de Oro*. La Paz: Imprenta Lavadenz.

Rafael, Vicente L. 1993. *Contracting Colonialism: Translation and Christian Conversion in Tagalog Society under Early Spanish Rule*. Durham: Duke University Press.

Redmond, Shana. 2014. *Anthem: Social Movements and the Sounds of Solidarity in the African Diaspora*. New York: New York University Press.

Reinaga, Fausto. 1970. *La Revolución India*. La Paz: Ediciones Amáuticas.

Renan, Ernest. 1884. Qu'est-ce qu'une nation? Accessed online, December 24, 2022: https://mjp.univ-perp.fr/textes/renan1882.htm.

Rivera Cusicanqui, Silvia. 1984. *"Oprimido pero no vencidos": Luchas de campesinado aymara y qhechwa 1900–1980*. La Paz: Hisbol-CSUTCB.

Rivera Cusicanqui, Silvia. 1987. *Oppressed but Not Defeated: Peasant Struggles among the Aymara and Qhechwa in Bolivia, 1900–1980*. Geneva: UN Research Institute for Social Development.

Rivera Cusicanqui, Silvia. 2008. "Colonialism and Ethnic Resistance in Bolivia." In Fred Rosen (Ed.), *Empire and Dissent: The United States and Latin America*. pp. 137–61. Durham: Duke University Press.

Rivera Cusicanqui, Silvia. 2012. "Ch'ixinakax utxiwa: A Reflection on the Practices and Discourses of Decolonization." *South Atlantic Quarterly* 111(1): 95–109.

Rodriguez, Juan Luis. 2016. "The National Anthem in Warao: Semiotic Ground and Performative Affordances of Indigenous Language Texts in Venezuela." *Journal of Linguistic Anthropology* 26(3): 335–51.

Rodriguez, Juan Luís. 2020. *Language and Revolutionary Magic in the Orinoco Delta*. London: Bloomsbury.

Rojas, Germán. 2013. "Canciller revela que no sabe cantar el Himno Nacional en aymara" [Chanciller Reveals That He Doesn't Know How to Sing the National Anthem in Aymara]. *Eju!* Accessed, December 25, 2022: eju.tv/2013/02/canciller-revela-que-no-sabe-cantar-el-himno-nacional-en-aymara/.

Rubel, Authur J. 1964. "The Epidemiology of a Folk Illness: Susto in Hispanic America." *Ethnology* 3(3): 268–83.

Samuels, David W. 2004. *Putting a Song on Top of It: Expression and Identity on the San Carlos Apache Reservation*. Tucson: University of Arizona Press.

San José, Diego Aitor. 2019. "Lucha de símbolos en el golpe de Estado de Bolivia: Biblias contra wiphalas." *El Diario* (November 13, 2019). Accessed online, December 27, 2022: https://www.eldiario.es/internacional/lucha-simbolos-bolivia-biblias-wiphalas_1_1253869.html.

Sandiford, Mark (with Zebedee Nungak). 2006. *Qallunaat! Why White People Are Funny.* Accessed online, December 28, 2022: https://www.nfb.ca/film/qallunaat_why_white_people_are_funny/.

Sapir, Eduard. 1910. "Song Recitative in Paiute Mythology." *Journal of American Folklore* 23(90): 455–72.

Schegloff, Emanuel and Harvey Sacks. 1973. "Opening Up Closings." *Semiotica* 8: 289–327.

Schiwy, Freya. 2008. "Indigenous Media and the End of the Lettered City." *Journal of Latin American Cultural Studies* 17(1): 23–40.

Shankar, Shalini and Jillian Cavanaugh. 2012. "Language and Materiality in Global Capitalism." *Annual Review of Anthropology* 41: 355–69.

Shankar, Shalini and Jillian Cavanaugh (Eds.). 2017. *Language and Materiality.* Cambridge: Cambridge University Press.

Silverstein, Michael. 1976. "Shifter, Linguistic Categories, and Cultural Description." In Keith Basso and Henry Selby (Eds.), *Meaning in Anthropology.* pp. 11–55. Alburquerque: University of New Mexico Press.

Silverstein, Michael. 1979. "Language Structure and Linguistic Ideology." In Paul Clyne, William F. Hanks, and Carol L. Hofbauer (Eds.), *The Elements: A Parasession on Linguistic Units and Levels.* pp. 193–247. Chicago: Chicago Linguistic Society.

Silverstein, Michael. 1984. "On the Pragmatic 'Poetry' of Prose: Parallelism, Repetition, and Cohesive Structure in the Time Course of Dyadic Conversation." In Deborah Schiffrin (Ed.), *Meaning, Form, and Use in Context: Linguistic Applications.* pp. 188–99. Washington: D. Georgetown University Press.

Silverstein, Michael. 1993. "Metapragmatic Discourse and Metapragmatic Function." In John Lucy (Ed.), *Reflexive Language: Reported Speech and Metapragmatics.* pp. 33–58. Philadelphia: University of Pennsylvania Press.

Silverstein, Michael. 2000. "Whorfianisim and the Linguistic Imagination of Nationality." In Paul Kroskrity (Ed.), *Regimes of Language: Ideologies, Polities, and Identities.* pp. 85–138. Santa Fe: School of American Research Press.

Silverstein, Michael. 2004. "'Cultural Concepts' and the Language-Culture Nexus." *Current Anthropology* 45(5): 62–645.

Silverstein, Michael. 2023. *Language in Culture: Lectures on the Social Semiotics of Language.* Cambridge: Cambridge University Press.

Smalls, Krystal. 2012. "We Had Lighter Tongues: Making and Mediating Gullah/Geechee Personhood in the South Carolina." *Language and Communication* 32(2): 147–59.

Solis, Gabriel. 2015. "The Black Pacific: Music and Racialization in Papua New Guinea and Australia." *Critical Sociology* 41(2): 297–312.

Spedding, Alison. 2004. *Kawsachun coca: Economía campesina cocalera en los Yungas y el Chapare*. La Paz: PIEB.

Spitulnik, Debra. 1996. "The Social Circulation of Media Discourse and the Mediation of Communities." *Journal of Linguistic Anthropology* 6(2): 161–87.

Stern, Steve. 1987. *Resistance, Rebellion, and Consciousness in the Andean Peasant World, 18th to 20th Centuries*. Madison: University of Wisconsin Press.

Swinehart, Karl. 2012a. "The Enregisterment of Colla in a Bolivian (Camba) Comedy." *Social Text* 30(4 [113]): 81–102.

Swinehart, Karl. 2012b. "Metadiscursive Regime and Register Formation on Aymara Radio." *Language and Communication* 32(2): 102–13.

Swinehart, Karl. 2012c. "Tupac in Their Veins: Hip-Hop Alteño and the Semiotics of Urban Indigeneity." *Arizona Journal of Hispanic Cultural Studies* 16(2012): 79–96.

Swinehart, Karl. 2018. "Gender, Race, Class, and Region in 'Bilingual' Bolivia." *Signs and Society* 6(3): 607–21.

Swinehart, Karl. 2019a. "Decolonial Time in Bolivia's *Pachakuti*." *Signs and Society* 7(1): 96–114.

Swinehart, Karl. 2019b. "The *Ch'ixi* Blackness of Nación Rap's Aymara Hip-Hop." *Journal of the Society for American Music* 13(4): 461–81.

Terkourafi, Marina. 2010. *The Languages of Global Hip-Hop*. New York: Bloomsbury Press.

Thomson, Sinclair. 2004. *We Alone Shall Rule: Native Andean Politics in the Age of Insurgency*. Madison: University of Wisconsin Press.

Thomson, Sinclair et al. 2018. *The Bolivia Reader: History, Culture, Politics*. Durham: Duke University Press.

Ticona Alejo, Esteban. 2005. "La rebelión Aymara y popular de Octubre 2003. Una aproximación desde algunos barrios paceños." In Pablo Dávalos (Ed.), *Pueblos Indígenas, Estado y Democracia* [Indigenous Peoples, State and Democracy]. pp. 185–96. Buenos Aires: CLACSO.

Tockman, Jason and John Cameron. 2014. "Indigenous Autonomy and the Contradictions of Plurinationalism in Bolivia." *Latin American Politics and Society* 56(3): 46–69.

Torero, Alfredo. 1975. "Lingüística e historia de la Sociedad andina." *Lingüística e indigenismo moderno de América: Trabajos presentados al XXXIX Internacional de Americanistas* 5: 221–59.

Tucker, Joshua. 2013. *Gentleman Troubadours and Andean Pop Stars: Huayno Music, Media Work, and Ethnic Imaginaries in Urban Peru*. Chicago: University of Chicago Press.

Uprimny, Rodrigo. 2011. "The Recent Transformation of Constitutional Law in Latin America: Trends and Challenges." *Texas Law Review* 89: 1587–609.

Urla, Jacqueline. 1995. "Outlaw Language: Creating Alternative Public Spheres in Basque Free Radio." *Pragmatics* 5(2): 254–61.

Urla, Jacqueline. 2012. *Reclaiming Basque: Language, Nation, and Cultural Activism*. Reno: University of Nevada Press.

Volosinov, Valentin. 1986. *Marxism and the Philosophy of Language*. Cambridge, MA: Harvard University Press.

Wardaugh, Ronald. 2010. *An Introduction to Sociolinguistics*. Malden, MA: Wiley.

Wertheim, Suzanne. 2003. "Language Ideologies and the 'Purification' of Post-Soviet Tatar." *Ab Imperio* 1: 347–69.

Winchell, Mareike. 2022. *After Servitude: Elusive Property and the Ethics of Kinship in Bolivia*. Berkeley: University of California Press.

Woolard, Kathryn. 1992. "Language Ideology: Issues and Approaches." *Pragmatics* 2(3): 235–49.

Woolard, Kathryn and Bambi Schiefflin. 1994. "Language Ideology." *Annual Review of Anthropology* 23: 55–82.

Wroblewski, Michael. 2022. *Remaking Kichwa: Language and Indigenous Pluralism in Ecuador*. London: Bloomsbury.

Yapita, Juan de Dios. 2014. "Aruskipt'asipxañanakasakipunirakispawa, una palabra aymara" ["Aruskipt'asipxañanakasakipunirakispawa, an Aymara word"]. First published in *Página Siete*, March 18, 2014, Accessed online via *Ukhamawa. blogspot*, December 26, 2022: https://ukhamawa.blogspot.com/2014/03/aruskiptasipxananakasakipunirakispawa.html.

Younging, Gregory. 2018. *Elements of Indigenous Style: A Guide for Writing by and about Indigenous Peoples*. Edmonton: Bush.

Index

Academy of Quechua Language 53
adolescence 102
African Americans 95–6, 116–17
agglutinative languages 5, 129
akhulli (see also chewing coca) 58, 65
anchor (ideological, discursive) 42, 45, 65, 107
Áñez, Jeanine 146
anti-Indian racism 8–9, 103–4
Apaza, Julián (see Tupak Katari)
archaicisms 44–6, 129
Aristotle 19
assimilation by analogy 141
assimilation, phonological 46
audience design 31
authority 42, 53–4, 77
Autonomous Indigenous Municipalities 124
Aymara Education Council (CEA) 59
Aymara, dehispanicized 11, 16, 30, 34
Aymara, morphology 5, 97
Aymara, number of speakers 1
Aymara, territory 4
ayni (mutual aid) 42–3

Bánzer dictatorship 105
Bertonio, Ludovico 43
Bésiro-Chiquitano language 125
blackness 95–7
Bolivian Communist Party (PCB) 122

Cabildo de Ayllus y Comunidades Originarias de Jesús de Machaqa (CACOJMA) 133
caciques apoderados 59, 133
CEPOS (see First Peoples' Education Councils)
ch'ixi 100, 150
Chatino language 126–7
chola (urban Indigenous woman) 27
chronotope 66, 84

citizenship, postmulticultural 124
coca 22–4, 58, 112–16
coca, chewing 58, 65, 71, 85, 112–13
coca, cocaleros (coca growers) 23, 70, 113
cocaine 22–4
Cocteau Twins 88
codeswitching 71–5
community centers 97
Conciencia de Patria (CONDEPA) 26
Confederación Sindical Única de Trabajadores Campesinos Bolivianos (CSUTCB) 36, 60, 123, 125
Confederation of Rural Teachers of Bolivia (CONMERB) 60
constituent assembly, in Venezuela 125
constituent assembly 13, 123–4
Constitution of Bolivia (2009) 13, 121, 123–4
Constitution of Bolivia (2009), official languages 125
constitutional reform in Latin America 125
corpus planning 37
correction 45, 77
Coulthard, Glen 149

decolonization 52
deictics, deixis 70, 109–12
dialogism 71–5
Dictionaries 43–4
discrimination, linguistic 103

enregisterment 10, 117
ethnopoetics 19
eugenics 145–6

figures of personhood 20, 24, 70
film, in Aymara language 28
First Peoples' Education Councils (CEPOs) 60

folktales 26
Foucault, Michel 54
fractal recursion 8

Gas War, October 2003 12, 55, 62–3, 97, 105–7
General languages of Indians 43
glossolalia 88
Guaraní language 125
Guaranis 13
Guarayu language 125

Habermas, Jürgen 29
Hardman, Martha 5
hip-hop 15
hip-hop, fashion 106–7
hip-hop, first Bolivian rap 101
hip-hop, Global hip-hop 100
Hip-hop, in Bolivia 101
hip-hop, mixing 116
Hip-hop, scene in El Alto 91–3, 95
Hymes, Dell 19

iconicity 31, 118–19
iconization (see rhematization)
Indianism 35
Inka Empire (see Tawantinsuyu)
interactional text 112
Intercultural Bilingual Education (IBE) 27
Inuits 157 n.13
Inuktitut language 157 n.13

Jakobson, Roman 5–6, 19
Jesuits 35, 36
Jesús de Machaca, Uprising 1921 132
journalism 30

Katarismo 35
Kichwa (Ecuador) 125

Laime Pairumani, Félix 56
language contact, Aymara and Quechua 51–2
language contact, Aymara and Spanish 46
language ideology 5, 78
language purism, discourse purism 37, 45
language purism, idiom of purism 37, 45
language shift 1–2, 50–1, 102–3

Ley de Exvinculación de Tierras (1874) 132
liberation theology 36
literacy 15, 60
Llanki, Faustino 132
Llanki, Marcelino 132
loanwords, archaic Spanish 46
loanwords, from Quechua 51–2
loanwords, phonologically assimilated 45–7
Loza, Remedios 27

matrix language 52, 57, 75, 153
mediatization 28–30, 58
Mesa, Carlos (President) 12
metalanguage, metalinguistic function 5, 73, 77, 78
metamoves (ideological, discursive) 65
metapragmatics 17, 20, 58, 78, 81–5
monitoring of speech (*seguimiento*) 40–9
Morales, Evo 12–13
morphology 5, 97, 109–12, 129
Movement to Socialism-Political Instrument for the sovereignty of Peoples (MAS-IPSP) 13, 123
Movimiento Indianista Tupak Katari (MITKA) 125
Movimiento por la Soberanía (MPS) 78, 84
Movimiento Revolucionario Tupak Katari (MPTK) 36
Movimiento Universitario Julián Apaza (MUJA) 125
Moxeño language 125
multisited ethnography 18, 93, 150
music-language 87
music, Andean 25, 90, 98, 104, 116
music, of protest 118
music, relation to language 87

Nación Rap 97
National Anthem, of Bolivia 125
National Anthem, of Mexico 126–7
national anthem, of South Africa 140–1
National Anthem, of Venezuela 125–6
nationalism 11, 58, 115–16, 140–1
Navajo language 140
neologism 48

official Languages of Bolivia 13
oppressed languages 1

pachakuti 14
Palenque, Carlos 26
participant roles (Goffman) 70
participant roles, and verbal deixis 111
participant roles, principal 70
Partido Indio de Aymaras y Keswas 35
Partido Indio de Bolivia (PIB) 35
Pink Tide 13
poetic function 6, 19
poetics, alignments 103, 109–12
poetics, parallelism 103, 111–2
proceso de cambio 1–2
professionalization 149–50
prosody, in radio broadcast 49
public shere, print capitalism and 29

q'ara 20–1, 78–81
Quechua 129
Qullasuyu 129

racial ideology 21, 81, 103–4
Radio Illimani 25
Radio Pacha Qamasa 27, 55, 61
Radio San Gabriel 15, 26, 61
Radio San Gabriel, founding 35
Radio y Televisión Popular (RTP) 26
radio, history in Bolivia 25–8
radio, miners radio 26
Real Academia Española 10
register 10, 98
Reinaga, Fausto 35, 117
reported speech (see represented speech)
represented speech 72
Revolution, Bolivian National Revolution 1952 26
rhematization 20–1, 56–7, 119
Rivera Cusicanqui, Silvia 100, 122, 133, 149–50
rural migration 91, 102–3, 149

Sánchez de Lozada, Gonzalo (President) 12, 62, 105
Scat (Jazz, vocal improvisation) 88
semilingualism 8, 53
Shakur, Tupac (2Pac) 21–2, 118
Sisa, Bartolina 107
social movements 12, 105–7, 132, 140
South Africa 140
speaker (category) 1, 38
speech chain 41
speech chain, baptismal events 157 n.14
standard language ideology 10, 15
stenography 41

Tawantinsuyu (Inka Empire) 129
technologies of the self (Foucault) 54
television, in Aymara language 28
theology of enculturation 36
translation 128–9, 135, 138
Tribuna del Pueblo 26
Tupac (2Pac) (see Shakur)
Tupak Amaru II 22, 107
Tupak Katari 12, 22, 70, 106–8

urban indigeneity 149

Volsinov, Valentin 73

Warao language 125–6
Warisata (school) 60
Washington Consensus 13
Water War 12, 106
whiteness 21, 95, 117
Willka, Pablo Zárate 146
wiphala (flag) 121, 125
Wu Tang Clan 98, 116, 118

Yapita, Juan de Dios 2, 45

www.ingramcontent.com/pod-product-compliance
Lightning Source LLC
Chambersburg PA
CBHW052122300426
44116CB00010B/1765